Lisa Smith has written an inspiring bo
based upon the life, writings and sermons of George Whitefield. Lisa has drawn many important applications from Whitefield's life for our times. I love learning from great men and women of the past and Lisa has made that easier by searching through the writings about and by Whitefield to discover principles that served him well and would serve us well. The emphasis upon the New Birth as a new creation and not justification alone but also sanctification is powerful. There are many other insights Lisa presents us in the book—all important for growing in sanctification. I thank Lisa for her work to write *Hammer & Fire*. I encourage you to read it and apply its insights so that along with the promises of God "you may become partakers of the divine nature" (2 Peter 1:4b).

—**RANDY CLARK,** president of Global Awakening Theological Seminary and overseer of the apostolic network of Global Awakening

George Whitefield is a complex and often misunderstood figure in the history of Christianity. Combining a scholar's depth of knowledge with a fervent believer's confessional ardor, Lisa Smith's *Hammer & Fire* serves as a historically grounded devotional text that can introduce a new generation of Christian readers to George Whitefield's evangelistic zeal.

—**GEOFFREY REITER,** associate professor and coordinator of literature, Lancaster Bible College

The book *Hammer & Fire* illumines some of the noteworthy and very personal details of Whitefield's life and ministry. It adds new insights into the spiritual life and ministry. His ardent spiritual life was the wellspring and mainspring of how God used him. The book will spawn challenging questions and discussion for Christians who want to be used by God and for His glory.

—**ROB ANTONUCCI,** assistant director for the J Christy Wilson Jr. Center for World Missions, Gordon-Conwell Theological Seminary

In *Hammer & Fire,* Smith examines the roots of George Whitefield's zeal for God and effectively translates them into practical, valuable truths for modern Christian life. She gracefully weaves Whitefield's personal religious experience, reflections on Scripture, and witness of God's powerful work in revival into a discipleship primer that both inspires and ministers to the reader. Her study questions for each chapter will drive these lessons home in personal or group reflection. Whitefield comes alive as we grasp that the cultural influences he faced are not so radically different from those we encounter in the 21st century—and Smith urges that the same God who used Whitefield to grow His Kingdom can and will use obedient Jesus-followers today.

—RACHEL S. STAHLE, faculty mentor at Kairos University and author
   of *The Great Work of Providence: Jonathan Edwards for Life Today*

The "Grand Itinerant," George Whitefield, was all about fervent, zealous, and authentic piety, whether preaching in front of massive crowds or communing with God in solitude. Little wonder that he was the chief mover of the Great Awakening! Whitefield's unwavering, lifelong vocation was to convert and edify, to convict the lost and animate believers, and to serve neighbors in need. *Hammer & Fire* draws on Whitefield's life and career with extracts from his writings to awaken readers from indifference, anxiety, and uncertainty and point them toward a life of consuming spiritual zeal and practice. With discernment and clarity, Smith applies Scripture- and Spirit-focused wisdom to lessons and encouragement from Whitefield's struggles and victories, but she isn't afraid to address his failings when it came to conflict and enslavement. The title, drawn from Jeremiah 23:29 (one of Whitefield's favorites), says it all: "Is not my word like fire, declares the LORD, and like a hammer that breaks the rock in pieces?" Readers seeking to awaken or stir the fire and hammer of spiritual passion will be strongly challenged, encouraged, and directed.

—MICHAEL DITMORE, professor of English, Pepperdine University

Hebrews 13:7–8 states, "Remember your leaders who spoke the word of God to you. Consider the outcome of their way of life and imitate their faith. For Jesus Christ is the same yesterday, today, and forever." In Dr. Smith's well-researched and accessible treatment of George Whitefield, she considers the life and thought of George Whitefield and bridges the historical gap between his ministry and our lives. Moving between history and devotion, this volume occupies a unique space, supplementing other academic investigations of the Grand Itinerant. She allows Whitefield's own writings to speak into the 21st century by presenting the evangelist's thought with a view to transplanting the same passion in our personal lives that drove the Great Awakening. Dr. Smith follows the building blocks of Whitefield's brand of evangelical spirituality that produced his Christian maturity and provides an outline for any contemporary Christian to embrace the same passion and depth Whitefield exemplified.

—**CHRISTIAN CUTHBERT,** senior pastor of Union Church (Vernon, CT) and editor of *The Wartime Sermons of Jonathan Edwards: A Collection*

Smith's carefully researched and beautifully crafted volume provides the reader with an excellent introduction to the life and ministry of the great 18th century evangelist, George Whitefield. It also invites readers to experience for themselves the same kind of spiritual renewal and passion to serve God that captured Whitefield's heart when he was a student at Oxford. Far more than an introduction to a celebrated preacher, Smith provides a spiritual feast for readers who are hungry to know God more fully and to serve God more faithfully.

—**GARTH M. ROSELL,** senior research professor of church history, Gordon-Conwell Theological Seminary

In this direct-address devotional, Lisa Smith blends spiritual encouragement with nuanced analysis of the life and works of George Whitefield. Smith's integration of primary historic documents provides opportunities for connection between a reader's own devotional practice and that of George Whitefield. Personal anecdotes from Smith in the book serve as a case study for the value of the words of Whitefield—sourced from personal journals and public-facing sermons alike—for modern spiritual practice.

—**ANASTASIA ARMENDARIZ,** librarian for Special Collections and the Malibu Historical Collection, Pepperdine University

Smith has succeeded in writing a personal and accessible biography of George Whitfield. She is not content, however, with simply telling the story of Whitfield's life or even of his work. Through her narrative, as well as his own journal entries, she allows us to meet Whitfield the man who was shaped by his relationship with God. As I read this book, Whitfield became a warm and real person rather than a force, as he appears in so many scholarly works. But the book goes further, as she finds ways to connect her own faith to Whitefield's story. Smith successfully weaves together devotional themes that will prove helpful for every Christian with a scholarly biography of the greatest revivalist preacher this country has ever known.

—**DANIEL R. SPANJER,** author of *Advent is the Story: Seeing the Nativity throughout Scripture*

HAMMER
& FIRE

HAMMER
& FIRE

Lessons on Spiritual Passion from the Writings and Life of
GEORGE WHITEFIELD

LISA SMITH

SQUARE HALO BOOKS

In Christian art, the square halo identified a living person
presumed to be a saint. Square Halo Books is devoted to publishing
works that present contextually sensitive biblical studies and
practical instruction consistent with the Doctrines of the Reformation.
The goal of Square Halo Books is to provide materials
useful for encouraging and equipping the saints.

©2023 Square Halo Books, Inc.
P.O. Box 18954 | Baltimore, MD 21206
www.SquareHaloBooks.com

ISBN 978-1-941106-32-7
Library of Congress Control Number: 2023942470

Printed in the United States of America

To the students
I've had the privilege
to mentor—your passion
for God inspires me.
I pray this book
inspires you.

NINE
SERMONS

UPON THE

Following SUBJECTS;

VIZ.

I. The LORD our Righte-
ousness.

II. The Seed of the Wo-
man and the Seed of the
Serpent.

III. Persecution every Christian's LOT.

IV. *Abraham's* offering up
his Son *Isaac*.

V. *Saul's* Conversion.

VI. The *Pharisee* and *Publican*.

VII. Christ, the Believer's
Wisdom, Righteousness,
Sanctification, and Re-
demption.

VIII. The Holy Spirit convincing the World of Sin,
of Righteousness, and of
Judgment.

IX. The Conversion of *Zac-
cheus*.

To which are annexed,

Several Prayers on various Occasions.

By GEORGE WHITEFIELD, *A.B.*
Late of Pembroke-College, Oxford.

LONDON:

Printed ; and Sold by SAM. MASON, Bookseller in
Woodstreet ; and GAB. HARRIS, *Jun.* Bookseller
in *Gloucester*. MDCCXLII.
Where also may be had,
All Mr. *Whitefield's* Tracts that are in Print.

TABLE OF CONTENTS

A

CONTINUATION

Of the REVEREND

Mr. *WHITEFIELD's*

JOURNAL,

From a few Days after his RETURN to

GEORGIA

To his ARRIVAL at

FALMOUTH,

on the 11th of MARCH, 1741.

CONTAINING

An ACCOUNT of the Work of GOD at
*Georgia, Rhode-Island, New-England, New-
York, Pennsylvania* and *South-Carolina.*

The Seventh JOURNAL.

The SECOND EDITION.

LONDON:

Printed by W. STRAHAN; and Sold by J. ROBINSON, in
Ludgate-Street; at the *Tabernacle*, near *Upper Moorfields*;
and by Mr. JOHN SIMS, near *Hoxton.* MDCCXLIV.
(Price One Shilling.)
SCC

ACKNOWLEDGMENTS

I am grateful for the opportunity to thank those who made this project possible. Heartfelt thanks to Steve Smith and Carolyn Taketa for reading drafts of the book and offering enormously helpful input and encouragement. Thanks to Ned Bustard for championing the project (and for the fabulous cover design), and to Théa Rosenburg for improving the work with her editing. My gratitude to Elizabeth Parang, Sally Bryant, and Melissa Pichette at Payson Library, Pepperdine University, for their herculean efforts in acquiring texts and advising me on bibliographic matters. And profound thanks and love to Ryan, my intrepid companion on countless Whitefield adventures, to Alex and Abby for their love and support, and to all my family and friends for their consistent encouragement and understanding during my immersion in the eighteenth-century world of George Whitefield.

Decembr 3th 1766
near 7 at night

Dr Madm

        I have just now
heard that You are married, therefore take the
first opportunity of wishing Your whole self
much joy — That You both may live together as
Heirs of the grace of life on earth, and after
death be translated to sit down at the marriage feast of the supper of the Lamb in heaven, is the hearty prayer of, Dr Madm

        Your real friend and servt
        for X's sake

        Whitefield

A NOTE ON THE TEXTS

From his entrance into professional ministry in his early twenties, George Whitefield was a public figure. In fact, he was an international celebrity. The extent of his popularity, his own awareness of his public persona, and the zeal of his friends to preserve and, where they deemed necessary, rehabilitate his reputation meant that most of Whitefield's writings have been heavily edited over the years. This note explains how I have attempted to offer readers what I consider to be the most "original" versions of Whitefield's works.[1]

Between 1738 and 1741, Whitefield published seven separate journals, covering events in his life and ministry from December 1737 through March 1741. In 1740, Whitefield released the autobiographical *A Short Account of God's Dealings with the Reverend Mr. George Whitefield*, which describes his life from birth through his ordination for professional ministry. In 1747, Whitefield published *A Further Account of God's Dealings with the Reverend Mr. George Whitefield*, which details the early years of his itinerant preaching ministry.

In 1756, Whitefield edited his seven journals and two autobiographical texts and republished them all as *The First Two Parts of his Life, with his Journals, Revised, Corrected, and Abridged*. In the revised version, Whitefield attempts to mollify his critics by toning down some of his more zealous sentiments. In this book, I use the first editions of his journals and autobiographical writings, not the revised version of 1756.

Whitefield was an incessant letter-writer to his numerous international contacts, but while several collections of his letters have been published, we currently do not have an authoritative, scholarly edition of Whitefield's correspondence.[2] I use the collections of Whitefield's letters that we do have, including the largest, John Gillies' six-volume *Works of the Reverend George Whitefield*, published in 1771–1772, shortly after Whitefield's death in 1770. Unfortunately, Gillies edited the more than 1400 letters in his collection, often removing the names of recipients, and many of the letters are no longer extant. I fill in the recipient's name in square brackets when scholars have made an identification.

Whitefield's sermons were sometimes published individually and often in sermon collections. For this book, I use the first editions of all sermons. In the same way, I use the first editions of all pamphlets and published letters.

I have accessed the writings reprinted here through two databases available at most university libraries and some public libraries. *Eighteenth Century Collections Online,* published by Gale, a division of Cengage, offers works published in Britain and many other English-speaking countries between 1701 and 1800. *Early American Imprints, Series I: Evans,* published by Readex, a division of NewsBank, offers writings published in America during the seventeenth and eighteenth centuries.

To make the eighteenth-century writings accessible to modern readers, I have silently modernized spelling and punctuation, adjusted paragraphing, added subtitles where needed, and expanded some contractions. Square brackets denote insertions for clarity, and endnotes offer additional information on people, places, and events that appear in the documents. Complete bibliographic information for all texts can be found in the bibliography.

Is not my word like fire,
declares the LORD, and like a hammer
that breaks the rock in pieces?
—Jeremiah 23:29

O how did the Word fall like
a Hammer and like a Fire!
—George Whitefield, journal

December, 1813.

The kingdom of
Heaven suffereth
violence, and the
violent take it by
force.

Matt. xi. 12.

E

M Ford

INTRODUCTION

A commemorative coin from the 250th remembrance of the death of George Whitefield in 2020 sits on my desk. On the front is a picture of the man himself, while on the back are the words "America's Spiritual Founding Father" along with his birth and death dates, 1714–1770. Modern readers might be surprised to see Whitefield identified as the spiritual founding father of America, especially since he is lesser known today than such historical Christian leaders as Jonathan Edwards or Charles Finney. But a quarter century before America became a nation, English clergyman George Whitefield landed on its shores for a transcolonial preaching tour that drew practically every colonist to the sound of his voice and engulfed American Christianity in an overpowering, transformative tide of fervent spiritual revival. In Whitefield's own words, written from a preaching stop in Philadelphia in 1740, "Jesus manifests forth his glory daily in these parts. . . . His word is like a fire and a hammer: last week I saw many quite struck down. . . . America, ere long, will be famous for Christians."[1] Over a ministerial career that spanned more than three decades, Whitefield became known throughout America and the rest of the eighteenth-century English-speaking world for his spiritual passion as his preaching struck listeners with the power of a hammer and ignited their hearts with the spiritual zeal of a blazing inferno.

To say Whitefield tirelessly promoted the kingdom of God throughout the western world during his lifetime is not an overstatement. Whitefield preached an estimated 18,000 sermons, delivered during seven trips to America, fourteen visits to Scotland, three tours of Ireland, and exhaustive travels throughout England and Wales.[2] Scholars estimate so many copies of his written works were printed in the first eight years of his ministry that at least one copy of his writings was available for every twenty men, women, and children in England and America.[3] He drew crowds estimated at more than 20,000 in some locations, appeared almost continually in American and English news-papers during the 1740s, and was the subject of more than 150 printed attacks for his unconventional spirituality in the English press in 1739–1740 alone.[4]

The spiritual passion that drove Whitefield's life and ministry was recog-nized by his contemporaries. Remarked one, "Mr. Whitefield's eloquence is unrivalled, his zeal inexhaustible." Noted another, "He is the most extraordi-nary man in our times. He has the most commanding eloquence I ever heard in any person—his abilities are very considerable—his zeal unquenchable."[5] Close friend Benjamin Franklin (1706–1790), who once admitted he never gave Whitefield the "satisfaction" of truly converting, nonetheless conceded, "His integrity . . . and indefatigable zeal in [accomplishing] every good work I have never seen equaled, I shall never see exceeded."[6]

Whitefield unequivocally identified his love for Jesus Christ as the source of the passion behind both his life and ministry. As he once disclosed in a letter to a friend regarding his preaching, "I look to Jesus for this, and for everything."[7] And his zeal for God was truly lifelong. As an Oxford student not yet twenty years old, Whitefield declared the principle that would come to characterize him: "How dangerous it is to be a lukewarm Christian . . . there is nothing to be done without breaking from the world, denying ourselves daily, taking up our cross, and following Jesus Christ."[8] Thirty-six years later, during his final preaching tour of America and only months before he died, the now veteran preacher closed his last will and testament with the same sentiment:

> I am more and more convinced of the undoubted reality and infinite importance of the grand gospel truths which I have from time to time delivered, and am so far from repenting my delivering them in an itin-erant way, that had I strength equal to my inclination, I would preach them from pole to pole—not only because I have found them to be the power of God to the salvation of my own soul, but because I am as much assured that the great Head of the Church has called me by his word, providence, and Spirit to act in this way, as that the sun shines at noon day.[9]

Whitefield authentically embodied Paul's admonition in Romans 12:11 to "never be lacking in zeal, but keep your spiritual fervor, serving the Lord."[10]

The fact that he died the morning after delivering sermons in two different New Hampshire towns and an extemporaneous exhortation from the house in Massachusetts where he was staying seems a fitting conclusion to the "spiritual fervor" of Whitefield's life and vocation.

ENCOUNTERING GEORGE WHITEFIELD

Whitefield's spiritual passion, revealed through his compelling words as well as his uniquely zealous and effective life and ministry, is what inspired this book. In a historical moment when Christians are struggling with a culture that is alternately antagonistic and smugly dismissive of authentic Christian faith, as well as a church that can at times seem lost, irrelevant, or even damaging to its own, we long to encounter heroes of the faith who, despite their own human frailty, demonstrated lives of genuine spiritual passion and impacted their generation for God. George Whitefield is that kind of hero.

As I mention in the introduction to my book *Godly Character(s): Insights for Spiritual Passion from the Lives of 8 Women in the Bible,* Whitefield first inspired me to pursue God with abandon when I discovered his personal journals as a graduate student in early American literature.[11] Since that time, I have studied and taught a multitude of eighteenth-century religious writers as an English professor, but Whitefield still stands alone for both his extraordinarily passionate love for God and the striking power and emotion of his writing. Even today, two and one-half centuries after his death, his journals, autobiographical texts, and printed sermons still have the power to move me and spark spiritual passion in my own heart when I read them. This book is my attempt to bring the most impactful of Whitefield's writings and life events to the modern reader.

Hammer & Fire combines the best of a biography with a selection of compelling written works to learn what Whitefield can teach us on the topic of increasing our passion for God. Each chapter weaves together seminal events from Whitefield's life and ministry with his own personal writings to uncover practical truths about eight aspects of spiritual passion: igniting the fire, embracing purpose, building a foundation, adopting a lifestyle, sharing the journey, facing opposition, responding to culture, and sustaining the fire.

Each chapter opens with a basic introduction to the topic under discussion, after which a significant event from Whitefield's life is recounted to illustrate how we as Christians can grow in that aspect of pursuing God. Incidents such as his conversion, the inauguration of his preaching ministry, his encounters with both support and criticism, and his responses to the culture around him are included, with a focus on his early life and ministry. A related excerpt from one of Whitefield's own writings is offered next to reveal additional insights. Writings include passages from his journals and autobiographical works, private and published letters, and reprints of his most popular sermons, all of which are updated to be accessible for modern readers. Lastly, the book closes with questions for personal or group study that encourage interaction with and application of the ideas in the chapter.

My hope for this book is that readers will encounter Whitefield's passion for God and learn what he has to teach us about increasing our spiritual desire through times of fruitfulness and success as well as periods of dryness, doubt, and opposition. Amid the challenges of travel, the pain of criticism, the fatigue of itinerant preaching, and the joys of witnessing the spread of the gospel, Whitefield maintained, shared, and defended his singular zeal for the Lord, and he ceaselessly encouraged others to do the same. His life and writings offer the perfect classroom for learning how to spark, sustain, and multiply love and enthusiasm for Jesus.

GEORGE WHITEFIELD'S EXTRAORDINARY TIMES

Like most historical figures, Whitefield comes to life the most engagingly when we understand just a bit about the distinctive events and forces that shaped him and how his life experiences connect to our own cultural moment. Whitefield's passion for God was forged in the unique times that were the eighteenth century—an era of intense transition, innovation, progress, and competition in the West. Enlightenment thought had produced significant paradigm shifts in scientific enterprise, political institutions, and religious ideology. When combined with the exponential growth of worldwide trade and commerce, political and social revolutions, colonization and human trafficking, and warfare and conquest, the result was a century that launched the

West into the modern age. Whitefield's time, like our own, was thus a hotbed of shifting values and viewpoints. Three cultural forces stand out as the most impactful in Whitefield's life.

First, Whitefield was influenced by the growing consumer culture within the expanding and interconnected worldwide British empire. Put simply, westerners were beginning to discover the power of marketing and branding techniques to create large, international trade markets, and Whitefield adopted the nascent ideology eagerly and effectively. Preaching outdoors where literally thousands of listeners could hear him, making alliances across denominational and international lines, and using a "press agent" of sorts to print local newspaper notices of his preaching stops, Whitefield was extremely progressive in his awareness of the emerging consumer ethos as well as in his willingness to publicize his name and ministry throughout the growing British realm. He was truly the first modern international celebrity.[12]

Second, the emerging influence and importance of the English colonies in North America in international politics, commerce, and philosophical thought impacted Whitefield in significant ways. As both a market for and producer of consumer goods and ideas, America was entering its period of western impact. Whitefield was a strong supporter of the American colonies, donating money to burgeoning American universities such as Princeton University and Dartmouth College and siding with the colonies in their successful attempt to have the Stamp Act of 1765 repealed. He ultimately made seven preaching tours of the colonies and died in 1770 in the manse of the Old South Presbyterian Church in Newburyport, Massachusetts, where he was buried in the crypt beneath the pulpit. Whitefield predicted his formidable influence in America in early 1741 at the end of his second preaching tour of the colonies: "All things concur to convince me that America is to be my chief scene for action."[13]

Third, the birth of the Protestant religious movement now known as evangelicalism had perhaps the greatest influence on Whitefield and was, in turn, irrevocably impacted by him. Emphasizing the need for a conversion experience, the centrality of the Bible and Jesus' salvific death on the cross, and the outworking of the gospel in acts of service to society, evangelicalism combined the theological underpinnings of Puritanism with the progressive, optimistic values of the Enlightenment.[14] The resulting religious movement was vigorous, appealing, and influential in western society and is still present with us today in Protestant non-denominational churches, modern worship music, and Christian humanitarian ministries. Whitefield was at the forefront of this developing movement, tirelessly preaching the necessity of being spiritually born again; enthusiastically raising funds for his primary ministry venture, an orphanage in Savannah, Georgia, he named Bethesda; and connecting with other emerging evangelicals throughout the western world.[15]

One of the most explosive products of the evangelical movement in Great Britain and America was a religious revival now known as the First Great Awakening. Peaking during the early 1740s when Whitefield was in his mid-twenties, the Awakening was a volatile combination of demonstrative born-again conversions, controversial innovative religious practices, shocking church splits and restructurings, and Enlightenment-inspired theology and doctrine. Thousands flocked to hear outdoor preaching, individuals concerned for their souls sought spiritual counsel with ardent emotion, countless small religious gatherings for prayer and spiritual study sprouted up in every city, and books on religious subjects crammed the presses.[16]

Whitefield is traditionally viewed by scholars as one of the chief promoters and initiators of the First Great Awakening and as absolutely central to the revival on both sides of the Atlantic. The first sermons he preached in England beginning in 1736 drew large crowds and sparked conversions and powerful manifestations of the Holy Spirit in many. He had personal connections in all the important regions touched by the revival—Scotland, Wales, Ireland, England, and America—and maintained those associations by frequent letters and visits. His truly indefatigable commitment to itinerant preaching took him to practically every city where revival flared, and his equally unflagging dedication to writing and publishing during the years of the Awakening made him the best known and most celebrated of the revivalists.

Even in America, Whitefield played a dominant role in the revival, despite the fact that he was an English Anglican clergyman who never settled permanently in the colonies. His arrival in Lewes, Delaware, on October 30, 1739, for a preaching tour of the colonies consolidated the movement in America as

Whitefield traveled unceasingly for fifteen months up and down the eastern seaboard, preaching to overflow crowds, connecting revival supporters, and experiencing sensational results from his ministry. During the key years of the Awakening in America, Whitefield preached more often and in more locations than did any American-born revivalist; he also published more original writings.[17]

In all three of these divergent yet powerful eighteenth-century forces—the developing consumer culture within the expanding British empire, the increasingly important role of the American colonies, and the inception of evangelicalism and its sparking of the First Great Awakening—Whitefield was both a product of his times and an influencer of his age. His central role in what many consider to be the inauguration of the modern era makes him uniquely qualified to speak across the centuries to our current culture and to our own longing to see God move passionately in our hearts and in our generation.

Next to the commemorative Whitefield coin on my desk is a printed image of a Methodist Love Feast ticket from 1813. Love Feasts were extended times of fellowship, prayer, shared meals, and worship instituted by Methodist founder and Whitefield's college friend John Wesley (1703–1791) right around the time of Whitefield's entrance into public ministry. Although the ticket is from a period much later than that of Whitefield, it nonetheless could have belonged to him if only for the verse printed on it: "From the days of John the Baptist until now, the kingdom of heaven has been forcefully advancing, and forceful men lay hold of it."[18] If anyone in history pursued Jesus with the spiritual forcefulness alluded to in that verse and thus deserved to carry the ticket into a Christian Love Feast, it was the Reverend George Whitefield. My hope is that as we encounter Whitefield's writings and transformative life experiences in these pages, the spiritual passion he displayed unceasingly throughout his lifetime will reach across the centuries to both instruct and inspire us to pursue Jesus Christ with ever-increasing fervency and love.

GEORGIUS WHITEFIELD,
Artium Magister, Verbi divini Minister
inter Anglos maxime
notus.

CHAPTER I

Igniting the Fire

Fire begins with a spark. Campfires, forest fires, bonfires, signal fires—each originates with a potent flash of ignition. So, too, does spiritual fire. Burning zeal for God and his purposes must be ignited in our hearts before we can embark upon a life of spiritual passion.

But what creates the spark that ignites spiritual fire in a human heart? According to the Bible, it is the touch of God the Father, offered to each of us through the mediation of his Son Jesus Christ, in the person of the Holy Spirit who indwells the Christian. As a "smoking firepot with a blazing torch" when he confirms his covenant with Abraham, as "flames of fire from within a bush" when he calls Moses to lead his people out of Egypt, as a "pillar of fire" by night which guides the Israelites in the desert, and as a "fire" that falls upon Mount Sinai causing it to smoke and tremble, God is revealed many times in the Old Testament as "a consuming fire."[1] Likewise in the New Testament, as "tongues of fire" in the upper room when the Holy Spirit descends upon the followers of Jesus, God is "a consuming fire."[2] Jesus expresses his own burning desire in Luke 12:49 when he cries out, "I have come to bring fire on the earth, and how I wish it were already kindled!" Thus, we understand and appreciate the fiery passion behind the words of our Bridegroom Jesus to his bride the church in Song of Songs 8:6: "Place me like a seal over your heart, like a seal on your arm; for love is as strong as death, its jealousy unyielding as the grave. It burns like blazing fire, like a mighty flame." Our God is a God of passion and fire who ignites this same fierce, explosive love in the hearts of his followers.

God first sparks in us this flame of burning love at salvation, forgiving our sins and indwelling us with his Holy Spirit. This work of God effectually removes us from the kingdom of darkness and death and places us in God's eternal kingdom of light and life through the intercessory death of Jesus Christ. As we know from Colossians 1:13–14, "[God] has rescued us from the domin- ion of darkness and brought us into the kingdom of the Son he loves, in whom we have redemption, the forgiveness of sins."

George Whitefield both experienced and appreciated the power of God to ignite a flame of passion in the human heart at salvation. After describing his own conversion in his first autobiographical writing, he assures the reader, "And if you have felt the powers of the world to come and been made a partaker of the Holy Ghost, [I] know you will rejoice and give thanks for what God has done for my soul."[3]

After conversion, as we follow Jesus over a lifetime, God continually re- ignites and grows our initial spark of spiritual passion into a raging, blazing inferno. Pursuing ever-deepening intimacy with God, transforming our minds more and more comprehensively according to his word, and displaying in- creasingly fruitful Spirit-directed obedience and ministry to others requires that the flame of God's love within us consistently increases to motivate us to deeper, fuller, more challenging, and more enriching places in the spiritual life, enabling us to overcome the obstacles that arise before us. In Whitefield's words, we pray that "the Man Jesus Christ is formed within [us] and brought forth and arrived unto the measure of his fullness who fills all in all!"[4]

Of course, we play a role in *nurturing* the heart-scorching flame of love that God sparks and grows in us—sustaining, sharing, and protecting our flame of passion for God—and this will be the subject of the subsequent chapters of this book. As the apostle Paul advises his spiritual son Timothy, "I remind you to fan into flame the gift of God."[5] But the first work is God's: igniting eternal, life-changing spiritual passion within us.

THE PROCESS OF IGNITION

While the process God uses to ignite spiritual passion in a human heart is unique and often surprising for each individual, God always begins with the same first step: drawing our heart to himself by awakening us and making us conscious of his existence, his purposes for us, and his love. As God reminds the people of Israel through the Old Testament prophet Hosea, "When Israel was a child, I loved him, and out of Egypt I called my son. . . . I led them with cords of human kindness, with ties of love."[6] God unleashes his overwhelming love upon a heart, powerfully awakening that heart and drawing it to himself.

God's initial action toward igniting spiritual passion can be seen in several incidents in Whitefield's life when he was just a young man growing up in Gloucester, England. Whitefield experienced God's irresistible tug on his heart first through several prophetic encounters, the initial one occurring while he was reading a play to his sister. Interrupting himself, Whitefield exclaimed, "Sister, God intends something for me which we know not of." Whitefield records these words in his autobiography, continuing, "How I came to say these words I know not. God afterwards showed me they came from him."[7]

At this point in his life, Whitefield had attended some school, worked in the family-owned tavern, and was seeking an apprenticeship in business since his family did not have the financial means to send him to a university. Soon after this experience, Whitefield and his mother learned of an opportunity for young men to discharge the expenses of attending college by working as servitors to wealthy students, assisting them with household and personal tasks. Within a week of discovering this information, Whitefield returned to his studies, hoping to someday attend Pembroke College at Oxford University.

Not long after his return to school, nearing his seventeenth birthday, Whitefield experienced his second prophetic encounter with God: "Near this time, I dreamed that I was to see God on Mount Sinai, but was afraid to meet him. This made a great impression upon me, and a gentlewoman to whom I told it said, 'George, this is a call from God.'"[8] This incident was quickly followed up by an even more compelling sense of God's calling to the ministry: "One night, as I was going on an errand for my mother, an unaccountable but very strong impression was made upon my heart that I should preach quickly."[9] When he recounted this thought to his mother, she derided it, causing Whitefield to comment wryly in his autobiography, "God has since shown her from whom that impression came."[10]

About one year later, when Whitefield was eighteen years old, he began his studies at Pembroke College at the University of Oxford. Although his pursuit of religion up until that point had been mostly haphazard and inconsistent, his powerful encounters with God had awakened his heart, and his time at Oxford would change his life forever.

RESPONDING TO GOD

When God begins to awaken our heart to himself to ignite spiritual passion in us, he does so with the hope that we will respond to his overtures. Just as an earthly lover yearns for his beloved to meet his tender advances with reciprocal affection, so, too, God longs for us to notice his movements in our heart and respond. At Oxford, Whitefield began responding to God, and his experience teaches us both the best and the worst choices we can make when reacting to God's stirrings in our heart.

The best choice Whitefield made in response to God's work was to choose to prioritize and pursue him. While at Oxford, Whitefield began seeking God by praying, fasting, serving the poor, attending church, and studying the Bible. Soon, Whitefield made the acquaintance of Charles Wesley (1707–1788) who, along with his elder brother John, was leading a movement of students whom detractors derisively called "Methodists" because of their commitment to consistently and "methodically" practice the spiritual disciplines. Through Charles, Whitefield began reading helpful spiritual books and growing in his understanding of God. From these writings, Whitefield realized for the first time that he must be born again to enter God's kingdom. In his words, "From that moment, but not till then, did I know that I must be a new creature."[11] His responsive pursuit of God had led him to recognize the need for his own heart to be ignited with the spark of God's passionate spiritual fire.

Like Whitefield, we also should make the wise choice to pursue God in response to his awakening of our heart. This pursuit will look different for each of us. For some, it might include studying the Bible to learn who God is and how he acts. For others, it could involve changing our daily schedules so we can spend time in God's presence, learning to hear his voice and understand his heart. For still others, it may include acts of service, changes to how we spend our money, or the forsaking of ungodly habits. For all of us, however, our choice to respond to God by pursuing him is crucial because it gives God "proof that we are serious and sincere in seeking inward renewal, for ... that evidence of sincerity is something God regularly requires as a condition of answering our prayers," as theologian J.I. Packer explains.[12] Our responsive pursuit of God shows him we are in earnest and places us in the position to continue to grow in receiving his awakening love.

However, Whitefield also shows us the most serious potential pitfall of responding to God by seeking him: believing our pursuit of him will in and of itself create the spark of God's love in our hearts. While pursuing God reveals our sincerity and puts us in the place where God can continue to draw us to himself, God alone is still the only one who can ignite spiritual fire within our hearts because spiritual passion comes from the Holy Spirit. In fact, like the law of God in the Old Testament, our focused pursuit of God should lead us not to a sense of self-sufficiency, but instead to a deep recognition of our own total and unqualified need for God to ignite our hearts with his own fiery passion. Packer, again, recommends "balance" in recognizing that "personal change will not occur without the use of means ... [but] no use of means will change the heart without God's blessing."[13]

After learning of his need to be born again spiritually, Whitefield fell into the trap of believing his own efforts would produce his conversion and ignite fire for God in his heart. Over the course of nearly a year, Whitefield pursued salvation by fasting until he was physically ill, allowing his body to suffer the cold without reprieve, isolating himself from even his Christian friends, and eventually suffering a seven-week bout of severe illness that left him unable even to continue with his studies. Recalling this period several years later, he identifies it as a time of deception by Satan: "When the Holy Spirit put into my heart good thoughts or convictions, [Satan] always drove them to extremes."[14]

Finally, Whitefield realized he could not spark spiritual fire himself. In a moment of surrender, he fell upon his bed and cried out to God desperately, "I thirst!" God answered with his saving grace, igniting Whitefield's heart with passionate holy love. Whitefield identified this moment as his conversion, the instant he became truly born again. As he recalls, "I was delivered from the burden that had so heavily oppressed me.... Now did the Spirit of God take possession of my soul and, as I humbly hope, seal me unto the day of redemption."[15]

Whitefield's experiences with God's awakening movements upon his heart, his response of fervent pursuit, his mistaken attempts to ignite the flame of God's love by his own efforts, his eventual acceptance of his own need for God's mercy, and his plea for God to touch him with his saving grace reveal the general outline of how God works to redeem us and ignite spiritual passion in us. Whitefield received God's spark of fiery love and would go on to stoke that flame throughout his lifetime. However, he never forgot the moment he first felt the blaze of God's love in his heart and its intense, enduring effects. More than twenty years after the experience, this is how he remembers it:

> But, oh, with what joy, joy unspeakable, even joy that was full of and big with glory, was my soul filled when the weight of sin went off and an abiding sense of the pardoning love of God and a full assurance of faith broke in upon my disconsolate soul! Surely it was the day of my espousals, a day to be had in everlasting remembrance. At first, my joys were like a spring-tide and, as it were, overflowed the banks. Go where I would, I could not avoid singing of psalms almost aloud; afterwards, it became more settled and, blessed be God, [except for] a few casual intervals, has abode and increased in my soul ever since.[16]

Whitefield's testimony should give us confidence to approach God boldly and ask him for the spark of spiritual passion for which we long. As Jesus states unequivocally in Matthew 7:7–8: "Ask and it will be given to you; seek and you will find; knock and the door will be opened to you. For everyone who asks receives; the one who seeks finds; and to the one who knocks, the door will be opened." God loves to spark his passionate fire in a human heart as we respond to his promptings and pursue him.

THE IMPORTANCE OF THE PROCESS

Whitefield's conversion reveals one final point about how God ignites our hearts with his fiery love: the process itself is important. Readers might find it surprising that Whitefield spent almost an entire year seeking true conversion after he learned that he needed to be born again. Modern Christians tend to assure potential converts that once they learn the truth of the new birth, they can without hesitation accept it and receive salvation.

In the eighteenth century, however, the *process* of conversion was viewed as just as significant as was an individual's ultimate decision to follow Christ. Unlike today, even revivalist preachers such as Whitefield did not assume salvation would occur for a person during just one religious meeting. Most believed that the process could take weeks, months, or even years until a person truly recognized their own absolute sinfulness, their inability to save themselves, and the perfect and unique sufficiency of Jesus' sacrifice for their sins.[17] Potential converts were encouraged to study the Scriptures, grow in practicing the spiritual disciplines, read Christian books, and search their hearts to learn the true depth of their sinfulness and abject need for Jesus.

Although Whitefield himself admitted that he was deceived by Satan into going to unhealthy extremes and relying too much on his own efforts during his conversion process, he did recognize the spiritual benefits he gained from his struggles. Three blessings stood out to Whitefield, and they are instructive for us as modern Christians when we consider our own view of how one reaches the point of deciding to become a follower of Jesus.

First, because of his spiritual labors, Whitefield knew that when he did become a true believer, he had made an informed, authentic decision that was based solely on a resolute belief in the righteousness of Christ and not his own human works. In a letter to a friend written just one week after his ordination to the ministry, Whitefield pronounces, "Indeed we may flatter ourselves that we may go to heaven without undergoing the pangs of the new birth, but we shall certainly find ourselves desperately mistaken in the end. . . . Let us therefore never cease praying and striving till we find this blessed change wrought in us and thereby we ourselves brought off from relying on any or all outward ordinances for salvation." Whenever Whitefield spiritually counseled individuals, he encouraged them to expend consistent effort to seek salvation "for nothing will do but that."[18]

Whitefield also appreciated the relationship he began to develop with God as he sought his own conversion over the many trying months. Although tempted often to give up the fight, Whitefield recalled how God had strengthened

and comforted him. He writes, "During this, and all other seasons of temptation, my soul was inwardly supported with great courage and resolution from
above. Every day God made me willing to renew the combat."[19] His experience
of learning the ways of God during his struggle for salvation prepared him for
a deep, solid relationship with Jesus once he converted.

Lastly, Whitefield knew his "outward and inward trials" during conversion were helpful for setting him on the path of spiritual passion for which
he would become known.[20] He writes that his hardships "inured me to contempt, lessened self-love, and taught me to die daily."[21] When we labor through
challenges and temptations to achieve a goal, a very real spark of passion is
created in us. As Augustine of Hippo (354–430) remarks when describing his
own lengthy conversion process in his *Confessions,* "Everywhere the greater
joy is ushered in by the greater pain."[22] In modern parlance, no pain, no gain.
Whitefield believed that his early conversion work bore fruit throughout his
lifetime, convinced that God allowed the difficulties so that "his future blessings might not prove my ruin."[23]

As we see from Whitefield's experience, time and effort expended in the
conversion process is not wasted, but ensures an informed decision to follow
Christ, acquaints one with the ways and character of God, and acts as a jump
start to a life of spiritual passion. Whitefield thoroughly believed in the eternal
benefits of fervently seeking salvation:

> If you are awakened to a sense of the divine life and are hungering and
> thirsting after that righteousness which is by faith only in Jesus Christ
> and the indwelling of his blessed Spirit in your heart, think it not abso-
> lutely necessary to pass through all the temptations that have beset me
> round about on every side. It is [true] in the spiritual as in the natural
> life—some feel more, others less, but all experience some pangs and
> travails of soul . . . . If God deals with you in a more gentle way, yet so as
> that a thorough work of conversion is effected in your heart, you ought
> to be exceeding thankful. Or if he should lead you through a longer
> wilderness than I have passed through, you need not complain. The
> more you are humbled now, the more you shall be exalted hereafter.
> One taste of Christ's love in your heart will make amends for all.[24]

Now we will turn to Whitefield's own words as he tells the story of his personal conversion experience.

WHITEFIELD'S NEW BIRTH

In our first excerpt of Whitefield's writing, the Grand Itinerant recounts the story of his spiritual struggles and eventual conversion to Christ as described in his autobiographical work *A Short Account of God's Dealings with the Reverend Mr. George Whitefield.* The text, which was written as he sailed to the American colonies in the fall of 1739 for a preaching tour, relates the events of his life from his birth to his ordination as an Anglican clergyman. Already famous in both Great Britain and America for his dramatic and effective preaching at the time of the writing, Whitefield sent the autobiography back to London to be published. By penning an autobiography before his twenty-fifth birthday, Whitefield revealed his strong sense of his own destiny and calling from God as well as his awareness of the media's power to both broadcast and intensify interest in him and his message.

In these excerpts, Whitefield describes his shock at learning that he must be born again to enter God's kingdom, followed by his intense though misguided efforts to attain this new birth by his own strength. His subsequent physical collapse leads him to recognize his need for God to spark spiritual fire in his heart and redeem him, and he cries out for help, finally receiving salvation. I believe you will be captivated by Whitefield's account of how he came to embrace the fire of God's love through new birth in Jesus Christ.

AUTOBIOGRAPHY

A Short Account of God's Dealings with the Reverend Mr. George Whitefield[25]

Discovering the New Birth

For above a twelvemonth, my soul longed to be acquainted with some of [the Methodists], and I was strongly pressed to follow their good example when I saw them go through a ridiculing crowd to receive the holy Eucharist at St. Mary's Church. At length, God was pleased to open a door. . . .

I thankfully embraced the opportunity [to meet Charles Wesley], and, blessed be God, it was one of the most profitable visits I ever made in my life. My soul at that time was thirsty for some spiritual friends to lift up my hands when they hung down and to strengthen my feeble knees.[26] He soon discovered it, and, like a wise winner of souls, made all his discourses tend that way. And when he had put into my hands Professor Franke's *Treatise Against the Fear of Man* and a book entitled *The Country Parson's Advice to his Parishioners* (the last of which was wonderfully blessed to my soul), I took my leave.[27]

In a short time he let me have another book entitled *The Life of God in the Soul of Man*,[28] and though I had fasted, watched, and prayed, and received the sacrament[29] so long, yet I never knew what true religion was till God sent me that excellent treatise by the hands of my never to be forgotten friend. At my first reading it, I wondered what the author meant by saying, "That some falsely placed religion in going to church, doing hurt to no one, being constant in the duties of the [prayer] closet, and now and then reaching out their hands to give alms to their poor neighbors." "Alas!" thought I, "if this be not religion, what is?" God soon showed me. For in reading a few lines further that "true religion was a union of the soul with God and Christ formed within us," a ray of divine light was instantaneously darted in upon my soul, and from that moment, but not till then, did I know that I must be a new creature. . . .

I now began, like [the Methodists], to live by rule and to pick up the very fragments of my time that not a moment of it might be lost. Whether I ate or drank, or whatsoever I did, I endeavored to do all to the glory of God.[30] Like them, having no weekly sacrament (although the rubric required it) at our own college, I received every Sunday at Christ Church. I joined with them in keeping the stations by fasting Wednesdays and Fridays and left no means unused which I thought would lead me nearer to Jesus Christ.

Regular retirement [to study and pray], morning and evening, at first I found some difficulty in submitting to, but it soon grew profitable and delightful. As I grew ripe for such exercises, I was from time to time engaged to visit the sick and the prisoners and to read to poor people, till I made it a custom, as most of us did, to spend an hour every day in doing acts of charity. . . .

Striving for Salvation

From my first awakenings to the divine life, I felt a particular hungering and thirsting after the humility of Jesus Christ. Night and day, I prayed to be a partaker of that grace, imagining that the habit of humility would be instantaneously infused into my soul. But as Gideon taught the men of Succoth with thorns,[31] so God (if I am yet in any measure blessed with true poverty of spirit) taught it me by the exercise of strong temptations.

I observed before how I used to be favored with [a sense of] devotion; those comforts were soon withdrawn and a horrible fearfulness and dread permitted to overwhelm my soul. One morning in particular, rising from my bed, I felt an unusual impression and weight upon my breast, attended with inward darkness. I applied to my friend Mr. Charles Wesley; he advised me to keep upon my watch and referred me to a chapter in Kempis.[32]

In a short time, I perceived this load gradually increase till it almost weighed me down and fully convinced me that Satan had as real a possession of, and power given over, my body as he had once over Job's.[33] All power of meditating or even thinking was taken from me. My memory quite failed me. My whole soul was barren and dry, and I could fancy myself to be like nothing so much as a man locked up in iron armor. . . . God only knows how many nights I have lain upon my bed, groaning under the weight I felt and bidding Satan depart from me in the name of Jesus. . . .

While my inward man was thus exercised, my outward man was not unemployed. I soon found what a slave I had been to my sensual appetite and now resolved to get the mastery over it by the help of Jesus Christ. Accordingly, by degrees I began to leave off eating fruits and such like and gave the money I usually spent in that way to the poor. Afterward, I always chose the worst sort of food, though my place furnished me with variety. I fasted twice a week. My apparel was [humble]. I thought it unbecoming a penitent to have his hair powdered. I wore woolen gloves, a patched gown, and dirty shoes, and though I was then convinced that the kingdom of God did not consist in meats and drinks, yet I resolutely persisted in these voluntary acts of self-denial because I found them great promoters of the spiritual life. For many months, I went on in this state, faint, yet pursuing, and travelling along in the dark, in hope that the Star[34] I had (before once) seen would hereafter appear again. . . .

Henceforward, [Satan] transformed himself into an angel of light[35] and worked so artfully that I imagined the good and not the evil Spirit suggested to me everything that I did. [Satan's] main drift was . . . when the Holy Spirit put into my heart good thoughts or convictions, he always drove them to extremes. For instance, having, out of pride, put down in my diary what I gave away, Satan tempted me to lay my diary quite aside. When Castaniza[36] advised to talk but little, Satan said I must not talk at all. So that I, who used to be the most forward in exhorting my companions, have sat whole nights almost without speaking at all. Again, when Castaniza advised to endeavor after a silent recollection and waiting upon God, Satan told me I must leave off all forms [of prayer] and not use my voice in prayer at all. The time would fail me to recount all the instances of this kind in which he had deceived me. . . .

Receiving the Spark of God's Love

Soon after this, the holy season of Lent came on, which our friends kept very strictly, eating no flesh during the six weeks, except on Saturdays and Sundays.[37] I abstained frequently on Saturdays also and ate nothing on the other days (except on Sunday), but sage tea without sugar and coarse bread. I constantly walked out in the cold mornings till part of one of my hands was quite black [from frostbite]. This, with my continued abstinence [from food] and inward conflicts, at length so emaciated my body that at Passion week, finding I could scarce creep up stairs, I was obliged to inform my kind tutor of my condition, who immediately sent for a physician to me. . . .[38] This fit of sickness continued upon me for seven weeks. . . .

About the end of the seven weeks and after I had been groaning under an unspeakable pressure both of body and mind for above a twelvemonth, God was pleased to set me free in the following manner. One day, perceiving an uncommon drought and a disagreeable clamminess in my mouth, and using things to allay my thirst, but in vain, it was suggested to me that when Jesus Christ cried out, "I thirst," his sufferings were near at an end.[39] Upon which, I cast myself down on the bed, crying out, "I thirst! I thirst!" Soon after this, I found and felt in myself that I was delivered from the burden that had so heavily oppressed me! The spirit of mourning was taken from me, and I knew what it was truly to rejoice in God my Savior and for some time could not avoid singing psalms wherever I was, but my joy gradually became more settled and, blessed be God, has abode and increased in my soul (having a few casual intermissions) ever since!

Thus were the days of my mourning ended. After a long night of desertion and temptation, the Star, which I had seen at the distance before, began to appear again, and the Day-star arose in my heart. Now did the Spirit of God take possession of my soul, and, as I humbly hope, seal me unto the day of redemption.[40]

CHAPTER II

Embracing Purpose

Once the spark of God's love is ignited in our heart, our life has purpose. We are now part of God's grand narrative, his overarching plan for the world he created. Our time on earth has eternal significance and value as we step into the role God uniquely created us to play in his everlasting kingdom.

Throughout the Bible, we see God reveal and enact a sense of purpose in the lives of his followers. As a young man, Joseph received dreams from God that he would one day be a leader in his family and region. Despite his brothers' attempts to derail his life by selling him into slavery, God sustained Joseph and elevated him to a position of authority in Egypt so he could later save his family from a famine. Esther, although she was an exile in the kingdom of Persia, received a powerful word from her uncle Mordecai that prompted her to step forward and risk her life to convince King Ahasuerus to protect her people from violence planned against them. Paul received his commission to preach the gospel to the Gentiles from both the Lord Jesus directly and the prophet Ananias, launching him into one of the greatest missionary careers in the New Testament.[1]

But sometimes we don't feel like we have any eternal purpose or significance. Those are people in the Bible, we say to ourselves, but do *I* actually have a divine purpose? Am *I* really crucial to God's kingdom? Yes, you are. We are *all* absolutely essential and irreplaceable in the kingdom of God since every member of the body of Christ has a role to play and a purpose to fulfill. The apostle Paul's words to the Corinthian believers are true for us as well: "But in fact God has placed the parts in the body, every one of them, just as he wanted them to be. . . . Now you are the body of Christ, and each one of you is a part of it."[2] According to Paul, we are all "called according to [God's] purpose" for we are "created in Christ Jesus to do good works, which God prepared in advance for us to do."[3] No one is unimportant or expendable.

Embracing God's purpose for our life stokes our spiritual passion because purpose inspires and motivates us to push past obstacles and delays, focuses and directs us to follow God's path, and produces striking fruitfulness and joy in our lives and ministries. A sense of purpose is like the jet engine that propels a plane—it inspires us, strengthens us, sustains us, and gives us confidence. George Whitefield knew what it felt like to embrace God's purpose for his life. On the day he was ordained to vocational ministry, he testified, "Let come what will, life or death, depth or height, I shall henceforward live like one who this day, in the presence of men and angels, took the holy sacrament upon the profession of being inwardly moved by the Holy Ghost to take upon me that ministration in the church."[4] Whitefield's sense of his divine purpose propelled him forward into a lifetime of accomplishing the "good works" God had prepared for him to do.

UNDERSTANDING PURPOSE

As Jesus identified in the two greatest commandments,[5] God's purpose for all Christians is in one sense identical and general in that we are all called first and foremost to be in a love relationship with God himself and to share God's love with others by caring for them as we would for ourselves. This is the overall purpose for each follower of Jesus Christ.

Beyond this shared overall purpose, God has unique, personalized purposes for each of us that will unfold throughout our lives. These individual purposes create an infrastructure of sorts into which fit the specific "good works" that God planned for us to do that Paul mentions in Ephesians 2:10. The means to accomplish these "good works" is the potent mix of spiritual gifts, abilities, resources, desires, life circumstances, and personality traits that make up each of us. Thus, our unique, individual purposes are achieved when we use who God created us to be to accomplish the "good works" he has planned for our lives.

A few examples may illustrate how our unique purposes, "good works," and who God made us to be work together. King David exhibited the unique purposes of leadership, worship, and shepherding throughout his life. Into that infrastructure fit his specific "good works," such as defeating the giant Goliath and ruling as king of Israel (leadership), writing many of the psalms (worship), and caring for the men who followed him during his exile as well as nurturing the spiritual health of the people of Israel (shepherding). David's personal mix of courage and musical skills (abilities and spiritual gifts), his boyhood experiences protecting his flock as a shepherd (life circumstances), his hunger for knowing God intimately (desire), and his heritage as an Israelite (resources) all enabled David to accomplish the "good works" within his unique purposes of leadership, worship, and shepherding.

One of my unique purposes from God is teaching. At different times in my life, I've pursued the "good works" of training my children as I raised them, instructing fellow Christians in the church, and teaching students at a university. My spiritual gift of teaching, professional training as an educator, extroverted personality, and desire to be a positive influence in people's lives combine to help me accomplish these "good works" within my purpose of teaching. Similarly, caring for and nurturing others is one of my friend Samantha's unique purposes from God. Over the years, she has engaged in God's "good works" for her by devoting herself full-time to raising her children, hosting countless events for family and friends at her beautiful home, and working within the county court system to advocate for foster children. Samantha's ability to design welcoming physical spaces, love of cooking and conversation, and spiritual gift of counseling make her successful in accomplishing her "good works" within her unique purpose of caring for others.

Whitefield's writings shortly after his conversion reveal his unique purposes that were later worked out in the "good works" he accomplished through his personal mix of gifts and skills, training, desires and personality, life experiences, and resources. Examining this time in his life helps us understand more of the process we can follow to identify God's unique purposes for ourselves. We pick up Whitefield's story during those foundational and often turbulent early adult years as he finishes his studies at Oxford, prepares for his ordination as an Anglican minister, and begins his professional ministry.

WHITEFIELD PURSUES PURPOSE

After his lengthy illness and dramatic conversion, Whitefield left school and traveled to his hometown of Gloucester, England, to recuperate. Between living in Gloucester and visiting his relatives in nearby Bristol, Whitefield was away from school for about nine months. He used the time to rest, pray, read spiritual books, plan sermons, fellowship with friends, and consider the appropriate timing for his ordination. It was during this period that two of Whitefield's individual life purposes emerged.

The first of God's unique purposes for Whitefield was the message he would believe resolutely, preach and defend zealously, and steward faithfully throughout his lifetime: the necessity of being born again spiritually through faith in Jesus Christ. Whitefield's first biographer, his Scottish friend and colleague the Rev. John Gillies (1712–1796), notes that there is a "uniformity of sentiment" found in all of Whitefield's writings and sermons.[6] In an early letter, Whitefield expounds:

> But what shall I write to you about? Why, of our common salvation, of
> that one thing needful, of that new birth in Christ Jesus, that ineffable
> change which must pass upon our hearts before we can see God and of
> which you have heard me discourse so often. Let this, my dear friends,
> be the end of all your actions.[7]

Whitefield would often refer to the "one thing needful" in his preaching and writing.

The necessity of the new birth was not a view held by all ministers in Whitefield's day. In fact, while many Christians outside the Church of England, usually called Dissenters or Nonconformists, preached the doctrine of the new birth, most Anglican ministers of the official Church of England believed infant baptism produced regeneration by the Holy Spirit. Whitefield and John Wesley, both Anglican clergymen themselves, met with Church of England leaders in late January 1739 to attempt to convince their colleagues of the necessity of being born again, but they were unsuccessful.[8] Perhaps, then, it is not surprising that in his first printed sermon, which asserts the necessity of the new birth, Whitefield calls out his brethren in ministry and wishes they "would more frequently entertain their people with discourses of this nature."[9]

The "good works" Whitefield accomplished within the infrastructure of his purpose of stewarding the message of the new birth were the many sermons he preached internationally, the numerous writings he published, and the countless personal conversations he records on the topic. Typical is an entry in his first published journal for January 15, 1737, while he was on board the *Whitaker,* sailing on his first journey to the American colonies. He notes that while preaching a sermon on the Holy Spirit, he "took occasion to show the nature and necessity of the new birth, a subject on which I delight to dwell."[10]

At the same time Whitefield became focused on the doctrine of the new birth, he received his second personalized purpose from God: a love for and loyalty to all sincere Christians regardless of denominational preference. Again, Whitefield was unique in this emphasis as most Christians of the day maintained an effectual separation from those with differing theological or ecclesiastical viewpoints. During his recuperation period with family, Whitefield records in his autobiography the impact of his decision to accept all believers: "I bless God the partition wall of bigotry and sect-religion was soon broken down in my heart, for as soon as the love of God was shed abroad in my soul, I loved all of whatever denomination that loved the Lord Jesus in sincerity of heart."[11] Several years later, Whitefield expresses to a friend his desire for unity among Christians by writing, "Oh that my heart glowed with the love of God and men! I would breathe nothing but love. I would love all that love the Lord Jesus, of whatsoever denomination. May the Lord heal our divisions."[12]

The "good works" within this purpose of unbiased love for all Christians were often seen in Whitefield's overseas ministry. For example, in America, Whitefield shocked Dissenters with his eager acceptance of them as he effectively connected all revivalist preachers throughout the colonies, regardless of denominational affiliation. He wrote to some divinity students he had preached to in Northampton, Massachusetts, "Though you are not of the Church of England, yet if you are persuaded in your own minds of the truth of the way wherein you now walk, I leave it. However, whether Conformists or Nonconformists, our main concern should be to be assured that we are called and taught of God."[13]

Sadly, Whitefield sometimes suffered for his commitment to ecumenicalism. In Scotland, members of the Dissenting Associate Presbytery vehemently attacked Whitefield in public and print because he preached in all Scottish churches, even non-Dissenting Church of Scotland parishes. The Associate Presbytery officially broke with Whitefield over the issue, but Whitefield was not deterred from his purpose of loving and working with all followers of Christ. He is famously remembered for assuring his Scottish critics, "If the Pope himself would lend me his pulpit, I would gladly proclaim the righteousness of Jesus Christ therein."[14]

Whitefield received his two purposes of championing the doctrine of being born again spiritually and accepting all Christians regardless of denomination as he recovered from his conversion among friends and family. This time was precious to him and changed him significantly; as he recalls, "My understanding was enlightened, my will broken, and my affections more and more enlivened with a zeal for Christ."[15] But the question of when he should seek ordination and begin his professional ministry was also on Whitefield's mind at this time. As he sought the Lord for the timing for his entrance into ministry, he received his third individual divine purpose.

BECOMING THE GRAND ITINERANT

While still in Gloucester, Whitefield received a dream from God that he met the Anglican bishop of Gloucester, and the bishop gave him some gold coins. Not long after this dream, the bishop summoned Whitefield to his residence and promised Whitefield he would ordain him whenever he was ready. This surprised Whitefield since he was technically under the age of twenty-three, the minimum age of men the bishop typically was willing to ordain. The bishop then gave Whitefield some money to buy a book, which reminded Whitefield of his dream and his "heart was filled with a sense of God's love."[16]

Whitefield sought guidance about ordination from God and Christian friends very seriously after that meeting, experiencing "agony in prayer when under convictions of my insufficiency for so great a work," but ultimately felt led by God to receive ordination to the ministry in the summer of 1736 at the age of twenty-two.[17] After ordination, Whitefield returned to Oxford, completed his bachelor's degree several weeks later, and remained at Oxford in his first paid ministry position. Although Methodism had declined at Oxford since Whitefield and John and Charles Wesley had left, Whitefield believed God had called him to minister there for a time. He recalls in one of his auto-biographical writings, "The Lord Jesus supported my soul and made me easy by giving me a strong conviction that I was where he would have me to be."[18]

It was at Oxford that Whitefield began to progress toward finding his third purpose from God, and that purpose would establish the direction of his pro-fessional ministry. His friends John and Charles Wesley had traveled to the American colony of Georgia in October 1735 to minister and preach, and they wrote letters to Whitefield of the ministry opportunities in the new colony. Whitefield notes that their letters "fired my soul . . . For I felt at times such a strong attraction in my soul towards Georgia that I thought it almost irresist-ible."[19] Whitefield prayed and sought the counsel of friends, ultimately decid-ing to travel to the colony himself to minister. To do so, he had to reject what he called a "very profitable" ministry position in London, but he had "resolved" to minister in Georgia.[20]

More than one year later in February 1738, Whitefield embarked for Georgia to minister. During his two-month stay in the colony, Whitefield preached, met both European settlers and Native Americans, connected with other Anglican ministers and trustees of the colony, and began to consider founding an or-phanage in Georgia. On his return voyage home, Whitefield wrote joyfully to a friend in England, "God has done for me more abundantly than I could dare ask or think. The seed of the glorious gospel has taken root in the American ground and, I hope, will grow up into a great tree."[21]

The ministry trip to Georgia changed Whitefield's life and gave him his third purpose—traveling and preaching throughout the world instead of being settled permanently in one Church of England parish. Refusing the many positions offered to him to minister at one settled church location in England, Whitefield chose to be officially appointed minister to the colony of Georgia in January 1739.[22] This position allowed him to preach itinerantly and raise money for the orphanage Bethesda that he would establish in Savanah, Georgia. Like his other two purposes, rejecting a settled position in one church location to work as an itinerant preacher was a unique approach to ministry in his time. By pursuing this purpose, Whitefield enjoyed constant access to new audiences for his gospel message and countless opportunities to connect with Christian brothers and sisters in many countries. But he was also exposed to the challenges and dangers of both eighteenth-century travel and a lack of a consistent, supportive, in-person community. He became an incessant letter-writer in order to stay connected to friends and family. Despite the difficulties of itinerant preaching, Whitefield embraced this third purpose from God with alacrity and excitement. As he wrote to a friend just two years after his trip to Georgia, "The whole world is now my parish. Wherever my Master calls me, I am ready to go and preach his everlasting gospel."[23]

Obviously, Whitefield's numerous international preaching tours were the "good works" that he accomplished within his purpose of working as a traveling preacher. But this third purpose also forced Whitefield to innovate. In most places in which he preached, the crowds were so large that the church buildings could not contain them, and many would be turned away. Thus, Whitefield made the radical decision to preach outdoors to whomever would listen. Even a clergyman as progressive as John Wesley took some convincing of the appropriateness of this tactic.[24] Just three years after his ordination, Whitefield wrote to a friend of his first field preaching experience: "Today, my Master by his providence and Spirit compelled me to preach in the churchyard at Islington. Tomorrow, I am to repeat that mad trick, and on Sunday to go out into Moorfields. The word of the Lord runs and is glorified."[25] Whitefield would continue the practice of outdoor preaching when necessary throughout his entire public ministry.

To complete the many "good works" God prepared for him to do within his three unique purposes of sharing the message of the new birth, uniting and honoring all Christians regardless of denominational affiliation, and preaching itinerantly throughout the English-speaking West, Whitefield relied on his unique resources, personality traits and passions, training, and life experiences. His legendary public speaking abilities, training as a minister, spiritual gift of preaching, desire to spread the gospel, resources of those united to him in ministry and life, and high emotional intelligence enabled him to fulfill his purposes.

Embracing God's purposes for his life fueled Whitefield's spiritual passion. As he embarked on his first ministry trip to Georgia in 1738, he revealed how confident he had grown in his sense of purpose in a letter to his London friend and publisher James Hutton (1715–1795): "You know, sir, what a design I am going upon and what a [young man] I am for so great a work, but I stand forth as David against Goliath in the name of the Lord of Hosts, and I doubt not but he that has and does will still deliver unto the end. God give me a deep humility, a well-guided zeal, a burning love, and a single eye, and then let men or devils do their worst."[26] Whitefield stepped into his young adult years fueled by the spiritual zeal that accompanies a life of purpose.

Whitefield's sense of purpose clearly fired his passion for God and his ministry, but how exactly did he recognize and embrace his unique purposes from God? What was his process of discovery? A closer look at this pivotal time in Whitefield's life reveals for us three helpful steps to becoming people of purpose and passion.

Time Alone with God

Whitefield spent his years of recuperation, ordination preparation, and early ministry engaged in many activities, but three were important for his growth in understanding his unique purposes in God. First, Whitefield devoted significant time to being alone with God, praying, meditating, and reading the Bible and Christian books. This is how he describes the moments he shared with Jesus:

Oh, what sweet communion had I daily vouchsafed with God in prayer after my coming again to Gloucester! How often have I been carried out beyond myself when sweetly meditating in the fields! How assuredly have I felt that Christ dwelt in me and I in him, and how did I daily walk in the comforts of the Holy Ghost and was edified and refreshed in the multitude of peace![27]

Spending quality time alone with God is key to helping us understand and embrace his purposes for us. First, it allows God space to share his heart with us. We discover what is important to him, how he sees us, and what is on his agenda for us and our life. Second, as we connect with the God of all passion, our own heart is moved with passion for him and who he is. Our affections are stirred and our hope is strengthened. Third, we gain concrete direction on choices we can make to move ahead with the plans he has for us, allowing him to guide and lead us. Finding time to be alone with God is never easy, but it is necessary for a life of spiritual passion.

The time we spend alone with God doesn't always have to be a "mountaintop" experience to be valuable. Every moment alone with God matters. Whitefield himself admits, "Not that I was always upon the mount; sometimes a cloud would overshadow me, but the Sun of Righteousness quickly arose and dispelled it, and I knew it was Jesus Christ that revealed himself to my soul."[28] Whitefield's times alone with God opened his heart to discover and embrace God's purposes for his life.

WHOLEHEARTED COMMITMENT

The second step Whitefield took to discover his divine purposes was to intentionally commit himself wholeheartedly to God. While we will never commit ourselves perfectly to anything this side of heaven, including God, we should value and embrace those times when we feel led by the Holy Spirit to explicitly testify to God that we trust him with our entire life and future. Feeling motivated to overtly pledge yourself and your years to God is not a sign that you have backslidden or lost your spiritual fervor, but instead is an indication that the Holy Spirit is stirring your heart to move you to a deeper, more intimate, more dedicated place in your relationship with Jesus. Such times can be virtual crossroads in your life when you profess your love and affection to the One who fully committed himself to you by shedding his blood for your redemption. Times of trusting God wholeheartedly with your future are precious moments that move God's emotions, shape your heart, and encourage you and other believers to rejoice. Most importantly, these times enflame your spiritual passion by moving you to a new place in your relationship with your Beloved.

For Whitefield, dedicating himself wholeheartedly to God involved three concrete actions. First, after he converted, Whitefield was careful to leave behind areas of sin that he had struggled with before his conversion, such as the desire to attend stage plays. Although as modern Christians we usually do not view attending the theater as sinful, during the eighteenth century, Christians often abstained from that form of entertainment, believing it was either an unhelpful use of time or, worse, a source of worldly thinking and values. For Whitefield, since he had acted in plays as a youth, his choice to refrain from attending the theater was significant for him. He even went so far as to extract passages from a book explaining why Christians should not attend the theater and have the collection published by a local printer. Whitefield considered this act to be an opportunity for him to "give a public testimony of my repentance as to seeing and acting plays."[29]

Whitefield's second concrete action to commit himself wholeheartedly to God was to devote time and energy to acts of service and ministry. Whitefield visited and encouraged prisoners in every town he resided in. Although it was a simple and lowly form of ministry, for Whitefield, it was another way for him to show his love to Jesus. As he wrote to a friend just a few years after his ordination, "Not that I expect in the least to be justified by any or all the works I either can or shall do. No, the Lord Christ is my righteousness, my whole and perfect righteousness, but then I would show forth my faith. I would declare to the world the sincerity of my love by always abounding in the works of my Lord."[30] He even had a dream about ministering to prisoners when he first arrived in Gloucester that was fulfilled several months later.[31] Whitefield believed these early experiences with ministry, though humble, were important for revealing his commitment to God, preparing him for future ministry, and stirring up his own spiritual passion.[32] As he recalls, "I cannot say any one of the prisoners was effectively [brought to salvation]; however, much evil was prevented, many were convinced, and my own soul was much edified and strengthened in the love of God and man."[33]

While turning from sin and performing acts of service were important for Whitefield as he committed himself completely to Jesus, trusting God with his future was the third concrete step he took. Whitefield made a point of intentionally placing himself and his future years entirely in God's hands, telling God explicitly that he was surrendering everything to him. He recalls times in these early years when he felt so moved in his heart by God's "infinite majesty that I would be constrained to throw myself prostrate on the ground and offer my soul as a blank in his hands to write on it what he pleased."[34] Six months after his ordination, he writes to his friend Charles Wesley, "I trust God will give me strength to throw myself blindfolded into his hands and permit him to do with me whatsoever seems good in his sight."[35]

Whitefield found that his own passion for God intensified during his moments of wholehearted commitment to his Savior. Once during his early ministry, he and a local man stood in a field during a lightning storm. Watching the lightning "run upon the ground and shine from one part of the heaven to the other," Whitefield found himself longing for his own heart to be enflamed with the fiery passion of Jesus:

> I and another ... were in the field praying to, praising of, and exulting
> in our God and longing for that time when Jesus should be revealed
> from heaven in a flame of fire! Oh, that my soul may be in a like frame
> when he shall actually come to call me! For I think I never had been
> happier than that night.[36]

These moments of dedicating himself to Jesus were pivotal for Whitefield in embracing his own unique purposes from God. He spent much of his early ministry sharing with all who came to him "the necessity of renouncing all in affection in order to follow Jesus Christ."[37]

Thus, by committing himself wholeheartedly to Jesus by turning from sin, serving others, and trusting God with his future, Whitefield put himself in the place in which he could discover God's unique purposes for his life. But the Holy Spirit also has a pivotal role to play in this process of discovery.

FAITH IN GOD'S TIMING

The third crucial part of Whitefield's process of discovering his God-given purposes was to be patient, trusting God for his perfect timing. One example of this is Whitefield's start as a preacher, the role that would come to define him internationally. During the two weeks prior to his ordination, he sought the Lord in order to prepare himself for the ordination service and to compose a sermon to preach in the afternoon of his ordination day, a common practice at the time. Surprisingly, he found himself unable to compose a sermon. When seeking wisdom on the matter from veteran members of the clergy, Whitefield was criticized by one for depending too heavily on the Holy Spirit, but encouraged by another to keep waiting on God. Turning to Ezekiel 3:26–27, Whitefield read God's words to the prophet Ezekiel: "You will be silent … but when I speak to you, I will open your mouth." Whitefield received this as confirmation to wait, spending the remainder of his preparation time reading the stories of the apostles and prophets and asking God to assist him in following in their footsteps.[38]

Since he had no prepared sermon, Whitefield did not preach during the afternoon of his ordination. Instead, he read prayers to prisoners, noting he was "willing to let the first act of my ministerial office be an act of charity." The next morning, as he spent time in prayer, he felt God release him to compose sermons and preach:

These words, "Speak out, Paul," came with great power to my soul. Immediately, my heart was enlarged. God spoke to me by his Spirit, and I was no longer [silent]. I finished a sermon I had in hand some time before, I began another, and preached the Sunday following to a very crowded audience with as much freedom as though I had been a preacher for some years.[39]

Waiting for God's timing to commence preaching was significant for Whitefield. Preaching would become the central feature of his ministry, the clearest display of his spiritual gifting, and the foundation of his personal legacy. Learning to follow God's timetable early in his career for the use of such an important spiritual gift was a key component for Whitefield as he discovered his unique purposes, and it is an essential step for us as well as we seek our own purposes from God. Whitefield ends his description of his time recuperating, preparing for ordination, and beginning his ministry succinctly: "Thus did God, by a variety of unforeseen acts of providence and grace, train me up for and at length introduce me into the service of his church."[40]

You may already know your individual purposes from God, or you may still be searching for some or all of them. Regardless, the process Whitefield followed to discover his purpose can be applied by all of us. Spending time alone with God is a foundational spiritual practice for every Christian; you can begin tomorrow learning to spend time with Jesus through print, digital, or in-person

resources on the topic. Making a wholehearted commitment to God happens
as you repent and turn from sin, perhaps by finding an accountability group;
serve others, maybe by joining a ministry at your church or local charity or-
ganization; and trust God with your future, possibly by meditating on and declaring his biblical promises. Lastly, accepting God's timing requires humility,
patience, and faith, but as you grow to value his game plan for your life, you
will more easily understand God's unique purposes for you. Whitefield was
young in years as a Christian when he sought the Lord to give him purpose and
increase his spiritual passion, so we can take encouragement from his example
and press in to learn what God has in store for each of us.

STARTING STRONG

Whitefield was, before everything else, a preacher *par excellence*, so it is
only fitting that in a chapter examining his God-given purposes, we encounter
an excerpt from his first published sermon, *The Nature and Necessity of our
New Birth in Christ Jesus, in Order to Salvation.* Printed in 1737, the sermon was
extremely popular, hitting its third edition by the end of the year. The publisher
even offered a discount for bulk orders for "those who give them away."[41]

The complete text opens with a preface in which Whitefield offers his hope
that if the sermon "be thereby made instrumental towards the convicting any one
sinner or confirming any one saint, I shall not be solicitous about the censures
that may be passed, either on the simplicity of the style or on the youth of the
author."[42] Whitefield then addresses four sub-topics: 1) what it means to be "in
Christ," 2) what it means to be a "new creature," 3) the reasons "we must be new
creatures [before] we can be in Christ," and 4) how the doctrine of the new birth
applies to listeners who are not true Christians—specifically, those who have
only an outward spirituality, those who believe they are morally good enough
on their own, and those who have only a partial obedience and commitment to
Christ.[43] Finally, Whitefield ends with a powerful encouragement to pursue true
salvation wholeheartedly despite the effort it requires and the reproach of others
because those who come to Christ "have a real title to all the glorious promises of
the gospel and are infallibly certain of being as happy, both here and hereafter,
as an all-wise, all-gracious, all-powerful God can make them."[44]

Interestingly, this first published sermon of Whitefield's reveals his three unique, God-given purposes: sharing the doctrine of the new birth, embracing and loving all believers regardless of denomination, and carrying his ministry throughout the world. First, the subject of the sermon is spiritual rebirth in Jesus by faith, the topic that would come to define his ministry. Second, the sermon garnered the attention of both Dissenters and Anglicans; in fact, Whitefield notes in his autobiography that it "sold well to persons of all denominations."[45] Third, Whitefield preached the sermon in several cities in England, presaging his future lifelong itinerant preaching ministry. In fact, Whitefield recalls that the sermon "under God began the awakening at London, Bristol, Gloucester, and Gloucestershire"—all the locations in which it was preached.[46] Whitefield's individualized purposes thus were already producing good works in his early years of ordained ministry, stoking the fire of spiritual passion in the young evangelist.

The Nature and Necessity of our New Birth in Christ Jesus also caused its share of controversy among Church of England ministers, thanks to a preface in which Whitefield calls out his fellow Anglican clergymen for allowing their congregations to "rest satisfied with the shell and shadow of religion" instead of exhorting them to pursue the "nature and necessity of that inward holiness and vital purity of heart."[47] But that is a story for another chapter. For now, I hope you enjoy Whitefield's passionate call to new birth in Jesus in this, an excerpt from his first published sermon.

SERMON

The Nature and Necessity of our New Birth in Christ Jesus, in Order to Salvation[48]

Preface

The importunity of friends, the aspersions of enemies, the great scarcity of sermons on this subject among the divines of our own church, and not any overweening conceit, I trust, of the worth of the performance, were, amongst diverse others, the reasons that induced me to permit the publication of this very plain discourse.

What reception it may meet with from the public it behooves me, for my own sake, to be very little concerned about. But I humbly hope that as God was pleased to give it surprising success when delivered from the pulpit, so the same gracious Being will continue to cooperate with it from the press. And then, if it be thereby made instrumental towards the convicting any one sinner or confirming any one saint, I shall not be solicitous about the censures that may be passed, either on the simplicity of the style or on the youth of the author.

I hope it will be permitted me to add my hearty wishes that my reverend brethren, the ministers of the Church of England (if such a one as I may be worthy to call them brethren), would more frequently entertain their people with discourses of this nature than they commonly do. And that they would not, out of a servile fear of displeasing some particular persons, fail to declare the whole will of God to their respective congregations, nor [allow] their people to rest satisfied with the shell and shadow of religion, without acquainting them with the nature and necessity of that inward

holiness and vital purity of heart which their profession obliges them to
aspire after, and without which no man living can comfortably see the Lord.
[George Whitefield]

2 Corinthians 5:17
If any man be in Christ, he is a new creature.

Introduction

The doctrine of our regeneration, or new birth in Christ Jesus, though
one of the most fundamental doctrines of our holy religion [and] though so
plainly and often pressed on us in sacred Writ, that he that runs may read,[49]
nay, though it is the very hinge on which the salvation of each of us turns
and a point too in which all sincere Christians of whatever denomination
agree, yet is so seldom considered and so little [experientially] understood
by the generality of [Christians], that were we to judge of the truth of it by
the experience of most who call themselves Christians, we should be apt to
imagine they had not so much as heard[50] whether there be any such thing
as regeneration or no.

It is true, men, for the most part, are orthodox in the common articles
of their creed: they believe there is but one God and one Mediator between
God and man, even the Man Christ Jesus,[51] and that there is no other name
given under heaven whereby they can be saved besides his.[52] But then tell
them they must be regenerate, they must be born again, they must be renewed in the very spirit, i.e., in the inmost faculties of their minds, [before]
they can truly call Christ Lord, Lord or have any share in the merits of his
precious blood, and they are ready to cry out with Nicodemus, "How can
these things be?"[53] Or with the Athenians, on another occasion, "What will
this babbler say? He seems to be a setter-forth of strange doctrines," because we preach unto them Christ and the new birth.[54]

That I may therefore contribute my mite towards curing the fatal mistake of such persons who would thus put asunder what God has insepa-
rably joined together and vainly expect to be justified by Christ (i.e., have
their sins forgiven) unless they are also sanctified (i.e., have their natures

changed and made holy), I shall beg leave to enlarge on the words of the text in the following manner.

First, I shall endeavor to explain what is meant by being in Christ: "If any man be in Christ."

Secondly, what we are to understand by being a new creature: "If any man be in Christ," says the apostle, "he is a new creature."

Thirdly, I shall produce some arguments to prove why we must be new creatures [before] we can be in Christ.

Fourthly and lastly, I shall draw some inferences from what will have been delivered and then conclude with a word or two of exhortation from the whole.

The Meaning of Being In Christ

And first, then, I am to endeavor to explain what is meant by this expression in the text, if any man be in Christ.

Now a person may be said to be in Christ two ways. First, only by an outward possession, and in this sense, everyone that is called a Christian or baptized into Christ's church may be said to be in Christ. But that this is not the sole meaning of the apostle's phrase now before us is evident because then everyone that names the name of Christ[55] or is baptized into his visible church would be a new creature. Which is notoriously false, it being too plain beyond all contradiction that comparatively but few of those that are born of water are born of the Spirit likewise,[56] or, to use another scriptural way of speaking, many are baptized with water which were never, effectually at least, baptized with the Holy Ghost.[57]

To be in Christ, therefore, in the full import of the word, must certainly mean something more than a bare outward profession or being called after his name. For as this same apostle tells us, "All are not Israelites that are of Israel,"[58] i.e., when applied to Christianity, all are not real Christians that are nominally such. Nay, that is so far from being the case that our blessed Lord himself informs us that many that have prophesied or preached in his name and in his name cast out devils and done many wonderful works shall, notwithstanding, be dismissed at the last day with a "depart from me, I know you not, workers of iniquity."[59]

It remains, therefore, that this expression if any man be in Christ must be understood in a second and closer signification, namely, to be in him so as to partake of the benefits of his sufferings.[60] To be in him not only by an outward profession, but by an inward change and purity of heart and co-habitation of his Holy Spirit. To be in him so as to be mystically united to him by a true and lively faith and thereby to receive spiritual virtue from him as the members of the natural body do from the head or the branches from the vine. To be in him in such a manner as the apostle, speaking of himself, acquaints us he knew a person was—"I knew a man in Christ," says he, i.e., a true Christian—or as he himself desires to be in Christ when he wishes in his epistle to the Philippians that he might be found in him.[61]

This is undoubtedly the full purport of the apostle's expression in the words of the text, so that what he says in his epistle to the Romans about circumcision may very well be applied to the present subject, namely, that he is not a real Christian who is only one outwardly, nor is that true baptism which is only outward in the flesh.[62] But he is a true Christian who is one inwardly, whose baptism is that of the heart, in the Spirit, and not merely in the water, whose praise is not of man, but of God. Or, as he speaks in another place, neither circumcision or uncircumcision avails anything of itself, but a new creature.[63] Which amounts to what he here declares in the verse now under consideration, that if any man be truly and properly in Christ, he is a new creature.

What is a New Creature?

What we are to understand by being a new creature was the next and second general thing to be considered.

And here it is evident at the first view that this expression is not to be so explained as though there was a physical change required to be made in us, i.e., as though we were to be reduced to our primitive nothings and then created and formed again. For supposing we were, as Nicodemus ignorantly imagined, to enter a second time into our mother's womb and be born.[64] Alas, what would it contribute towards rendering us spiritually new creatures since that which was born of flesh would be flesh still; i.e., we should be the same carnal persons as ever, being derived from carnal parents and consequently receiving the seeds of all manner of sin and corruption from them?

No, it only means that we must be so altered as to the qualities and tempers of our minds that we must entirely forget what manner of persons we once were. As it may be said of a piece of gold that was in the ore after it has been cleansed, purified, and polished that it is a new piece of gold. As it may be said of a bright glass that has been covered over with filth, when it is wiped and so become transparent and clear, that it is a new glass. Or as it might be said of Naaman when he recovered from his leprosy and his flesh returned unto him like the flesh of a young child, that he was a new man,[65] so our souls, though still the same as to essence, yet are so purged, purified, and cleansed from their natural dross, filth, and leprosy by the blessed influences of the Holy Spirit that they may properly be said to be made anew.

How this glorious change is wrought in the soul cannot easily be explained. For no one knows the ways of the Spirit save the Spirit of God himself.[66] Not that this ought to be any argument against this doctrine, for as our blessed Lord observed to Nicodemus when he was discoursing on this very subject: "The wind," says he, "blows where it [will], and you hear the sound thereof, but know not whence it comes and whither it goes," and if we are told of natural things and we understand them not, how much less ought we to wonder if we cannot immediately account for the invisible workings of the Holy Spirit?[67]

The truth of the matter is this: the doctrine of our regeneration or new birth in Christ Jesus is dark and hard to be understood by the natural man.[68] But that there is really such a thing and that each of us must be spiritually born again before we can enter into the kingdom of God, or, to keep to the terms made use of in the text, must be new creatures before we can be in Christ, I shall endeavor to show under my [third point].

Why We Must be New Creatures to be In Christ

[My] third general head, in which I was to produce some arguments to prove why we must be new creatures in order to qualify us for being savingly in Christ.

And here one would think it sufficient to affirm that God himself in his holy word has told us so. For, not to mention many texts that might be produced out of the Old Testament to prove this point (and, indeed, by the way, one would wonder how Nicodemus who was a teacher in Israel and who was therefore to instruct the people in the spiritual meaning of the law should be so ignorant of this grand article as we find he really was by his asking our blessed Lord when he was pressing on him this topic, "How can these things be?"[69] Surely he could not forget how often the psalmist had begged of God to make him a new heart and renew a right spirit within him.[70] As, likewise, how frequently the prophets had warned the people to make them new hearts and new minds and so turn unto the Lord their God.).

But not to mention these and such like texts out of the Old Testament, this doctrine is so plainly and often repeated in the New that as I observed before, he that runs may read. For what says the great prophet and instructor of the world himself? Except a man (i.e., everyone that is naturally engendered of the offspring of Adam) be born again of water and the Spirit, he cannot enter into the kingdom of God. And lest we should be apt to slight this assertion and, Nicodemus-like, reject the doctrine because we cannot immediately explain how this thing can be, our blessed Master therefore affirms it, as it were, by an oath. "Verily, verily, I say unto you," or, as it may read, I the Amen, who am truth itself, say unto you, that it is the unalterable appointment of my heavenly Father, "that unless a man be born again, he cannot enter into the kingdom of God. . . ."[71]

But I proceed to a second argument to prove why we must be new creatures in order to be rightly in Christ, and that shall be taken from the purity of God and the present corrupt and polluted state of man.

Now God is described in Holy Scripture (and I speak to those who profess to know the Scripture) as a Spirit, as a Being of such infinite sanctity as to be of purer eyes than to behold iniquity, as to be so transcendently holy that it is said the very heavens are not clean in his sight and the angels themselves he charges with folly.[72] On the other hand, man is described (and every regenerate person will find it true by his own experience) as a creature altogether conceived and born in sin; as having no good thing dwelling in him; as being carnal, sold under sin, nay, as having a mind which is enmity with God, and such like.[73] And since then there is such an infinite disparity, can anyone conceive how such a filthy, corrupted, polluted wretch can dwell with an infinitely pure and holy God before he is changed and rendered, in some measure, like him? Can he that is of purer eyes than to behold iniquity dwell with it? Can he, in whose sight the heavens are not clean, delight to dwell with uncleanness itself? No, we might as well suppose light to have communion with darkness[74] or Christ to have concord with Belial.[75] But I pass on.

A third argument to make good the apostle's assertion in the text, which shall be founded on the consideration of the nature of that happiness God has prepared for those that unfeignedly love him.

To enter indeed on a minute and particular description of heaven would be vain and presumptuous since we are told that eye has not seen, nor ear heard, neither has it entered into the heart of man to conceive the things that are there prepared for the sincere followers of the holy Jesus.[76] However, this we may venture to affirm in the general, that as God is a Spirit, so the happiness he has laid up for his people is spiritual likewise, and, consequently, unless our carnal minds are changed and become spiritualized, we can never be made [suitable] to partake of that inheritance with the saints in light. . . .

Fourth and last argument, I shall offer to prove that we must be new creatures [before] we can be in Christ, namely, because Christ's redemption will not be complete without it.

If we reflect indeed on the first and chief end of our blessed Lord's coming, we shall find it was to save us from our sins, to be a propitiation for our sins, to give his life a ransom for many.[77] But then, if the benefits of our dear

Redeemer's death were to extend no further than barely to procure forgiveness of our sins, we should have as little reason to rejoice in it as a poor condemned criminal that is ready to perish by some fatal disease would have in receiving a pardon from his judge. For Christians would do well to consider that there is not only a legal hindrance to our happiness as we are breakers of God's law, but also a moral impurity in our natures which renders us incapable of enjoying heaven (as has been already proved) till some mighty change has been wrought in us. It is necessary therefore in order to make Christ's redemption complete that we should have a grant of God's Holy Spirit to change our natures and so prepare us for the enjoyment of that happiness our Savior has purchased by his precious blood. . . .

Encouragement to Pursue True Salvation

Proceed we now to the next general thing proposed, namely, to draw some inferences from what has been delivered. . . .

The sum of the matter is this: Christianity includes morality, as grace does reason, but if we are only mere moralists, if we are not inwardly wrought upon and changed by the powerful operations of the Holy Spirit and our moral actions proceed from a principle of a new nature, however we may call ourselves Christian, it is to be feared we shall be found naked at the Great Day [of Judgment] and in the number of those who vainly depend on their own righteousness and not on the righteousness of Jesus Christ, imputed to and inherent in them, as necessary to their eternal salvation. . . .

But would you know, oh vain man, whoever you are, what the Lord your God requires of you?[78] You must be informed that nothing short of a thorough, sound conversion will avail for the salvation of your soul. It is not enough to turn from profaneness to civility, but you must turn from civility to godliness. Not only some, but all things must become new in your soul. It will profit you but little to do many things, if yet some one thing you lack. In short, you must not be only an *almost*, but *altogether* a new creature or in vain you hope for a saving interest in Christ. . . .

But, beloved, I am persuaded better things of you and things that accompany salvation,[79] though we thus speak and humbly hope that you are fully and heartily convinced that nothing but the wedding garment of a new nature can gain admission for you at the marriage feast of the supper of the Lamb,[80] that you are sincerely persuaded that he that has not the Spirit of Christ is none of his, and that unless the Spirit which raised Jesus from the dead dwell in you here, neither will your mortal bodies be quickened by the same Spirit to dwell with him hereafter.

Let me therefore (as was proposed in the last place) earnestly exhort you in the name of our Lord Jesus Christ to act suitable to those convictions and to live as Christians that are commanded in holy writ to put off their former conversation concerning the old man and to put on the new man, which is created after God in righteousness and true holiness.

It must be owned, indeed, that this is a great and difficult work, but, blessed be God, it is not impossible. Many thousands of happy souls have been assisted by a divine power to bring it about, and why should we despair of success? Is God's hand shortened that it cannot save?[81] Was he the God of our fathers, is he not the God of their children also? Yes, doubtless, of their children also. It is a task likewise that will put us to some pain; it will oblige us to part with some lust, to break with some friend, to mortify some beloved passion which may be exceeding dear to us, and perhaps as hard to leave as to cut off a right hand or pluck out a right eye.[82] But what of all this? Will not being made a real living member of Christ, a child of God, and an inheritor of the kingdom of heaven abundantly make amends for all this trouble? Undoubtedly it will.

Lastly, setting about and carrying on this great and necessary work perhaps may, nay, assuredly will, expose us to the ridicule of the unthinking part of mankind who will wonder that we run not into the same excess of riot with themselves. And because we may deny our sinful appetites and are not conformed to this world,[83] being commanded in Scripture to do the one and to have our conversation in heaven in opposition to the other, they may count our lives folly and our end to be without honor.[84] But will not being numbered among the saints and shining as the stars forever and ever be a more than sufficient recompense for all the ridicule, calumny, or reproach we can possibly meet with here?

Indeed, was there no other reward attended to a thorough conversion but that peace of God which is the unavoidable consequence of it, and which, even in this life, passes all understanding,[85] we should have great reason to rejoice.

But when we consider this is the least of those mercies God has prepared for those that are in Christ new creatures, that this is but the beginning of an eternal succession of pleasures, that the day of our deaths, which the unconverted, unrenewed sinner must so much dread, will be, as it were, but the first day of our new births and open to us an everlasting scene of happiness and comfort; in short, if we remember that they who are regenerate and born again have a real title to all the glorious promises of the gospel and are infallibly certain of being as happy, both here and hereafter, as an all-wise, all-gracious, all-powerful God can make them, methinks, everyone that has but the least concern for the salvation of his precious, his immortal soul, having such promises, such a hope, such an eternity of happiness set before him, should never cease watching, praying, and striving till he find a real, inward, saving change wrought in his heart and thereby knows of a truth that he dwells in Christ and Christ in him, that he is a new creature in Christ, that he is therefore a child of God, that he is already an inheritor and will [before] long, if he endure to the end, be an actual possessor of the kingdom of heaven.

GEORGE WHITEFIELD. M.A.

Elisha Gallaudet *Sculp. NYork.1774.*

CHAPTER III

Building a Foundation

Receiving God's spark of perfect love in our hearts at salvation and embracing the purposes he has for us launches us onto the path of authentic spiritual passion. But these two steps are not enough by themselves to sustain fervent pursuit of Jesus through the challenges we will inevitably face: unexpected obstacles, painful heartaches, distracting successes, troubling doubts, and perhaps even outright persecution. Maintaining true zeal for God through both the trials and triumphs of life requires a strong, dependable, enduring foundation upon which to build our spiritual lives.

But what should this spiritual foundation consist of? Should it be made up of religious practices such as worship, service, and fasting? Can it be assembled from the "good works" we accomplish by using our spiritual gifts? Perhaps intense encounters with God will support an abiding passion? Or maybe a coterie of caring, supportive fellow believers can provide a sturdy base for lasting spiritual zeal?

If you're like me, you've already tried to build a robust, reliable foundation upon these elements and found them wanting. Our commitment to the spiritual disciplines inevitably falters, the deeds we do in Christ's name sometimes tilt toward appearing insignificant, spiritual experiences come and go, and even sincere believers fail to live up to our expectations. While all these components of the spiritual life definitely *contribute* to maintaining religious desire, none is sufficient as the *foundation* for a lifetime of love for God and others. We need something much more powerful, more durable, and, quite frankly, more enjoyable to sustain true spiritual passion.

In the summer of 1739, George Whitefield decided to make a second visit to America, this time planning an extensive preaching tour throughout all the colonies. During his eleven-week sea voyage, Whitefield laid a secure foundation that supported a lifetime of unflagging spiritual commitment and ministerial zeal. In this chapter, we will explore the key elements of Whitefield's spiritual foundation.

RECOGNIZING THE NEED

In August 1739, Whitefield boarded the *Elizabeth* for America, just a few months shy of his twenty-fifth birthday, having already experienced three years of public ministry in England. Ordained as the Anglican minister to the colony of Georgia and committed to an itinerant preaching lifestyle, Whitefield had encountered both success and challenges in his early professional years.

The success was substantial. In just three years of professional ministry, 1737–1739, Whitefield became the best-known preacher in England and something of a minor celebrity. People of all ages, denominations, and socio-economic status crammed into churches to hear his sermons. His preaching style was revolutionary. Instead of reading directly from a printed sermon, he spoke extemporaneously. Instead of offering only logical arguments and applications from the Bible, he incorporated analogies, personal stories, and questions for the audience. Instead of a dry, dispassionate delivery, he exhibited passionate emotion, dramatic gestures, and direct pleas for a response. People couldn't get enough.

To get a visual of what Whitefield's packed services looked like, listen to the man himself: "It was wonderful to see how the people hung upon the rails of the organ loft, climbed upon the [roof] of the church, and made the church itself so hot with their breath that the steam would fall from the pillars like drops of rain."[1] Outdoor sermons allowed for more listeners; crowds to hear his field preaching were counted sometimes as upwards of 30,000, estimates that modern acoustical studies have confirmed as possible.[2] Upon hearing Whitefield preach, Methodist leader John Wesley wrote to a mutual friend, "Oh how is God manifested in our brother Whitefield! I have seen none like him!"[3]

Whitefield was a print sensation as well, publishing his sermons, spiritual journals, and letters. His first published journal went through six editions in nine months, and the number of his printed works increased from ten in 1737 to almost ninety in 1739.[4] He also began appearing in the newspapers. Initially, Whitefield resisted the publicity, writing to a friend, "I suppose you have heard of my 'mighty deeds,' falsely so called, by reading the newspapers, for I find some back-friend has published abroad my preaching four times in a day, but I beseech[ed] . . . the printer never to put me into his news upon any such account again, for it is quite contrary to my inclinations and positive orders."[5] Whitefield overcame his hesitancy toward publicity, however, eventually using his close companion William Seward (1711–1740) as a "press agent" to advertise his upcoming sermons and better manage his public persona.[6]

Perhaps not surprisingly, what made Whitefield popular with the people made him worrisome to some of his colleagues in the Church of England, creating early challenges for the young evangelist. His dramatic extemporaneous preaching style, emphasis on the necessity of being spiritually born again, and candid descriptions of his personal spiritual experiences in his published journals were not business as usual for eighteenth-century Anglican clergy, and a few strongly opposed Whitefield and his approach to ministry.

For example, in 1739, just before Whitefield embarked for America, the Bishop of London, Edmund Gibson (1669–1748), published a fifty-five-page pastoral letter warning his parishioners of both complacency in faith on the one hand and unhealthy fanaticism on the other. His example of fanaticism, which was called "enthusiasm" in the eighteenth century, is Whitefield. Using fourteen pages to quote and critique passages from Whitefield's published journals, Gibson criticizes Whitefield for what he believes is unbiblical and radical behavior. Gibson accuses Whitefield of claiming he receives "extraordinary communications" from God, believing he has "a special and immediate mission from God," and inappropriately declaring the effects of his preaching to be "the sole work of a divine power."[7]

Whitefield certainly has a flair for the dramatic in his writing, but for Christian readers today, his statements in his journals that the Holy Spirit was actively working in and through him and his ministry would not seem particularly radical. In the eighteenth century, however, a more reserved and modest faith was expected, especially of ministers, and so Whitefield's bold declarations of God's blessing and power in his life were unique and, for some, inappropriate. Criticism of Whitefield personally, his spiritual practices, and his ministerial methods would continue throughout his lifetime, and we will look specifically at how he handled challenges to his ministry and reputation in a subsequent chapter.

Whitefield recognized the toll both ministerial success and opposition had already taken on him, so when he decided to make a second trip to America, he viewed the upcoming sea voyage as a time to temporarily "retire," to use his word, from public ministry and strengthen his spiritual foundation. One week before he sailed, he writes to a friend, "Pride and selfishness are the tempers of the devil. By the help of my God, I will never rest till my Master gives me power to overcome them. It is difficult, I believe, to go through the fiery trial of popularity and applause untainted. Blessed be God, I am now sweetly retired."[8] A few days later as he boarded the *Elizabeth,* another letter reveals his plan to use the time at sea to seek God: "As I am now retired from a public life, I trust I shall have time to try my heart and search out my spirit."[9] And Whitefield did just that. Less than one week after sailing, he records in his journal that he was "very earnest with God to give me grace to improve my present retirement to his glory, the good of his church, and the edification of my own soul."[10]

Whitefield kept a spiritual journal during his weeks at sea, and his entries for the voyage reveal how he spent the time searching his heart, deepening his intimacy with God, and forging a strong spiritual foundation upon which to erect a life of passionate love and ministry. By examining his journal, we discover first, the foundation he constructed and, second, its key components.

FOUNDED ON RELATIONSHIP

Like all of us, Whitefield had many options upon which to construct his foundation for spiritual passion: his uniquely powerful preaching gifts, his successful and popular ministry, his multitude of friends and admirers, and his respected status as a minister of the Church of England. However, Whitefield chose none of those, instead building a life of spiritual zeal upon a deep, intimate relationship with God.

Upon repenting of our sins and choosing to become a follower of Jesus, every believer receives the Holy Spirit and thus begins a relationship with God. God expects and desires that our friendship with him will grow and deepen over time into true intimacy. In fact, intimacy with us is so important to God that he actively searches for those who also desire and will intentionally pursue closeness with him: "For the eyes of the Lord run to and fro throughout the whole earth, to show himself strong on behalf of those whose heart is loyal to him."[11]

God wants a close relationship with us because he loves us, but he also knows that our friendship with him is the only secure foundation upon which to build both our lives and healthy spiritual passion. He recognizes that the temptations and challenges we face in this life will derail our zeal for him if we do not know him intimately as our lover and friend.[12] Whitefield realized this as well; even a casual glance at his writings for the early years of his ministry reveals that he consistently identified his relationship with God as the center and foundation of his life. As he exhorts Ebenezer Blackwell, a banker and Methodist in London, the month he boarded the *Elizabeth,* "Oh, my dear friend, [following Jesus] is worth being laughed at. It is worth ten thousand worlds.... Let Jesus Christ be the Alpha and Omega, the beginning and the end of all your thoughts, words, and actions."[13]

But what does a close relationship with God look like? What are the important traits of a divine friendship upon which we can erect a life of spiritual fervor? Whitefield's journal identifies for us three important characteristics: cherished, honest, and affectionate.

CHERISHED

When we cherish something, we highly value it. It is special to us, and we intentionally devote resources, attention, and even our physical presence to it. We spend time with those we love, we remove all distractions when we concentrate on a task of great importance, and we give financial assets to the causes that are dear to our hearts. As you look at your own life, what would you say you cherish the most?

As Christians, we know that God cherishes us. Jesus revealed this most clearly by dying on the cross for us, holding nothing back, enduring his "terrible baptism of suffering" for "the joy set before him," which is relationship with us.[14] Old Testament prophet Zephaniah reminds us that God takes "great delight" in his people and will "rejoice over [us] with singing," while the New Testament apostle Paul notes that nothing "in all creation, will be able to separate us from the love of God."[15]

Being cherished by God leads us to respond to him in the same way. As the apostle John declares in 1 John 4:19, "We love because he first loved us." Not surprisingly, God wants to be cherished by us in return. In the Old Testament book Song of Songs, our Bridegroom Jesus praises the bride his church because she has reserved herself only for him: "You are a garden locked up, my sister, my bride; you are a spring enclosed, a sealed fountain."[16] As our Creator and Savior, God desires to be the one we cherish the most in our lives.

Cherishing God is the first characteristic of Whitefield's friendship with the Lord that enabled it to function as a sturdy foundation for spiritual passion. Many letters written by Whitefield during the months leading up to his voyage to America reveal how deeply Whitefield valued his relationship with Jesus. For example, he shares with his close friend Welsh revivalist Howell Harris (1714–1773), "I have tasted that the Lord is gracious, I have felt his power." He confides to John Wesley, "Great comfort and joy in the Holy Ghost does God, of his free grace, give me. I find myself strengthened in the inner man day by day. I feel an intenseness of love and long that all should be partakers of it." The month before he embarked, he writes to a friend, "As for my own soul, God mightily strengthens me in the inward man and gives me often such foretastes of his love that I am almost continually wishing to be dissolved that I may be with Christ."[17]

Whitefield spent the eleven-week passage on board the *Elizabeth* as he did on land: enjoying time alone with Jesus, studying the Bible and other Christian books, praying for himself and his friends, seeking God for direction for his ministry, and searching his heart for unconfessed sin. A typical entry is found for September 15, in which he records, "Gave myself to reading the word of God and to prayer the greatest part of this week."[18] Cherishing God enabled Whitefield to enjoy God's love in his heart throughout the voyage. His last day on board, he rejoices, "Oh, how can I be thankful enough for this blessed voyage! I have been on board just eleven weeks, but they have seemed to me only as so many days. My inner man has been much bettered by it."[19]

Whitefield chose to cherish his relationship with God by devoting time and energy to it, valuing it, and rejoicing in the blessings and love that flowed from it. In what ways can we cherish Jesus more in our own lives? Do we need to adjust our habits, our spending, our use of time, our priorities? Any change in our lives is worth it to show God how much we cherish and value him, our first love.[20]

HONEST

A second noteworthy aspect of Whitefield's relationship with God is its honesty. It is often easy for us to share our successes and praises with God, but opening up to him about our failures and frailties can be challenging. Whitefield's journal entries during the voyage to America reveal that he was unafraid to share with God both his struggles with sin and his need for help in times of weakness.

First, Whitefield spent much of his prayer time on board asking God to reveal and forgive the unconfessed sin in his heart. He writes of one "glorious opportunity of spending many hours in close communion with God to ask pardon for the defects of my public ministry and to pray for strength to prepare me for future work and trials. My soul was frequently dissolved into tears."[21] Less than one week later, Whitefield records, "Frequently was enlightened to see the pride and selfishness of my heart and as frequently longed for that perfect liberty wherewith Jesus Christ sets his servants free."[22]

Whitefield also was unashamed to admit to Jesus his human weakness and ask for help. He confesses in one entry, "I had many inward strugglings. I could do nothing but lay myself down and offer my soul up to God."[23] He sought God often for assistance: "Endeavored to keep close to God by watching unto prayer for direction and help in time of need."[24]

Whitefield wanted God to be honest with him as well. Throughout his journal, Whitefield is grateful to God for his "loving correction."[25] He rejoices in what he has learned of God's character during the journey: "I have also been more enlightened to see into the mystery of godliness, God manifest in the flesh, and behold more and more of God's goodness in letting me have this time of retirement to search out my spirit. . . . It has been sweet and profitable to my soul."[26] Just two weeks before he landed in America, Whitefield writes this prayer in his journal: "Lord, I want to know myself and you. Oh, let not the hurry of business, which awaits me on shore, prevent my hearing the small, still voice of your Holy Spirit."[27]

We all must battle the temptation to share only our positive moments and attitudes with God and to hide the parts of ourselves that cause us embarrassment or disappointment. Shame, fear, and a sense of our unworthiness and weakness can lead us to close off parts of our hearts, never sharing with him our most profound hurts, fears, and insecurities. Sadly, this keeps our relationship with Jesus strictly on the surface, but our Divine Friend longs to connect with us on a deeply intimate level. He is not satisfied with only a casual relationship with us. He already knows our weaknesses, hurts, and anxieties, and he longs to meet us exactly at those points to heal, restore, and encourage us. God is pure love, and love desires to rush toward the one in need. As paradoxical as it may sound to us, pure love *receives* by *giving*. It's what love does, and it's what God longs to do in his relationship with us.

Ask yourself these questions as you consider how honest you are in your relationship with God. When was the last time I asked God for his help? Do I turn to God for comfort when I am disappointed? Do I feel comfortable asking God about aspects of his character or actions that confuse me? Can I share my feelings of anger with God in a productive way? Am I able to receive God's forgiveness when I confess to him my sin? Do I allow time and space for God to share with me what is on his heart?

God is a real person. He's not a philosophical construct or a prime mover. He will interact with us in an authentic, personal way if we are open to it. Whitefield shared his own heart honestly with God and rejoiced to find that God was longing and willing to do the same with him.

AFFECTIONATE

On a cold night in January, the solo pastor of the leading church in a mid-sized New England town left home for two weeks for ministry purposes. When he returned, he found that his wife had experienced an ongoing, life-transforming encounter with God during the time he was away. So powerful was this two-week encounter, that his wife spent whole nights enjoying a profound sense of God's presence and being overcome by his love. She excitedly shared with her husband the results of her experience: a release from concerns that had been troubling her such as her status and reputation in the town and a sense of being complete-ly secure and satisfied in the reality of God's love for her.

Her husband encouraged her to document the experience. Here is one small portion of her description:

But all night I continued in a constant, clear, and lively sense of the heavenly sweetness of Christ's excellent and transcendent love, of his nearness to me, and of my dearness to him, with an inexpressibly sweet calmness of soul in an entire rest in him. I seemed to myself to perceive a glow of divine love come down from the heart of Christ in heaven into my heart in a constant stream, like a stream or pencil of sweet light. At the same time, my heart and soul all flowed out in love to Christ, so that there seemed to be a constant flowing and reflowing of heavenly and divine love from Christ's heart to mine, and I appeared to myself to float or swim in these bright, sweet beams of the love of Christ, like the motes swimming in the beams of the sun or the streams of his light which come in at the window.

She relates that her experience not only centered her own heart in God's love, but also created in her a strong affection and compassion for others and a deep sense of humility.[28]

What an encounter with God! Perhaps you have had experiences like this yourself, when you felt the love and affection of God toward you, and your own heart went out to him and the ones he loves in responsive, mutual love. If you have, then you know how such emotional encounters can strengthen our hearts and our passion for God. The pastor in this story, moved by his wife's experience and those of others he knew, went on to write a lengthy theological treatise on the importance of affection in the spiritual life. He concludes, "I am bold to assert that there never was any considerable change wrought in the mind or conversation of any one person by anything of a religious nature that ever he read, heard, or saw that had not his affections moved."[29]

If you are a fan of American church history, you might have already guessed the identity of this pastor and his wife—Jonathan Edwards (1703–1758) and Sarah Pierpont Edwards (1710–1758). Sarah's encounter happened in January 1742, while the First Great Awakening was at its height in America. At the time, emotional encounters with God were being experienced by many Christians, and being derided by just as many, so Jonathan took it upon himself to defend these encounters in print and validate their significance, using his wife as an illustrative example.[30]

Understanding the proper place of affection in our relationship with God can be tricky. We worry that we will be at the mercy of intense highs and lows if we emphasize our emotions too much, or that we will become cold-hearted and robotic if we ignore our feelings. But the good news is that as Christians our emotions are just like every other aspect of our humanity such as our mind and will—corrupted by original sin, but fully redeemed and restored by the power of the Holy Spirit within us to function as a helpful part of our spiritual lives.

As we know from personal experience, affection is essential to form strong bonds with one another, and our connection with God is no different. For our relationship with God to function as a secure foundation for a life of spiritual passion, we have to *feel* something for him. As Jonathan Edwards argues, "He that has doctrinal knowledge and speculation only, without affection, never is engaged in the business of religion. Nothing is more manifest in fact than that the things of religion take hold of men's souls no further than they affect them."[31] If our affections are not moved by God, if we are not "affected" by him in the deepest place, we will struggle to maintain spiritual zeal through the challenges of life. Our feelings express what our hearts are experiencing in relationship with him—how we are touched by him, how he delights us, how we desire him. The affections for God we experience strengthen our intimacy with him.

Of course, our sanctified emotions toward God are at base the overflow of his love and affection toward us, made possible by the presence of the Holy Spirit within us. As God pours his life-changing love into us, we release that love and affection back to him. Whitefield explains the importance of the emotions in our relationship with God in a lengthy letter to the Bishop of Gloucester, written when Whitefield was just twenty-four years old:

> When we talk of the *sensible* operations of the Holy Ghost .... we do
> not mean that God's Spirit manifests itself to our senses, but that it may
> be perceived by the soul as really as any sensible impression made
> upon the body. Although the operations of the Spirit of God can no
> more be accounted for than how the wind comes and goes, yet may
> they be as easily felt by the soul as the wind may be felt by the body. My
> lord, indeed, we speak what we know.[32]

For Whitefield, what he *felt* in his encounters with God were really simply the
movements of God's Spirit upon his own spirit, allowing him to receive and
experience God's loving affection for him and enabling him to respond in reciprocal love and affection toward God. As Whitefield encourages a friend,
"Give [Jesus] your heart—your whole heart."[33]

The emotional component of his relationship with God fueled Whitefield's
passion for the spiritual life. While he never recommends stirring up fake feelings toward God, he does value and eagerly embrace the affections of God toward him, and just as eagerly releases his own responsive emotions back to the
Lord. As he writes on board the *Elizabeth*, "Had my heart warmed with a sense
of his love and distinguishing mercies. . . . and enjoyed such an unspeakable
peace and tranquility within that I was often filled with a holy confusion and
was obliged to retire to give my soul vent."[34] Ten days later, he records, "In the
evening, was so visited from above that my soul was quite confounded in the
sense of the divine goodness."[35] Allowing emotion a place in our relationship
with God uniquely fortifies our foundation for spiritual passion by encouraging and strengthening our hearts.

BUILDING A FOUNDATION IN COMMUNITY

Whitefield's cherished, honest, and affectionate relationship with God was
developed during his times alone with the Lord and provided him with a firm
foundation for his life of spiritual passion. But all healthy relationships also
have an outward-facing component, for just as water grows stagnant when it
has no outlet, so too do our closest relationships. During his voyage to America,
Whitefield's close friendship with Jesus was bolstered as he spent time fel-
lowshipping with his on-board community, praying for absent friends, and

seeking the Lord for direction and power for his public ministry.

Whitefield was joined on the *Elizabeth* by a small community he had gathered to assist him with the orphanage he was founding in Georgia. Referred to by Whitefield as his "family," the group consisted of thirteen adults, a young boy, and two small children.[36] His journal records that he intentionally made time throughout the voyage to pray, confess sin, worship, and take communion with the whole group or, at times, just a few members. These periods of fellowship were impactful for Whitefield. Near the end of the journey, he records, "Held a close [meeting] for some hours this evening with my whole family, wherein we opened our hearts, confessed our faults to, and prayed for one another."[37] Their gatherings were vulnerable and honest: "At night I prayed with strong cryings and many tears before all my family, for them and all those dear people who have recommended themselves to my prayers."[38]

Beyond his on-board family, Whitefield held in his heart his friends who were not with him in person, praying often for them. Typical is this journal entry during the voyage: "Had comfortable communion with God in interceding for our dear friends on shore."[39] Whitefield also appreciated the prayers others offered for him. He writes, "The assurance of [my friends'] prayers often lifts up my hands when they hang down and strengthens my feeble knees."[40]

Whitefield thought even beyond his friends and supporters, taking seriously the responsibility and privilege God had given him to love and bless anyone he encountered as a traveling preacher. He sought the Lord in prayer fervently and frequently for wisdom and direction for his ministry. He read spiritual books, studied biblical commentaries, and prepared sermons while on board.[41] When facing challenging times such as seasickness or slow progress because of weather conditions, he consistently understood such times as preparation for the rigors of ministry. One Sunday he notes, "The day was calm and clear, and though we do not go forward much in our course, yet I trust we shall every day be fitted more and more for those various turns of providence which I expect we shall meet with when we come to shore."[42] Whitefield's outward focus certainly strengthened his own personal spiritual foundation and was a natural by-product of a healthy friendship with God.

Hopefully, I have whetted your appetite to read some excerpts from Whitefield's journal that he composed during his eleven-week voyage to America. His entries from his time at sea form approximately the first twenty pages of his fifth published journal, which appeared in 1740. The remainder of the fifth journal records the explosive start of his historically successful colonial preaching tour, which will be featured in subsequent chapters. I believe you will enjoy encountering Whitefield's personal record of his journey across the Atlantic and how his spiritual foundation of an intimate relationship with God was deepened and strengthened.

JOURNAL

A Continuation of the Reverend Mr. Whitefield's Journal, From his Embarking after the Embargo, To his Arrival at Savannah in Georgia[43]

On board the Elizabeth, Capt. Stevenson, Commander, bound from England to Philadelphia.

TUESDAY, [AUGUST] 14. Blessed be God, I was much rejoiced at retiring from the world. Oh, that God may now fully show me myself.

Search, try, O Lord, my reins and heart,

If evil lurks in any part;

Correct me where I go astray,

And guide me in thy perfect way![44]

WEDNESDAY, AUGUST 15. Began to put those of my family who I thought were prepared for it into [fellowship groups]. In all, we are eight men, four women, one boy, and two children, besides Mr. Seward and myself. . . . Most of my other assistants have left good places and are willing freely to spend and be spent for the good of the orphan house. Several of them have already found, [and] all, I hope, are seeking, Christ. We seem perfectly settled already, and whatever storms God may permit to attack us without, I hope we shall have a constant calm within and among ourselves. Blessed be God, I find myself composed and perfectly resigned, nay, much rejoiced at my present situation. Oh, that I could always have no other will but God's!

THURSDAY, AUGUST 16. Had still greater reason to rejoice at the regulation of my family. Wrote several letters and began to have public prayers morning and evening and spent above an hour in examining and exhorting my fellow travelers, and went to bed almost forgetful that I had ever been out in the world. Forever blessed be God's holy name through Christ.

SATURDAY, AUGUST 18. Made but small advances in our way, there being little wind and that not very fair, till about six this evening, at which time it favored us very much. Was enlightened in reading God's word. Had my heart warmed with a sense of his love and distinguishing mercies. Was enlarged in praying several times with and for my friends and was very earnest with God to give me grace to improve my present retirement to his glory, the good of his church, and the edification of my own soul. Perceived also my bodily strength to increase and enjoyed such an unspeakable peace and tranquility within that I was often filled with a holy confusion and was obliged to retire to give my soul vent. Our Lord, I am sure, is with us in the ship. Oh infinitely condescending God!

MONDAY, AUGUST 20. Fair wind all night, by which our ship was carried to the Bay of Biscay[45] and went before the wind at the rate of six miles an hour almost the whole day. The wind being brisk and a great swell coming out of the bay, most of us grew sick and could do little else but lie down upon our beds. This rejoiced me much for I had a glorious opportunity of spending many hours in close communion with God to ask pardon for the defects of my public ministry and to pray for strength to prepare me for future work and trials. My soul was frequently dissolved into tears. A sense of my actual sins and natural deformity humbled me exceedingly, and then the freeness and riches of God's everlasting love broke in with such light and power upon my soul that I was often awed into silence and could not speak any more! A dear companion was with me and helped me to lament, pray, and give praise. Oh, the comforts of religious friendship! Sanctify it, oh Lord, to me, for your dear Son's sake.

TUESDAY, AUGUST 21. Contrary winds all day and the swell continued, which kept all my family as well as myself a little sickish. I conversed with God by prayer and his word most of the time and felt enlargements of heart in the evening. Oh, that by conversing with God I may be changed from glory to glory and fitted for whatever he has appointed for me to do or suffer during my pilgrimage here on earth!

SATURDAY, AUGUST 25. Endeavored to keep close to God by watching unto prayer for direction and help in time of need. Frequently was enlightened to see the pride and selfishness of my heart and as frequently longed for that perfect liberty wherewith Jesus Christ sets his servants free. The sea was calmer today than before. My family grew better, and we spent near two hours this evening in talking of the inward state of our souls and preparing for the reception of the blessed sacrament. Lord, grant that we all may have on the wedding garment.[46]

SUNDAY, AUGUST 26. Administered the holy sacrament early in the morning. Spent the remainder of the day in reading, intercession, etc. God was pleased to enlighten me in reading his holy word and gave me satisfaction in the behavior of those about me. The wind was still contrary and the sea rough, but I had a great calm and joy in my own soul. How can I be thankful enough for the glorious opportunities I now enjoy for improvement. Let all that is within me praise God's holy name.

FRIDAY, AUGUST 31. Very light winds for two days last past and an entire calm today. But I had many inward strugglings. I could do nothing but lay myself down and offer my soul up to God. At night, I prayed with strong cryings and many tears before all my family, for them and all those dear people who have recommended themselves to my prayers. Afterwards my soul received comfort. Oh, that the inward conflicts may purge, humble, and purify my polluted, proud, and treacherous heart! Let all that love me say amen.

I observe these inward trials always follow inward communications [from God]. For these two days last past, I have been much assisted. Lest I should be puffed up and that my mind may be prepared to receive greater degrees of light, God, out of love, has sent me a thorn in the flesh. Lord, grant this loving correction of yours may make me truly great! Amen, Lord Jesus, amen.

SATURDAY, SEPTEMBER 15. Had a pleasant prospect today of some of the western islands. Gave myself to reading the word of God and to prayer the greatest part of this week. Was visited with frequent inward trials. Had many things on my heart to write, but am as yet withheld. Ended the week comfortably with my family and was exceedingly strengthened in reading Professor Francke's account of the orphan house at Halle near Glauchau. It seems in many circumstances to be so exactly a parallel to my present undertaking for the poor of Georgia that I trust the orphan house about to be erected there will be carried on and ended with the like faith and success.[47] Amen, amen.

SATURDAY, SEPTEMBER 22. Underwent inexpressible agonies of soul for two or three days at the remembrance of my sins and the bitter consequences of them. Surely my sorrows were so great that had not God, in the midst of them, comforted my soul, the load would have been unsupportable! All the while, I was assured God had forgiven me, but I could not forgive myself for sinning against so much light and love. I felt something of that which Adam felt when turned out of Paradise; David, when he was convicted of his adultery; and Peter, when with oaths and curses he had thrice denied his Master.[48] I then, if ever, did truly smite upon my ungrateful breast and cry, "God be merciful to me, a sinner!" I ate but very little and went mourning all the day long.[49]

At length, my Lord looked upon me and with that look broke my rocky heart, and floods of contrite tears gushed out before my whole family, and indeed I wept most bitterly! When in this condition, I wondered not at Peter's running so slowly to the sepulcher when loaded with the sense of his sin.[50] Alas, a consideration of aggravated crimes quite took off my chariot wheels,[51] and I drove so exceeding heavily that was I always to see myself such a sinner as I am and as I did then without seeing the Savior of sinners, I should not so much as be able to look up.

This latter part of the week, blessed be the Lord, he has restored me to the light of his countenance[52] and enlarged my heart to write freely and praise him with joyful lips. Our ship being got southwardly into the trade winds[53] and the weather warm, I and some of my companions lay upon deck. We had the holy sacrament on the Festival of St. Matthew,[54] and though we are like to have a long, yet I trust it will be a profitable, voyage to our souls. Blessed be God that he does still chasten and correct me and not give me over unto eternal death. It is good for me to be thus afflicted, for thereby I get an [experiential] knowledge of God's laws. Praise the Lord, O my soul!

SUNDAY, SEPTEMBER 23. Had a sweet sacrament and Love Feast afterwards.[55] Was much strengthened, both in my morning and evening [spiritual] exercises, and felt such unspeakable comfort and warmth of heart towards my absent friends as made me for a while forget the anguish I lately felt; but at night, a sense of my sins weighed me down again, and I mourned in my prayer and was vexed. Alas, how are they mistaken that go out of the world to avoid temptations. I never am so much tempted as when confined on shipboard. A mercy this from God to keep me in action and prepare me for future blessings. Luther says he never undertook any fresh work, but he was either visited with a fit of sickness or some strong temptation. Prayer, meditation, and temptation are necessary accomplishments, in his account, for every minister. May I follow him as he did Christ![56]

SATURDAY, SEPTEMBER 29. Administered the holy sacrament this morning. Had fair winds and lay upon deck with my companions the greatest part of the week. Have been much strengthened and assisted in writing every day, an ample recompense for the trials of the last week. Thus does God sometimes humble and sometimes exalt, and by all his dispensations perfect the regenerate soul. . . . I see more and more the benefit of leaving written testimonies behind us concerning these important points [justification by faith alone]. They not only profit the present, but will also much edify the future age. Lord, open my mouth that I may henceforward speak more boldly and explicitly, as I ought to speak!

SUNDAY, OCTOBER 7. Administered the holy sacrament, had a Love Feast, and expounded, as usual. The wind blowing very fresh, the ship-men were obliged to attend the sails and so could not come to public worship. Sailed sometimes near nine miles an hour, for which we endeavored to praise the Lord. Had comfortable communion with God in interceding for our dear friends on shore, and at night felt such freedom in my spirit from a load I labored under as caused me to break out into many thanksgivings to God. Every day more and more convinces me that the Lord will fulfill the desires of them that fear him.[57] He is the Father of mercies; he is the God of all consolations;[58] he can create comfort out of nothing and bring light and order out of the greatest confusion. This my soul knows right well.[59] O my soul, be not slack to praise him and love him forever and ever!

FRIDAY, OCTOBER 12. Kept a family fast this day that we might afflict ourselves before our God to seek a right way for us and our little ones and for all our substance. I trust it was such a fast as the Lord would choose.

His divine presence was among us, and we had good reason to hope and believe that the Lord was entreated for us. Oh, that we may find more and more reason to say so when we come on shore. I dread going into the world. But wherefore do I fear? Lord, I believe (oh, help my unbelief)[60] that you will keep me unspotted from it.

SATURDAY, OCTOBER 13. Still God is pleased to send us contrary winds, but very warm and pleasant weather. The power of writing has been in a great measure taken from me, but God has been with me in reading, expounding, and my other exercises of devotion. I have experienced some blessed teachings of his Holy Spirit in convicting me of the pride, sensuality, and blindness of my own heart, and of the advantages Satan has gained over me by working on them. I have also been more enlightened to see into the mystery of godliness, God manifest in the flesh, and behold more and more of God's goodness in letting me have this time of retirement to search out my spirit. I would not but have come [on] this voyage for a thousand worlds—it has been sweet and profitable to my soul. The length and continuance of it highly delights me. Lord, I want to know myself and you. Oh, let not the hurry of business, which awaits me on shore, prevent my hearing the small, still voice of your Holy Spirit. Enable me, as you did your servant Enoch, whether in public or private life, to walk with you, my God![61]

SUNDAY, OCTOBER 14. Felt God's power with us, both at sacrament and public worship, morning and evening. Was enlarged in intercession and had reason to believe there was a sweet communion kept up between us and our friends on shore. The assurance of their prayers often lifts up my hands when they hang down and strengthens my feeble knees. The prospect of the many changes and trials which I must necessarily be exposed to and undergo sometimes fills me with fear and trembling, but when I reflect that God has stirred up the hearts of his choicest servants to pray for me, my fears vanish. Methinks I could then leap into a burning fiery furnace or bear to be thrown into a den of devouring lions. Lord, make me thus minded in the hour of trial! My dear friends, continue to pray for me, that my faith fail not.

SATURDAY, OCTOBER 19. On Tuesday and Wednesday had the roughest weather we have yet met with, but the latter part of the week has been warm and calm. All our fresh livestock of every kind is now gone, but through the divine bounty in raising us friends, we have not only food enough for ourselves, but some to spare to the ship's company.

My being on board is every day more and more comfortable. I experience fresh teachings and communications from God's Holy Spirit and have received some remarkable answers to prayer, both in respect to myself and family. We are most of us lusty as eagles and eat our bread with gladness and singleness of heart.[62] The Lord is pleased to fill me out of his divine fullness and to show me more of the glories of the upper world. I can never be thankful enough for this sweet retreat. How wonderfully does the great and infinitely wise God cause everything to work together for our good![63] I want a thousand tongues to praise him. Let everything that has breath praise the Lord.

SATURDAY, OCTOBER 27. Came within sight of land again today, but still are kept back [by adverse weather conditions]. Blessed be God I am quite resigned; I love my retirement too well to be fond of leaving it till the Lord wills. . . . The Lord has been especially gracious unto me, as he always is in the time of any necessity. He has been pleased to give me great freedom in writing and has vouchsafed me such plentiful communications from himself that I have abundant reason to cry out, "Surely God is in this place!"[64]

Lo! God is here! My soul, adore
And own how dreadful is this place!
Let all within thee feel his power,
In silence bow before his face;
To him let all thy thoughts arise,
Ceaseless accepted sacrifice![65]

SUNDAY, OCTOBER 28. Felt more of the divine assistance today than I have since I have been on board. I have been engaged in writing my extemporaneous sermon on the marriage of Cana.[66] The Holy Ghost brought many things to my remembrance, and though I have well drunk of divine comforts since my retirement already, yet I may say with the governor of the feast, "Lord, you have kept the good wine until now." Hasten that time, Oh Lord, when I shall drink it new in your heavenly kingdom![67]

Pennsylvania. Lewis Town.[68]

TUESDAY, OCTOBER 30. Had sweet communion with God last night. Prayed with, exhorted, and solemnly recommended my family to the grace of our Lord Jesus, expecting to go on shore this morning. Being near [Cape Henlopen],[69] a pilot came on board in whose boat brother Seward, myself, and another dear friend went to Lewis Town in order that we might go to Philadelphia by land and get a house in readiness before the ship arrived at that place. While in the boat, I hope each of our hearts was filled with a sense of God's love, and when we reached Lewis Town about evening, I took the first opportunity of retiring to vent my heart in praises and thanksgiving for his abundant mercies conferred on me and mine.

Oh, how can I be thankful enough for this blessed voyage! I have been on board just eleven weeks, but they have seemed to me only as so many days. My inner man has been much bettered by it. My knowledge, I trust, in spiritual things increased, my understanding enlightened to see my corruptions, and my heart much enlarged in writing letters and other things. The remembrance of my humiliations is sweet unto my soul, and the freedom which God has given me over some darling failings fills me with joy unspeakable and full of glory. My family also have great reason to be thankful. God has been pleased to work on many of their hearts, and I believe none of them repent leaving their native country. . . . I cannot say any remarkable conversions have been wrought on board, but many have had strong convictions. Lord, cause them to end in sound conversions! Amen.

But to return. About five in the evening, we landed at Lewis Town, situated in the southern part of the province of Pennsylvania and about 150 measured English miles from Philadelphia. . . . We supped very comfortably together and after prayers and singing with the family, I and my dear companions went to rest, admiring more and more the goodness and providence of the all-wise God. He is the great householder of the whole world, and I look upon all places and persons as so many little parts of his great family. I pray to him before I go, and I find in answer to my prayer, he always commands some or other of his household to take care of and provide for me. As here's the same sun, so here's the same God in America as in England.

I bless God all places are equal to me, so I am where God would have me to be; I hope I shall never account myself at home till I arrive at my heavenly Father's house above. My heart is there already. I long to shake off this earthly tabernacle. It sadly confines my soul. However, I desire patiently to tarry till my blessed change comes. I would not desire to reign till I have suffered with my Master. Heaven will be doubly sweet when I am worn out with distresses and persecutions for the sake of Jesus Christ. Lord, grant that I may continually be looking up to the glory which is to be revealed hereafter, and then deal with me as it seems good in your sight during my pilgrimage here.

> If rough and thorny be my way,
> My strength proportion to my day;
> 'Till toil and grief and pain shall cease,
> Where all is calm and joy and peace![70]

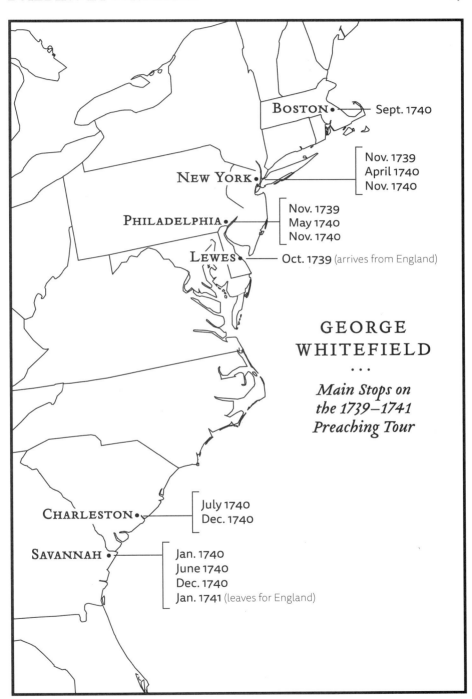

BOSTON • — Sept. 1740

NEW YORK • — Nov. 1739
April 1740
Nov. 1740

PHILADELPHIA • — Nov. 1739
May 1740
Nov. 1740

LEWES • — Oct. 1739 (arrives from England)

GEORGE
WHITEFIELD
• • •
*Main Stops on
the 1739–1741
Preaching Tour*

CHARLESTON • — July 1740
Dec. 1740

SAVANNAH • — Jan. 1740
June 1740
Dec. 1740
Jan. 1741 (leaves for England)

George Whitefield A.B.

CHAPTER IV

Adopting a Lifestyle

As fiery, purpose-driven lovers of God, secure in our foundation of intimate relationship with him, we now can consider what an individual lifestyle of spiritual passion might look like. It's time to ask ourselves, "How should my daily life reflect my passionate pursuit of Jesus?"

In my personal experience as a believer, I have learned three truths that are real for every fervent Christian. First, if our hearts are on fire for God, our lives will show it. Private feelings of love and devotion are always externally visible, revealed by such realities as how we treat and speak to others, how we spend our time and money, and how we view ourselves. The apostle Paul encourages his readers in Philippians 1:27a: "Whatever happens, conduct yourselves in a manner worthy of the gospel of Christ." Peter also recommends, "Live such good lives among the pagans that, though they accuse you of doing wrong, they may see your good deeds and glorify God on the day he visits us."[1] Jesus himself assures his followers that the world will know we love him if we love one another.[2]

Sometimes love just shows on our faces. I can remember one of the first weekends I spent with the woman who would become my son's wife. My son spent the entire weekend sneaking looks at his then-girlfriend and smiling broadly. I knew then he was lovestruck. In the same way, our outward lives will evidence the passion for God in our hearts.

However, the life and choices of each believer are unique, so despite our mutual zeal for God, the second trait we all share is that we each will display that passion in distinctive, personalized ways. My desire for God may fuel a singularly committed prayer life, yours may inspire an unstoppable energy for physically serving others, while someone else's may produce excellence and success in a career in the financial sector. As Jesus shares in the parable of the talents in Matthew 25:14–30, and as Paul explains in his comparison of the church to a human body in 1 Corinthians 12, we are each divinely-fashioned creations of God, called to reject judgment and criticism toward each other and instead rejoice in and celebrate every believer's uniqueness in Christ.

As a college professor, I have seen firsthand the variety of paths pursued by young Christians who are passionate about the Lord. Students I have mentored have become schoolteachers, full-time missionaries, graduate students, CEOs of their own start-up companies, journalists, and marketing strategists. They have founded houses of prayer, created Christian living communities, joined 24/7 worship ministries, and developed church children's programs. In every case, passion for loving God and his people has been channeled into unique, personalized lifestyles and callings.

The third truth I have seen evident in the daily lives of those who are passionate for God is that we all must leave space in our spirituality for growth and change. While we earnestly desire that our daily choices reflect our passion for Jesus, we recognize that we are all works in progress, and we will never be perfect. Because of this reality, we will mature and transform over the years as we seek to live out our spiritual zeal. Second Peter 1:5–8 encourages us to intentionally and consistently pursue spiritual growth:

> Make every effort to respond to God's promises. Supplement your faith
> with a generous provision of moral excellence, and moral excellence
> with knowledge, and knowledge with self-control, and self-control
> with patient endurance, and patient endurance with godliness, and
> godliness with brotherly affection, and brotherly affection with love for
> everyone. The more you grow like this, the more productive and useful
> you will be in your knowledge of our Lord Jesus Christ.[3]

The process of personal spiritual transformation will never be complete until we reach heaven.

If you examine your own life, I'm sure you can identify areas in which the Holy Spirit has produced growth in you over the years. Has your prayer life become deeper and more consistent? Have you developed more patience with those around you? Is your understanding of Scripture more nuanced than it was just a few years ago? Have you been asked to participate in your local fellowship group in ways that you wouldn't have considered earlier in life? If we are attentive, we can see how over time our passion for God has yielded richness and development in our daily lifestyle. We can rely on the power of God to help us mature and progress as fervent followers of Jesus.

Recognizing that our passion for God will be reflected in our lives by being evident, unique, and ever-growing gives us a strong basis for embracing a lifestyle of passion, but how can we delve even deeper into the ways our daily rhythms and activities can reflect our love for God? George Whitefield, just emerging in our story from his eleven-week sea voyage to the American colonies, is just the man to show us the way.

HAMMER AND FIRE

On October 30, 1739, after eleven weeks at sea, Whitefield and his onboard family landed at Lewes, Delaware, for an intercolonial preaching tour. Americans were eager to hear Whitefield preach, having read colonial newspaper accounts of his success in England as well as published copies of his journals and sermons. Although just twenty-five years old, Whitefield was walking into a supremely energized religious environment in which he was expected to play the central role.

Whitefield, for his part, embraced his primacy of place with enthusiasm and effectiveness. He spent fifteen months traveling 5,000 miles throughout the colonies, preaching more than 350 times in seventy-five cities and towns. Scholars estimate that close to one-quarter of all Americans heard him preach as he journeyed back and forth from his base in Savannah, Georgia, to the northernmost reaches of New England.[4] As in England, he appeared consistently in every American newspaper and sold a significant number of his writings.

As he also had done in England, Whitefield preached to shockingly large crowds—crowds that sometimes exceeded in size the number of inhabitants of the actual cities themselves. In Philadelphia, the second largest city in the colonies at the time with approximately 13,000 residents, he records in his journal drawing 20,000 listeners to his farewell sermon. In Boston, the largest colonial city with about 17,000 residents, one newspaper reports that 23,000 people assembled to hear him preach before he left the city. Even in New York City, the third-largest city with 11,000 residents but one of the less religious regions of the country, Whitefield drew 8,000 listeners.[5] Crowds of this size had never been seen before in the colonies.

The most noteworthy feature of these assemblies was the overt power of God moving on the hearts of Whitefield's listeners. In his journal for May 13, 1740, Whitefield records:

> Preached at Wilmington in the morning to about 5,000 and at White
> Clay Creek, about ten miles distant, in the evening to about 3,000. A
> great presence of God was in both places, especially at White Clay
> Creek. . . . The word, I believe, was both like a fire and a hammer, for
> many were exceedingly melted, and one cried out most bitterly as in
> great agonies of soul.[6]

In practically every place in which Whitefield preached, his passionate words drove his record crowds to either solemn silence, weeping, or crying out. Whitefield's assistant from his later years recalls in his memoirs, "He had a most peculiar art of speaking personally to you, in a congregation of four thousand people."[7] After a service, his residence would often be overrun by those touched by his words and seeking spiritual counsel. Listeners were converted in droves. Whitefield's preaching stops were thus distinguished not only by their size, but also by their power.

To get an idea of what it was like to attend a Whitefield sermon, we turn to one of the earliest American eyewitness accounts of Whitefield's preaching—a detailed three-page letter that appeared in the *New York Gazette* on November 26, 1739, shortly after Whitefield preached in that colony. The anonymous writer attended several of Whitefield's sermons, both in the fields and in churches, and is representative of many of Whitefield's listeners: he had read some of Whitefield's published sermons and journals, had heard both good and bad reports about the evangelist, and decided to attend the first service because of "curiosity."

In the eyewitness account, Whitefield himself and his uniquely dramatic preaching style strike the writer first, as was the case with most listeners. The writer describes Whitefield as "a man of a middle stature, of a slender body, of a fair complexion, and of a comely appearance. He is of a sprightly cheerful temper, acts and moves with great agility and life." His oratory skills are arresting: "He has a most ready memory and, I think, speaks entirely without notes. He has a clear and musical voice and a wonderful command of it. He uses much gesture, but with great propriety. Every accent of his voice, every motion of his body, *speaks,* and both are natural and [unpretentious]."

The spectacular impact of Whitefield's words on his listeners surprises the writer the most. He records, "All became hushed and still; a solemn awe and reverence appeared in the faces of most, a mighty energy attended the word. I heard and felt something astonishing and surprising. . . . I thought I saw a visible presence of God with Mr. Whitefield." At an evening sermon to about 2,000 people overflowing a Presbyterian church, the writer declares:

> I never in my life saw so attentive an audience. Mr. Whitefield spoke as one having authority. All he said was demonstration, life, and power! The people's eyes and ears hung on his lips. They greedily devoured every word. I came home astonished! Every [doubt] vanished. I never saw nor heard the like, and I said within myself, "Surely God is with this man of a truth."

The writer was not unique in his response to Whitefield's preaching. In every colony Whitefield visited, he enraptured audiences and convincingly fulfilled the outsized expectations of his American listeners. By the end of his tour, Whitefield had established himself as the premier evangelist in the colonies.

But the Grand Itinerant established something else during his travels in America: a *bona fide* intercolonial religious revival. Named the First Great Awakening by later historians and already growing in parts of England when Whitefield came to the colonies, the revival eventually touched every region in America during the 1740s. Whitefield was not the only evangelical revivalist to fan the flame, but he was the most well-known and, many would argue, the most effective. Just two months before he left America, Whitefield exults to a friend in England, "A glorious church is raising in America. The Lord mightily reveals his arm. It would please you to see his outgoings, his stately steps in the great congregation."[8] In fact, America exploded in flames of revival, fostered in large part by Whitefield's preaching.

The rest of this book will mine Whitefield's uniquely impactful 1739–1741 American preaching tour during the First Great Awakening for insights for how to live a life of spiritual passion. In this chapter, we will focus on Whitefield's last, yet arguably most important, regional preaching circuit of the tour—his remarkable visit to New England.

BATTING IN THE BIG LEAGUES

Whitefield had been in the American colonies almost eleven months when he set out for New England, leaving Charleston, South Carolina, by ship and landing in Newport, Rhode Island, on September 14, 1740. His six-week visit to the region was his only one of this tour.

New England at the time consisted of the colonies of Connecticut, Rhode Island, Massachusetts, and New Hampshire, although parts of what would become the state of Maine were already settled. The region was one of the first in the colonies established by English settlers, with Plymouth Plantation founded by Separatists in 1620 and Boston settled by Puritans in 1630. At the time of Whitefield's visit, Boston, Massachusetts, was the most populated colonial city with approximately 17,000 residents and a diverse mix of races, ethnicities, and lifestyles. Although still much smaller than a great European city like London that boasted closer to half a million residents, Boston was one of the leading cultural and commercial centers of America where one could find five of the eleven weekly newspapers publishing at the time and the oldest college in the colonies, Harvard.

New England was also strikingly religious. Over six hundred Congregational ministers, heirs of the founding Puritans, worked in the colony, producing the lowest ratio of clergymen to lay people in the western world.[9] New Englanders incorporated religion into both their personal lives and civic society, valued their spiritual past, and hoped and prayed for a new season of God's favor. Whitefield himself notes in his journal the extensive spirituality of the area, claiming that New England "certainly on many accounts exceeds all other provinces in America and, for the establishment of religion, perhaps all other parts of the world."[10]

The religious history and culture of the region made its residents among the most expectant for Whitefield's visit and perhaps the most important in terms of igniting religious faith and revival fervor. Several of Boston's leading Congregational ministers had been communicating with Whitefield by letter since his arrival in the colonies back in October 1739, and practically every New Englander had been following the Grand Itinerant's progress in the newspapers. At the time of Whitefield's arrival in New England, the five Boston newspapers had printed almost as many notices related to Whitefield and the Awakening as had all other colonial newspapers combined.[11] New England was thus the most spiritually prepared and expectant region that Whitefield visited on his preaching tour.

Whitefield's reception at Newport, Rhode Island, his first stop in New England, was eagerly noted by the Boston newspapers, with the earliest report appearing on September 22, 1740, in the *Boston Weekly Post-Boy:*

Newport, Rhode Island, Sept. 19. Last Lord's Day arrived here the Rev. Mr. George Whitefield from South Carolina, who preached two excellent sermons on Monday in the Church of England, in the forenoon from those words in Romans 14:17, and in the afternoon from John 17:3. On Tuesday, he preached twice, in the forenoon from 2 Corinthians 5:17 [and] in the afternoon from Luke 18:14. And in the evening of both the days, he entertained a vast number of people of several denominations, with exhortations in private families. Great numbers of people flocked from all quarters both in town and country to hear his sermons and exhortations, and many of them could not refrain shedding tears. He set out from hence for Boston on Wednesday morning.

From Newport, Whitefield preached his way north along the fifty miles to Boston, arriving there Thursday evening, September 18.

His reception in Boston was explosive. Audiences grew from 4,000 at his initial sermon, to double the number the next day, to approximately 15,000 on Boston Common the following day. Financial collections for his Savannah orphanage Bethesda exceeded amounts collected anywhere else, including London.[12] As in Rhode Island, he preached in public usually twice daily, counseled countless people who came to his lodgings, and delivered private exhortations in homes. At the close of his first week in Boston, Whitefield ends his journal entry by excitedly praying, "Oh, that the Lord may beat them down with the hammer of his word till the heart of stone be entirely taken away! Amen, Lord Jesus. Amen and Amen."[13]

On September 29, he left Boston to travel and preach in the outlying towns, returning to Boston on October 6 and noting in his journal that he had ridden 178 miles and preached sixteen times, yet "was not in the least wearied or fatigued."[14] After another week in Boston, he preached his farewell sermon on October 12, drawing 23,000 listeners, according to the *New England Weekly Journal* for October 14. Whitefield then returned south, preaching as he went, and arrived in Rye, New York, on October 29. His appraisal of New England was positive: "In short, I like New England exceeding well, and when a spirit of reformation revives, it certainly will prevail more than in any other place because they are simple in their worship, less corrupt in their principles."[15]

Whitefield's six-week New England circuit can function as a microcosm for how he lived a lifestyle of spiritual passion. Examining his journal entries written during the trip, we see that Whitefield revealed his passion for God in three important ways throughout his ministry in the region. In this chapter, each section will include a journal entry that illustrates the lifestyle trait being highlighted.

Work Hard

Open the dictionary to the word *hard-working,* and you just might see a picture of George Whitefield. The Grand Itinerant is remembered as one of the most diligent disciples in the kingdom of God, and his New England tour certainly underscored that fact. Whitefield's six weeks in the region included a nonstop daily itinerary of preaching and spiritual counseling, assembling and encouraging diverse groups of believers, meeting with civic officials, writing letters to his numerous American and international connections, spending time alone with God, and traveling to even the most difficult-to-reach towns over unforgiving terrain. He rested very little, often to the consternation of his friends and the detriment of his physical health.

Plain and simple hard work is sometimes overlooked in discussions of how to pursue God passionately. Often, we focus so emphatically on our spiritual gifts, calling, or natural talents and resources that simply putting our nose to the grindstone and expending effort for the kingdom of God never enters our minds. However, diligence must be one of the cornerstones of a zealous Christian life. Consider how the apostle Paul highlights the essential nature of hard work within God's economy of reaping and sowing in Galatians 6:7–10:

> Do not be deceived: God cannot be mocked. A man reaps what he sows. Whoever sows to please their flesh, from the flesh will reap destruction; whoever sows to please the Spirit, from the Spirit will reap eternal life. Let us not become weary in doing good, for at the proper time we will reap a harvest if we do not give up. Therefore, as we have opportunity, let us do good to all people, especially to those who belong to the family of believers.

Paul himself lived out these words, expending tremendous effort and energy to preach the gospel wherever he traveled.

Perhaps most significantly, our diligence reveals what truly matters to us. Think of what is non-negotiable for you, and then ask yourself, "How hard do I work for the people, events, or values that are important to me?" I imagine you work extremely hard for what you appreciate and cherish. How then can it be any different with the Lover of our souls? We will evidence our passion and love for Jesus with a lifestyle of diligence.

Whitefield's journal entry below is for just one day in his New England preaching tour, approximately halfway through his visit to the region, after he had returned to Boston from a week-long circuit around the city's environs. In the entry, we read of Whitefield counseling spiritually distressed visitors at his lodgings, delivering a powerful sermon on being spiritually born again, dining with the governor, preaching on Boston Common to 15,000 listeners, praying publicly for a struggling new minister, attending a funeral, preaching at a local charity building, preaching at a local workhouse, exhorting the many who gathered in the evening at his rooms, fulfilling a dinner obligation, and then retiring to sleep. Now that's a busy day! I hope you enjoy this glimpse into the life of the hard-working Rev. George Whitefield.

JOURNAL

A Continuation of the Reverend Mr. Whitefield's Journal, From a few Days after his Return to Georgia to his Arrival at Falmouth, on the 11th of March 1741[16]

THURSDAY, OCTOBER 9. Have been applied to this and every morning since my return [to Boston] by many souls under deep distress and was only grieved that I could not have more time with them. Preached this morning the public lecture at Dr. Sewall's meeting-house, which was very much crowded.[17] When I had left my lodgings, I had fixed upon and folded down a particular text, but when I came near the meeting-house, I found it much impressed upon my heart that I should preach upon our Lord's conference with Nicodemus.[18] I acquainted a friend with it. . . .

After sermon, I dined with the governor, who seemed more kindly affected than ever, and particularly told one of the ministers, who has lately begun to preach extemporaneously, that he was glad he had found a way to save his eyes.[19] Oh, that others would follow him! I believe they would find God ready to help and assist them.

In the afternoon, I preached on [Boston] Common to about 15,000 people; collected upwards of £200 for the orphans. Just as I had finished my sermon, a ticket was put up to me wherein I was desired to pray "for a person just entered upon the ministry, but under apprehensions that he was not converted." God enabled me to pray for him with my whole heart. And I hope that ticket will teach many others not to run before they can give an account of their conversion; if they do, they offer God strange fire.[20]

Went to a funeral of one belonging to the council, but do not like the custom at Boston of not speaking at the grave. When can ministers' prayers and exhortations be more suitable than when the corpse before them will silently, as it were, assist them, and with a kind of [silent] oratory bid the spectators consider their latter end? When the funeral was over, I went, as privately as possible, to the almshouse and enlarged on these words, "The poor received the gospel," for near half an hour.[21] Then I went to the workhouse, where I prayed with and exhorted a great number of people who crowded after me, besides those belonging to the house, for near an hour more.[22]

And then, hearing there was a considerable number more waiting for me at my lodgings (though some cried out, "Spare thyself"), God strengthened me to give them a spiritual morsel, and then I went and ate bread very comfortably at a friend's house whither I was invited, and soon after retired to my rest. Oh, how comfortable is sleep after working for Jesus! Lord, strengthen me yet a little longer and then let me sleep in you, never to awake in this vain world again. Still, I must entreat you, if most conducive to your glory and the good of souls, to make no long tarrying, oh my God!

FOLLOW THE SPIRIT'S LEADING

While hard work is imperative to sustaining a lifestyle of passionately loving God, all the effort in the world will not accomplish God's purposes if we are out of step with his Holy Spirit. Thus, a second daily choice we hope to make in our lives as Jesus' ardent disciples is to accurately and energetically follow the Spirit's leading in all that we say and do.

Even Jesus, the Anointed One of God, did not teach, heal, or act of his own volition; instead, as Peter declares in the house of the Roman centurion Cornelius in Acts 10:38, "God anointed Jesus of Nazareth with the Holy Spirit and power, and . . . he went around doing good and healing all who were under the power of the devil, because God was with him." In fact, when questioned by the Jewish leaders for healing on the Sabbath, Jesus retorts, "My Father is always at his work to this very day, and I too am working. . . . Very truly I tell you, the Son can do nothing by himself; he can do only what he sees his Father doing, because whatever the Father does the Son also does. For the Father loves the Son and shows him all he does."[23]

The first disciples of Jesus followed in his footsteps, recognizing their dependence upon the Holy Spirit and prioritizing his leading. Peter obeys the Spirit and shares the good news of Jesus with the Roman centurion and his household in Acts 10, Paul travels to Macedonia in response to a vision he receives in Acts 16, and Philip is physically carried off by the Spirit to Azotus after baptizing an Ethiopian official in Acts 8.[24]

Whitefield himself, like those early followers of Jesus, deeply valued the leading of the Holy Spirit. In the excerpt above, we notice that Whitefield abandoned his planned text for his sermon at Dr. Sewall's meetinghouse on the way to the church, feeling led by the Spirit to preach instead on Jesus' conversation with Nicodemus in John 3. This type of adjustment was standard practice for Whitefield—what text to preach from, which town to visit, how long to stay in one location—all of these decisions were made based on what Whitefield believed the Holy Spirit was directing him to do. Whitefield's entire itinerant preaching ministry could be said to be founded on following the Spirit's leading, and he spent much of his time alone with God seeking the Spirit's guidance and direction.

Whitefield's New England tour reveals for us one important aspect of reliance on the Holy Spirit: favor and fruitfulness in the kingdom of God result from following the leading of the Spirit. Whitefield attributed his success throughout his lifetime of ministry to the blessing that naturally results from obeying the Holy Spirit. We see this dynamic powerfully in one stop in Northampton, Massachusetts, during his New England preaching tour.

The church in Northampton was pastored by Jonathan Edwards, the Massachusetts pastor mentioned in Chapter 3 of this book along with his wife Sarah Edwards for their writings and experiences with religious affections. Edwards had garnered a bit of fame for himself several years before Whitefield's visit when a London press published his account of a 1734–1735 revival in his own parish titled *A Faithful Narrative of the Surprising Work of God*. The text had become standard reading among eighteenth-century Christians seeking revival.

Whitefield knew of Edwards and his *Faithful Narrative,* and just two weeks after he landed in America and before New England newspapers had even announced his arrival, Whitefield wrote a letter to Edwards, promising, "I hope, God willing, to come and see [you] in a few months."[25] Three months later, Edwards returned a response, sharing his own hope to connect with Whitefield when he visited New England: "I have a great desire, if it may be the will of God, that such a blessing as attends your person and labors may descend on this town, and may enter my own house, and that I may receive it in my own soul."[26]

During the second half of his New England tour as he made his way south from Boston, Whitefield decided to visit Northampton. Even though he seldom spent more than one day in the smaller towns, Whitefield chose to remain four days in Northampton. His time here reveals the powerful results keeping in step with the Spirit can produce when it is part of a lifestyle of spiritual passion.

During his stay in Northampton, Whitefield preached four times in Jonathan Edwards' meetinghouse and once in Edwards' home, and his impact on the congregation was radical.[27] Edwards, Whitefield writes in his journal, "wept during the whole time" of his penultimate sermon. "The people," he records, "were equally, if not more, affected. . . . And though their former fire might be greatly abated, yet it immediately appeared when stirred up."[28] In a letter to a colleague, Edwards reports, "The congregation was extraordinarily melted by every sermon; almost the whole assembly being in tears for a great part of sermon time."[29] Whitefield himself was moved by the Christians of the town: "My own soul was much lifted up towards God. . . . I have not seen four such gracious meetings together since my arrival. My soul was much knit to these dear people of God."[30]

Whitefield stayed in the Edwards home, and the fellowship he shared with the family also bore much fruit. Jonathan asked Whitefield to speak to his young children about salvation—they were twelve, ten, eight, six, four, and two years old at the time. Whitefield himself was impressed with the Edwards children and with the spiritual union shared by Jonathan and Sarah. He notes in his journal his own desire for a spiritually-compatible wife, recording that

Sarah "talked feelingly and solidly of the things of God."[31]

So strong was the bond formed between Jonathan Edwards and Whitefield that Edwards accompanied Whitefield for two additional days after the evangelist left Northampton, hearing him preach in the towns of Westfield, Springfield, Suffield, and Windsor. On the short journey, Edwards watched Whitefield argue passionately to thousands of listeners both in church buildings and outdoor settings for the necessity of being spiritually born again. Their time together ended at the home of Edwards' parents in East Windsor, where Edwards' father was a pastor. There, Whitefield parted from Jonathan with "some inward regret," but reminded himself that "we shall meet again in eternity."[32]

Jonathan Edwards' passion for God and revival was stoked by his time with Whitefield. Two months after Whitefield's departure from Northampton, Edwards sent a short letter to the evangelist updating him on the revival that he had ignited with his visit in both the town and Edwards' own household:

[Religion] has been gradually reviving and prevailing more and more ever since you were here. Religion is becoming abundantly more the subject of conversation; other things that seemed to impede it are for the present laid aside. I have reason to think that a considerable number of our young people, some of them children, have already been savingly brought home to Christ. I hope salvation has come to this house since you were in it with respect to one, if not more, of my children.

Edwards also asks for Whitefield's prayers, "That I may be filled with his Spirit and may become fervent as a flame of fire in my work."[33] Whitefield's following of the Spirit took him to Northampton for an extended time of ministry and opened a door for God to work through him as he exhibited a lifestyle of spiritual passion. Below is Whitefield's record of his time in Northampton.

JOURNAL

A Continuation of the Reverend Mr. Whitefield's Journal, From a few Days after his Return to Georgia to his Arrival at Falmouth, on the 11th of March 1741[34]

FRIDAY, OCTOBER 17. When I had taken a little refreshment, we crossed the ferry to Northampton where no less than 300 souls, as was supposed, were savingly brought home to the dear Lord Jesus about 5 or 6 years ago. Their pastor's name is Edwards, successor and grandson to the great Stoddard, whose memory will be always precious to my soul and whose books entitled *A Guide to Christ* and *Safety of Appearing in Christ's Righteousness* I would recommend to all.[35] Mr. Edwards is a solid, excellent Christian, but at present weak in body. I think I may say I have not seen his [equal] in all New England.

When I came into his pulpit, I found my heart drawn out to talk of scarce anything besides the consolations and privileges of saints and the plentiful effusion of the Spirit upon the hearts of believers. And when I came to remind them of their former experiences and how zealous and lively they were at that time, both minister and people wept much, and the Holy Ghost enabled me to speak with a great deal of power.

In the evening, I gave a word of exhortation to several that came to Mr. Edwards' house. My body was somewhat weak, my appetite almost gone, but my Lord gave me meat which the world knows nothing of.[36] Lord, evermore give me this bread. Amen and amen.

Hadfield and Northampton.

SATURDAY, OCTOBER 18. At Mr. Edwards' request, I spoke to his little children, who were much affected. Preached at Hadfield 5 miles from Northampton, but found myself not much strengthened. Conversed profitably on the way about the things of God with dear Mr. Edwards and preached about 4 in the afternoon to his congregation. I began it with fear and trembling,[37] feeling but little power in the morning, but God assisted me. Few dry eyes seemed to be in the assembly for a considerable time. I had an affecting [view] in my own heart of the glories of the upper world and was enabled to speak of them feelingly to others. I believe many were filled, as it were, with new wine.[38] And it seemed as if a time of refreshing was come from the presence of the Lord. Even so, come Lord Jesus, come quickly. Amen and amen.

Northampton.

SUNDAY, OCTOBER 19. Felt wonderful satisfaction in being at the house of Mr. Edwards. He is a son himself and has also a daughter of Abraham for his wife.[39] A sweeter couple I have not yet seen. Their children were dressed not in silks and satins, but plain, as becomes the children of those who, in all things, ought to be examples of Christian simplicity.

[Sarah Edwards] is a woman adorned with a meek and quiet spirit, talked feelingly and solidly of the things of God, and seemed to be such a helpmeet for her husband that she caused me to renew those prayers which, for some months, I have put up to God that he would be pleased to send me a daughter of Abraham to be my wife. I find, upon many accounts, it is my duty to marry. Lord, I desire to have no choice of my own. You know my circumstances; you know I only desire to marry in and for you. You did choose a Rebekah for Isaac, choose one for me to be a helpmeet for me in carrying on that great work committed to my charge.[40] Lord, hear me. Lord, let my cry come unto you.

Preached this morning, collected £59, and perceived the meeting begin sooner and rise higher than before. Dear Mr. Edwards wept during the whole time of exercise. The people were equally, if not more, affected, and my own soul was much lifted up towards God.

In the afternoon, the power increased yet more and more. Our Lord seemed to keep the good wine till the last.[41] I have not seen four such gracious meetings together since my arrival. My soul was much knit to these dear people of God, and though I had not time to converse with them about their experiences, yet one might see that, for the most part, they were a gracious, tender people. And though their former fire might be greatly abated, yet it immediately appeared when stirred up. Oh, that my soul may be refreshed with the joyful news that Northampton people have recovered their first love, that the Lord has revived his work in their dear souls and caused them to do their first works![42]

MONDAY, OCTOBER 20. Left Northampton in the evening.

LEAVE THE RESULTS TO GOD

Working hard and following the leading of the Holy Spirit are elements of a daily lifestyle of passion that we can lean into and accomplish. What happens after that, however, is anyone's guess. People's responses, the timing of events, our own thoughts and emotions, and how history remembers our words and actions are among the myriad of forces that can impact the results of our spiritual discipleship and that are usually beyond our personal control. Leaving to God these unpredictable, unmanageable aspects of life is the third key step in adopting a lifestyle of spiritual passion.

Realistically, this might be the most difficult principle to make a consistent part of a passionate life. The more our zeal for loving Jesus and others matures and deepens, the more we may struggle with leaving the results in God's hands. Our desire to see God's kingdom expand and our own hearts become more like his can reach such a fever pitch that we may begin to unconsciously put pressure on ourselves to actually *produce* certain outcomes. I've seen it happen countless times in my own life, and I'm sure you can recall similar instances yourself as well. We may end up battling discouragement or depression when we do not see others or even ourselves responding to God as we had hoped.

Sadly, in the most extreme situations, we even may blame ourselves or God when the expected results don't materialize and launch ourselves headlong into a crisis of faith.

The Old Testament story of Esther may encourage us. One of the Jews forced into exile in the Persian Empire, Esther becomes a wife of King Ahasuerus. When Esther's cousin Mordecai uncovers a plot to destroy all the Jews living in the empire, he calls upon Esther to ask the king for mercy for their people, a perilous venture for Esther since anyone who enters the king's presence unannounced risks execution. Nonetheless, Esther decides to approach the king with the support of the Jewish people, leaving the results of her actions in God's hands:

> Go, gather together all the Jews who are in Susa, and fast for me. Do not eat or drink for three days, night or day. I and my attendants will fast as you do. When this is done, I will go to the king, even though it is against the law. And if I perish, I perish.[43]

Thankfully, the king accepts Esther into his presence, and her entreaty saves her people. The Jewish holiday of Purim commemorates Esther's heroic actions.

In this story, the final result of Esther's passionate love for God and her people is resoundingly positive, and while this is not always the case, we can be inspired by Esther's willingness to trust God with the results of her actions. No matter what may happen in our lives, we can have confidence in the God who loves us. Keeping our eyes are on our Beloved and asking the Holy Spirit to increase our faith helps us reject the pressure to produce specific results ourselves and instead trust God to accomplish his perfect ends for his own glory, our good, and the advancement of his kingdom.

The good news is that when we leave in God's hands the results of our hard work and obedience to the Spirit, we enter a place of rest, delight, and, perhaps paradoxically, fruitfulness. We are free to let others have their own spiritual journeys, to wait patiently for the fulfillment of God's promises, to expend our resources without fear of lack, to embrace the needy and weak, and to exercise faith for the truly impossible. Releasing results to God moves us toward freedom and contentment, and actually can motivate us even more in our zealous pursuit of Jesus.

Whitefield experienced his own struggles with leaving the results of his passionate lifestyle in God's hands. His intense desire to see the unconverted saved, his craving for personal holiness and spiritual growth, and the enormous expectations placed upon him everywhere he preached to generate visible reactions in his listeners such as weeping or crying out sometimes produced in him dejection or even despair. Twice during his New England tour, Whitefield notes in his journal his battles with discouragement.

At the beginning of his tour, Whitefield writes that he experienced limited success when he preached in the New Hampshire towns of Hampton and Portsmouth. However, he encourages himself by rejoicing over the one individual who sought him out for spiritual counsel, leaving the rest of his listeners in God's hands, noting that "God's Spirit blows when and where it [will]."[44] When he returned two days later to the same towns, his words were met with much more receptivity, and he was joyful.

Two weeks later, as he traveled south in the second half of his tour, Whitefield experienced astounding success in his ministry in the Massachusetts towns of Worcester and Leicester, but the next day struggled with dejection over his own personal battle with sin as well as poor results in Cold Spring, Massachusetts. This time, he turned to the Lord for comfort and strength by "pouring out [his] complaints and petitions before the dear Lord Jesus."[45]

Whitefield shows us that it is perfectly natural to wish for positive results from our passionate pursuit of God and even to feel sadness when those results don't materialize in recognizable ways. However, when we turn to God for comfort and release the outcomes to him, we can experience "sweetness and freedom of soul" through our loving God.[46] Interestingly, one day after struggling with ministry in Cold Spring, Whitefield arrived in Northampton, where, as noted above, he would have some of his greatest preaching success and most delightful Christian fellowship of his New England tour. Whitefield's journal excerpts below reveal both his struggles and successes in leaving in God's hands the results of fervent ministry.

JOURNAL

A Continuation of the Reverend Mr. Whitefield's Journal, From a few Days after his Return to Georgia to his Arrival at Falmouth, on the 11th of March 1741[47]

Hampton, Portsmouth, and York.

WEDNESDAY, OCTOBER 1. Preached in the morning, though not with so much freedom as usual, at Hampton to some thousands in the open air. The wind was almost too high for me. Some, though not many, were affected. God's Spirit blows when and where it [will].[48] After dinner, rode in company with many to Portsmouth, a large town about fourteen miles from Hampton. Got there in about an hour and a half. Preached to a polite auditory and so very unconcerned that I began to question whether I had been preaching to rational, or brute, creatures. Seeing no immediate effects of the word preached, I was a little dejected, but God, to comfort my heart, sent one young man to me crying out in great anguish of spirit, "What shall I do to be saved?" Oh, how does God pity the weakness of his children! Why were you so cast down, O my soul?[49]

FRIDAY, OCTOBER 3. Preached this morning at Portsmouth to a far greater congregation than before. Instead of preaching to dead stocks, I had now reason to believe I was preaching to living men. People began to melt soon after I began to pray, and the power increased more and more during the whole sermon. The word seemed to pierce through and through and carried such conviction along with it that many who before had industriously spoken evil of me were ashamed of themselves. Mr. Shurtleff, the minister, when he afterwards sent me £97 collected at this time for the orphans, wrote thus, "You have left great numbers under deep impressions, and I trust in God they will not wear off, but that the convictions of some will be kept up and cherished till they have had their desired effect."[50] Amen and amen.

Hastened after dinner to Hampton. Preached to several thousands of people with a great deal of life and power. Collected £41 for my little ones and set out directly for Newbury, which we reached about eight at night, and was kindly entertained at a gentleman's house with all my friends. My heart was much enlarged and filled with joy, and in the way two old disciples came to me, acquainting me what sweet refreshing times God had vouchsafed them under my ministry. Lord, not unto me, not unto me, but unto your free grace be all the glory![51]

Worcester and Leicester.

WEDNESDAY, OCTOBER 15. I preached in the open air to some thousands [at Worcester]. The word fell with much weight indeed; it carried all before it. . . .

Was enabled much to rejoice in spirit. Preached in the afternoon at Leicester, 6 miles from Worcester, with some, though not so much, power as in the morning. Got to Brookfield by night and was upon the mount indeed. My soul was upon the wing. I was exceedingly enlarged and was enabled, as it were, to take the kingdom of God by force.[52] Oh! What precious hours are those, when we are thus strengthened, as it were, to lay hold on God.

Brookfield and Cold Spring.

THURSDAY, OCTOBER 16. Rose in great dejection of soul at the consideration of indwelling sin. Retired and wept before the Lord. Preached not with extraordinary freedom at first, but at last the word ran and melted many down. After dinner, was much enlarged again and strengthened to wrestle strongly with God for a revival of his work in these parts.

Preached at Cold Spring, 15 miles from Brookfield, at the house of Mr. L—nd to 3 or 400 people, but perceived little moving [of the Holy Spirit], except a few minutes. Spent the evening with my dear fellow travelers. Was somewhat cast down, but afterwards recovered sweetness and freedom of soul by retiring and pouring out my complaints and petitions before the dear Lord Jesus. Oh, the sovereign, distinguishing freeness of God's grace. If it was not for the consideration of that, my soul must be continually pierced through and through with many sorrows. Lord, for your mercy's sake, never [allow] me to let this consideration go. Amen, Lord Jesus, amen.

Reaping the Harvest

As passionate lovers of God, we sincerely desire that our zeal for the Lord will be evident and present in our daily life choices. Our words, actions, thoughts, and emotions should all point to the One we love before all others. Jesus himself, in his earthly ministry, announces to his disciples in Luke 12:49, "I have come to bring fire on the earth, and how I wish it were already kindled!" Our Savior's fiery passion ultimately led him to choose a harrowing and humiliating death on a cross to accomplish salvation for his beloved ones. As Jesus' devoted and ardent followers, we seek to model his passionate lifestyle on this earth. Working hard, following the Spirit's leading, and releasing the results to God will enable us to evidence our love for God and others in our daily life.

Whitefield displayed his commitment to consistent choices in line with a lifestyle of spiritual passion during his six-week preaching tour of New England, and the results of his choices were striking. On January 15, 1741, ten weeks after he left New England, Whitefield received several letters from Boston reporting the powerful effects of his ministry there. Government officials, ministers, and lay Christians all testified to how Whitefield's visit had stirred up desire for God among the people. Notable are the words of one merchant:

I can't break off till I just mention, to the glory of the grace of God and for your comfort and encouragement, the success your ministry of late has had among us. Impressions made seem to be abiding on the minds of many. The doctrines of grace seem to be more the topic of conversation than ever I knew them. Nay, religious conversation seems to be almost fashionable and almost everyone seems disposed to hear or speak of the things of God. Multitudes flock to the evening lecture, though it has sometimes been the worst of weather. Ministers seem to preach with more life, and the great [audiences] seem to hear with solemn attention, and, I hope, our Lord Jesus is getting to himself the victory over the hearts of many sinners.[53]

Whitefield's lifestyle of spiritual passion was an instrument of God's favor to the entire region of New England. May we receive encouragement from Whitefield's experience to pursue our own daily life of zeal for God.

CHAPTER V

Sharing the Journey

Igniting the fire of passion in our hearts, embracing God's purposes, building a foundation of relational intimacy with Jesus, and adopting a passionate lifestyle all work together to shape us into zealous lovers of God and his people. But no individual believer exists on earth in a vacuum. We are all part of God's worldwide body, and our membership in God's universal church is central to a life of spiritual passion. The final four chapters of this book will examine how we embrace lives of zeal for God within the context of the body of Christ as we share the journey, face opposition, respond to culture, and finish strong.

Sharing the journey of spiritual passion is key to a life of zeal for God. As humans, we naturally gravitate toward connection with others. In fact, we require relationships to become all that our Creator intends us to be because longing for intimacy is built into our DNA. In Genesis 2:18, God acknowledges that it is not good for Adam, the first created human, to be alone in the Garden of Eden, so he fashions Eve. God himself enjoys and models for us perfect harmony and fellowship, eternally existing as the three distinct yet united persons of Father, Son, and Holy Spirit. Thus, it is understandable that we, like our Edenic forbears, flourish when in healthy relationship with others.

As Christians, we are enabled to create strong, supportive connections through the presence of the Holy Spirit within us. The Holy Spirit of God, present in all believers, unites us, joining us in a way that is truly supernatural and beyond common interests, personality similarities, or basic like-mindedness. We literally share one Spirit Who creates among us an eternal bond that cannot be broken because it flows from the triune God himself. The apostle Paul confirms this truth in 1 Corinthians 12:12–13: "The human body has many parts, but the many parts make up one whole body. So it is with the body of Christ. Some of us are Jews, some are Gentiles, some are slaves, and some are free. But we have all been baptized into one body by one Spirit, and we all share the same Spirit."[1]

The presence of the Holy Spirit in all believers is great news for those of us who desire to pursue God passionately. We know, beyond a shadow of a doubt, that the zeal within us for God and his purposes will ignite, provoke, and strengthen passion for God in other Christians in such a way that we are both encouraged and refreshed. Recall how John the Baptist leaped in Elizabeth's womb and Elizabeth herself was filled with the Holy Spirit simply at the greeting of Mary the mother of Jesus in Luke 1:41. If you have ever experienced a spike in your desire and love for God after spending time with another fervent Christian, you know this truth.

Sharing the journey also sustains us when our passion falters. Obstacles, distractions, doubts, and fears will always assail us as we pursue Jesus, but the presence of God's fiery lovers in our life can strengthen and encourage us as nothing else can. The Holy Spirit enables us to rekindle the fire of passion in each other during times of struggle.

But how do we find fellow believers with whom we can share the journey of spiritual passion in a significant and transformative way? Sometimes, those connections are already around us, in our neighborhoods, schools, book clubs, church groups, workplaces, fitness clubs, or charitable endeavors. If you recognize someone in your life who shares your passion for God, reach out to them. It doesn't have to be a grand gesture; simply ask them to meet for coffee after church, text them an encouraging Bible verse, go see a movie you both will enjoy, or invite them to your Super Bowl party. Although it's hard to be the first to reach out, God delights in bringing people together who share a true desire for him. You can trust him to help you both move into a deep, inspiring friendship.

On the other hand, we sometimes feel like we don't have anyone around us who truly shares our passion for Jesus. God understands these times in our lives. Ask the Father to bring zealous believers into your life. He will. He loves to connect whole-hearted lovers of Jesus and lead them into sweet fellowship.

It's his plan for his family! Keep your eyes and heart open and see who the Lord leads into your life.

And, sometimes, God just surprises us. Recently, a friend gave me a book of poetry written by a friend of hers who lives in our town. Reading the poems, my heart was stirred by the Holy Spirit, and I felt a connection with the author, even though I did not know her. I asked my friend to introduce us, and, many emails and lunches later, the author and I have become close friends, shared many impactful times of prayer, and encouraged each other profoundly in loving Jesus. My new friend and I often marvel at the seemingly random way we connected, but the truth is, God wants to draw together believers who will encourage and bless each other, so we can be intentional and expectant in obeying the leading of the Spirit to connect with the other earnest Christians he highlights for us.

Regardless of how we find each other, we should always value our relationships with passionate believers. Those who bond in the Spirit over a shared zeal for Jesus are, honestly, rather hard to come by. If you have found a friend who shares your commitment to fervently pursue our Beloved, do not take that person for granted. They are a special gift from God, so prioritize that connection and invest your time and resources to deepen and extend the relationship. You will never, ever regret pouring yourself into friendship with a fellow lover of God who will share with you the journey of a life of spiritual passion.

Although George Whitefield excelled at the solitary work of preaching to a crowd, he also highly valued and pursued relationships with other zealous believers. In fact, creating a personal network of like-minded, fervent American Christians committed to revival was one of his goals for his 1739–1741 preaching tour. During the first few months of his arrival in America, while he traveled throughout the mid-Atlantic colonies of New Jersey, Pennsylvania, and New York, Whitefield gathered the members of the founding group of this network. A look at Whitefield's first passionate posse reveals for us three important aspects of sharing the journey of love for God.

A SHARED PURPOSE: PHILADELPHIA

Three days after landing at Lewes, Delaware, on October 30, 1739, Whitefield arrived at his first American preaching stop—Philadelphia, the city of brotherly love. As was his custom when entering any new city, Whitefield began connecting immediately with local believers, especially resident clergy. As an itinerant minister, Whitefield needed other pastors' permission to preach in their church buildings and valued their follow-up with those converted by his preaching. Several days after getting settled in a rented house in Philadelphia, he notes in his journal his first meetings with Christians from several denominations in the city:

> Read prayers and preached to a large auditory. Dined with the other [Anglican] churchwarden and had some close and edifying conversation about our justification by faith in Christ. Was visited in the afternoon by the Presbyterian minister. Went afterwards to see the Baptist teacher, who seems to be a spiritual man, and spent part of the evening most agreeably with two loving Quakers.[2]

The next evening, both the Presbyterian and Baptist ministers visited Whitefield at his house as did several women. Whitefield, viewing the visits as a "hint from providence," brought them all together for a time of exhortation and prayer.[3] Whitefield spent a week in Philadelphia, connecting with other believers and preaching both in Anglican churches and outdoor locations to large audiences, one of which was estimated at 6,000 listeners by the *Pennsylvania Gazette*.[4]

While Whitefield was pleased to meet any and all Christians in a given location, he was chiefly interested in making close alliances with those who shared his primary purpose: to combat the lifeless, traditional, culture-based Christianity widely practiced in the West by preaching the opportunity to receive a vibrant, passionate new life in Jesus through spiritual rebirth. At the time of Whitefield's visit to America, the institution of Christianity was central to the colonies, but many who practiced the faith did so only out of a sense of obligation and not sincere devotion. Attempting to awaken complacent American "Christians" who had never had a true conversion experience was Whitefield's primary mission during his 1739–1741 preaching tour.

Whitefield was saddened that most colonial churchgoers did not enjoy genuine, life-giving fellowship with God, complaining in his journal, "I fear many rest in a head knowledge, are close Pharisees, and have only a name [of Christian] to live.[5] It must needs be so when the power of godliness is dwindled away and where the form only of religion is become fashionable among people."[6] By connecting with American revivalists who were themselves advocating for an authentic, transformative conversion experience and spiritual life, Whitefield sought to create a colonial band of brothers who shared his evangelistic purpose. Fortunately for Whitefield, on November 10, 1739, one week into his stay in Philadelphia, the man who would become the first member of his American crew appeared on his doorstep, the Rev. William Tennent, Sr. (1673–1746).

A Pennsylvania Presbyterian minister originally from Scotland, William Tennent Sr. had faithfully preached the need for spiritual rebirth in his region, along with his three sons in professional ministry and other like-minded pastors. He had founded a seminary called the Log College more than a decade earlier, which emphasized evangelistic zeal along with the traditional seminary education. The Log College had become the epicenter of revival fire in the area, producing ministers who were known for their fervent pursuit of God instead of simply externally conforming to religious traditions and practices. Whitefield liked Tennent immediately and "conversed of the things of God for a considerable time" with him and a Swedish minister from the city.[7]

Whitefield's encounter with William Tennent Sr. reveals our first key point for connecting with others on the journey of passion for God—unite with those who share your sense of spiritual purpose. As the well-known passage of Hebrews 10:24–25 reminds us, "And let us consider how we may spur one another on toward love and good deeds, not giving up meeting together, as some are in the habit of doing, but encouraging one another—and all the more as you see the Day approaching." Christians who share our sense of purpose can encourage us when we are struggling and help us remain focused on the work we know God has called us to do.

Upon meeting Tennent and exchanging testimonies, Whitefield recognized that he and the "old grey-headed disciple and soldier of Jesus Christ," as

Whitefield calls Tennent in his journal, shared the same passion for testifying to the new birth in Christ. Whitefield also records that Tennent reminded him of his revivalist friends in Scotland and England. The ministers' shared sense of purpose caused Whitefield to exult in his journal, "Yet I doubt not but the Lord will appear for us as he did for [Elijah] and make us more than conquerors."[8] Whitefield had found his first ally in the colonies who would share with him the journey of spiritual passion. As we will see in the rest of this chapter, William Tennent Sr. would go on to connect the Grand Itinerant with many others in the region who also shared his powerful calling.

Iron Sharpens Iron: New York City

After ten days of ministry in Philadelphia, Whitefield left the city to travel to New York. He had received two requests from New York City resident Thomas Noble (d. 1746) to come preach, and Whitefield likened the "pressing invitation" to the call to Paul to come to Macedonia.[9] On the way, he stopped in New Brunswick, New Jersey, to meet the Rev. Gilbert Tennent (1703–1764), eldest son of William Tennent Sr. Pastor of a Presbyterian church in New Brunswick, Gilbert Tennent was Whitefield's equal in religious zeal and his elder in years of ministry.

As Tennent shared with Whitefield his experiences with the power and presence of God in his life and ministry, Whitefield knew he had found another American friend and supporter. Whitefield records in his journal that "God, I find, has been pleased greatly to [validate] his labors. He and his associates are now the burning and shining lights of this part of America."[10] Tennent joined Whitefield's entourage traveling to New York, and the group arrived in the city the next day where they were welcomed by Thomas Noble and others.

That evening, in the Wall Street Presbyterian Church, the first sermon of Whitefield's New York City visit was delivered, but not by the Grand Itinerant.[11] Instead, Gilbert Tennent preached the sermon, and it was a blockbuster. True to their shared purpose, Tennent spoke on Whitefield's favorite topic—the necessity of being spiritually born again and the insufficiency of external religious actions to result in true salvation.

Whitefield was strongly impacted by Tennent's sermon, specifically the uncompromising courage and conviction with which Tennent preached. His journal entry reveals his astonishment:

[I] never before heard such a searching sermon. He went to the bottom indeed and did not daub with untempered mortar. He convinced me more and more that we can preach the gospel of Christ no further than we have experienced the power of it in our own heart. Being deeply convicted of sin ... he has learned experimentally to dissect the heart of a natural man. Hypocrites must either soon be converted or enraged at his preaching. He is a Son of Thunder and does not fear the faces of men.[12]

Whitefield himself had confidently testified to the necessity of the new birth in his own ministry, but something about Tennent's bold preaching rocked Whitefield's world. His stunned reaction to Tennent's sermon is unique in his journals. At the end of the entry, Whitefield confesses, "My soul was humbled and melted down with a sense of God's mercies, and I found more and more what a babe and novice I was in the things of God."[13]

Tennent's inspiring influence on Whitefield was visible the very next day as Whitefield preached an afternoon sermon outdoors to approximately 2,000 people and an evening sermon in the Wall Street Presbyterian Church to a "very thronged and attentive audience." Whitefield's journal record of these two sermons hints at his invigorated courage: "In the field, some few mocked, but God gave me power to speak to them, and they grew more serious. At night, the people seemed exceedingly attentive, and I have not felt greater freedom in preaching, and more power in prayer, and a stronger witness of the Spirit since I came into America."[14] Gilbert Tennent's fearless preaching strengthened Whitefield's resolve to present the truth of the gospel audaciously and boldly.[15]

The friendship produced mutual blessings, however, as Whitefield convinced Tennent of the value of itinerant preaching, something not common in America at the time. In the summer of 1740, about six months after experiencing Whitefield's preaching tour of New York, Tennent conducted his own short preaching trip through parts of New Jersey, Delaware, and Maryland. A few months later in November, on his way home from his remarkably successful preaching tour of New England, Whitefield stopped in New Brunswick and persuaded Tennent to make his own preaching circuit of New England so Tennent could stir up the revival fires Whitefield had sparked.[16] Tennent's connection with Whitefield thus inspired the New Jersey preacher to take his powerful message on the road with his own traveling ministry.

The friendship between Whitefield and Tennent reveals for us a second tip for sharing the journey of spiritual passion: be intentional in your efforts to help other believers grow and be encouraged. Proverbs 27:17 suggests that "as iron sharpens iron, so one person sharpens another," and this verse, along with many New Testament passages, reminds us of our sacred obligation to bless, inspire, and, at times, admonish and correct fellow Christians. In the same way, our companions on the journey of spiritual zeal will stir up our passion for Jesus, remind us of God's promises when we are struggling, gently question our unwise choices, and stand by us when we are opposed. We will both be blessed as we mature as believers and as human beings, fervently pursuing the One we love.

The mutually beneficial relationship between Whitefield and Tennent also highlights the importance of diversity within our spiritual friendships. While Tennent and Whitefield shared a passion for God and for declaring the message of spiritual rebirth, they each had their own unique personalities and ministries: Tennent as an American Presbyterian pastor with a fiery approach to preaching and Whitefield as an English Anglican clergyman with an unwavering commitment to itinerant ministry. Neither man attempted to change the other, disparaged his friend's unique gifting and calling, or felt insecure in his own identity. Instead, both Whitefield and Tennent lived out their personal passion for God within the context of supportive friendship, fortifying the enthusiasm and sense of purpose they shared. Hopefully, as we travel the road of loving God with others, we, too, will be true to who God has called us to be as we support our sisters and brothers in Christ in their own unique spiritual journeys.

Joyful Celebration: New Jersey

Whitefield, Gilbert Tennent, and their friends left New York City and traveled back to Tennent's home in New Brunswick, New Jersey, arriving on Monday evening, November 19, 1739. The next day at Tennent's church, revivalist ministers and lay believers from around the region assembled for a time of worship, preaching, fellowship, and testimony. Whitefield records in his journal that it was a "large assembly gathered together from all parts" that increased in energy as the meetings progressed.[17] Whitefield preached three times, with his first sermon lasting almost two hours. This one-day worship extravaganza points to the third key aspect of sharing with others the journey of spiritual passion—the importance of joyful communal celebration.

As followers of Jesus, we want to be people of heavenly joy. Joy encourages our heart, reinforces our passion for God, and makes our journey on this earth highly pleasurable; as Nehemiah 8:10b exhorts us, "The joy of the Lord is your strength." Peter reminds persecuted believers in the first century that their faith in Jesus produces in them "an inexpressible and glorious joy."[18] Jesus our King, anointed by God the Father with the "oil of joy," fulfilled his calling on this earth with a joyful heart: "For the joy set before him he endured the cross, scorning its shame, and sat down at the right hand of the throne of God."[19]

Our heavenly joy on this earth is magnified, deepened, and expanded when it is shared among brothers and sisters who are passionately in love with God. Together, we triumphantly celebrate who God is, what he has done, and who we are becoming as his children. As the apostle John writes in 2 John 1:12, "I have much to write to you, but I do not want to use paper and ink. Instead, I hope to visit you and talk with you face to face, so that our joy may be complete."

Whitefield's experience during the whole of this one-day celebration at Tennent's church was one of surpassing joy, primarily because of the Christians who joined him there. He exults in his journal entry for the day:

> To me, the meeting seemed to be like the meeting of the twelve tribes
> [of Israel] when they came from different parts to worship the Lord
> at Jerusalem.... With these ministers and many other disciples of our
> dear Lord Jesus, I took sweet counsel. We ate our bread with gladness

and singleness of heart and comforted ourselves with this consideration—that though we must be separated from each other on earth, yet we should sit down to eat bread with Abraham, Isaac, and Jacob in the kingdom of heaven. Hasten, O Lord, this blessed time![20]

The celebration was also a time of fruitfulness. Whitefield notes that "several were brought under strong convictions, and our Lord's dear disciples were ready to leap for joy."[21]

Whitefield, Tennent, and the group traveled together and preached throughout the region for three more days, eventually parting on November 23. Whitefield returned to Philadelphia, feeling gratitude for the shared journey and writing, "Oh, how can I express my thankfulness for this little excursion! The Lord has done great things for us in it, whereat the people of God are much rejoiced."[22] Whitefield stayed in Philadelphia slightly less than one week and experienced tremendous success in preaching, his farewell sermon drawing "the greatest number of people that was ever seen gathered here and computed at no less than 10,000 people," according to one Philadelphia newspaper.[23] Whitefield left the city to travel to Savannah, Georgia, preaching as he went.

The Fruit of a Shared Journey

Whitefield's four-week circuit through the mid-Atlantic colonies was his first experience sharing his journey of passion for God with American Christians during his 1739–1741 preaching tour. For Whitefield, the connections were delightful, encouraging, and transformative beyond his hopes and expectations. As he wrote in his journal at the end of his tour, "We had sweet communion with each other and spent the evening in concerting what measures had best be taken for promoting our dear Lord's kingdom. . . . A notable war, I believe, is commencing between Michael and the dragon; we may easily guess who will prevail. The seed of the woman shall bruise the serpent's head."[24] Whitefield believed he had found truly zealous Christians with whom he shared a common purpose, a commitment to growth and accountability, and a desire to joyfully celebrate the coming kingdom of God.

His friends felt the same way. Whitefield received a letter from the Rev. Ebenezer Pemberton of the Wall Street Presbyterian Church in New York while he was still in Philadelphia in which the minister remarks that Whitefield had been "the means of awakening some among us to a serious sense of practical religion, and may be the beginning of a good work in this secure and sinful place."[25] William Tennent Sr. appreciated how Whitefield had stirred up his own spiritual passion, writing, "As to myself, I have been thereby somewhat quickened and . . . was honored with intimate communion with the King, our dear and glorious Emmanuel, and am, if not deceived, rendered more able to follow the footsteps of the flock."[26]

Gilbert Tennent became one of Whitefield's closest American friends. In a letter to Whitefield dated just one week after they parted, Tennent shares his sincere affection:

I think I never found such a strong and passionate affection to any stranger as to you when I saw your courage and labor for God at New York. I found a willingness in my heart to die with you or to die for you. . . . I hope your coming here (my dear brother) has been (through grace) of some service to my soul, for thereby my esteem of the Scripture has been excited and my love to Christ's kingdom and Christ in some manner inflamed.[27]

Two weeks later, Whitefield updated Tennent by writing, "The hand of the Lord brought wondrous things to pass before we left Pennsylvania."[28] One month later, Whitefield wrote again to Tennent from Savannah, Georgia, noting the inspiration Tennent gave him even from afar: "But what think you? I am sometimes doubting whether I shall have sufficient matter given me to preach upon. Methinks I hear you say, 'Oh, you of little faith! Why do you doubt? As the day is, so shall your strength be.'"[29] Their friendship and mutual encouragement would continue for many years.

A CLARION CALL

Whitefield was significantly impacted by sharing the journey of spiritual passion with his first cadre of on-fire American Christians. Their supportive encouragement and example strengthened his determination to fulfill his calling to preach the gospel of new birth in Jesus Christ to colonial listeners who were trapped in empty religious ritual and tradition. We see this fresh resolve perhaps most clearly in a new sermon he wrote and preached in Philadelphia just days after he returned to that city from his travels to New York with his new friends.

Published as *The Wise and Foolish Virgins* and based on Jesus' parable in Matthew 25:14, the sermon is a fiery, uncompromising declaration of the difference between two groups of "virgins" waiting for a bridegroom in the parable—the "wise virgins," or true Christians who carry in their lamps the oil of the Holy Spirit, and the "foolish virgins," or non-believers who have no oil in their lamps because they have relied on the superficial performance of religious duties for salvation. Whitefield pulls no punches as he candidly and fervently appeals to his audience to consider their current spiritual choices and eternal destination. Surely, Gilbert Tennent and friends were proud.[30]

SERMON

The Wise and Foolish Virgins: A Sermon Preached at Philadelphia, 1739[31]

Matthew 25:13
Watch, therefore, for ye know neither the day nor the hour in which the Son of Man comes.[32]

Preparing for the Bridegroom

The apostle St. Paul, in his epistle to the Hebrews, informs us, "That it is appointed for all men once to die; after that," says he, "comes judgment."[33] And I think if any consideration be sufficient to awaken a sleeping, drowsy world, it must be this: that there will be a day wherein these heavens shall be wrapped up like a scroll, this element melt with fervent heat, the earth and all the things therein be burnt up, and every soul and every nation and language summoned to appear before the dreadful tribunal of the righteous Judge of [living] and dead, to receive rewards and punishments, according to the deeds done in their bodies. . . .

For what says our Lord in the parable of which the words of the text are a rendition or conclusion, and which I intend to make the subject of my present discourse? "Then," that is, at the day of judgment, which he had been discoursing of in the foregoing and prosecutes in this chapter, "shall the kingdom of heaven" (i.e., the state of professing Christians in the gospel church) "be [compared to] ten virgins, which took their lamps and went forth to meet the bridegroom." In which words is a manifest allusion to a custom prevailing in our Lord's time among the Jews at marriage solemnities, which were generally at night, and at which it was customary for the persons of the bride-chamber to go out in procession with many lights to meet the bridegroom.

By the bridegroom then here spoken of, you are to understand Jesus Christ. The church (i.e., true believers) are his spouse. He is united to them by one Spirit, even in this life, but the solemnizing of these sacred nuptials is reserved till the day of judgment, when he shall come to take them home to himself and present them, before men and angels, as his purchase to his Father, without spot or wrinkle or any such thing.

By the ten virgins, we are to understand the professors of Christianity in general. All are called virgins because all are called to be saints. Whosoever names the name of Christ is obliged by that very profession to depart from all iniquity. The pure and chaste in heart are the only persons that will be so blessed as to see God.[34] As Christ was born of a virgin, so he can dwell in none but virgins' souls, made pure and holy by the cohabitation of his Holy

Spirit. But what says the apostle? "All are not Israelites that are of Israel"—all are not true Christians that are called after the name of Christ.[35] No, says our Lord, in the second verse, "Five of these virgins were wise" (i.e., true believers), "and five were foolish" (i.e., formal hypocrites).

But why are five said to be wise and the other five foolish? Hear what our Lord says in the following verses, "They that were foolish took their lamps and took no oil with them, but the wise took oil in their vessels with lamps." They that were foolish took their lamps (i.e., the lamp of an outward profession [of faith]). They would go to church, say over several manuals of prayers, come perhaps even into a field to hear a sermon, give at a collection, and receive the sacrament [of communion] constantly, nay, more often than once a month.

But then here lay the mistake: they had no oil in their lamps, no true principle of grace, no living faith in their hearts, without which though we should give all our goods to feed the poor and our bodies to be burnt, it would profit us nothing.[36] In short, they were exact, nay, perhaps superstitious bigots as to the form [of religion], but all the while, they were strangers to and in effect denied the power of godliness in their hearts. They would go to church, but at the same time, think it no harm to go to a ball or an assembly, notwithstanding they promised at their baptism to renounce the pomps and vanities of this wicked world. They were so exceeding fearful of being righteous overmuch that they would even persecute those that were truly devout if they attempted to go a step farther than themselves.

In one word, they never effectually felt the powers of the world to come. They thought they might be Christians without so much inward feeling, and, therefore, notwithstanding their high pretensions, had only a name to live....

"But the wise," says our Lord, verse 4, "took oil in their vessels with their lamps." Observe, the wise, that is, the true believers, had their lamps as well as [did] the foolish virgins, for Christianity does not require us to cast off all outward forms. We may use forms and yet not be formal. For instance, it is possible to worship God in a set form of prayer and yet worship him in Spirit and in truth. And, therefore, brethren, let us not judge one another. The wise virgins had their lamps; herein did not lie the difference between them and the foolish, that one worshiped God with a form and the other did not. No, as the Pharisee and publican went up to the temple to pray, so these wise and foolish virgins might go to the same place of worship and sit under the same ministry.

But then the wise took oil in their vessels with their lamps; they kept up the form, but did not rest in it. Their words in prayer were the language of their hearts, and they were no strangers to inward feelings. They were not afraid of searching doctrine, nor affronted when ministers told them they deserve to be damned. They were not self-righteous, but were willing that Jesus Christ should have all the glory of their salvation. They were convinced that the merits of Jesus Christ were to be apprehended only by faith, but yet were they as careful to maintain good works as though they were to be justified by them. In short, their obedience flowed from love and gratitude and was cheerful, constant, uniform, universal, like that obedience which the holy angels pay our Father in heaven. . . .

Arrival of the Bridegroom

For verse 5, "While the Bridegroom tarried" (i.e., in the intermediate space of time which passed between our Lord's ascension and his coming again to judgment), "they all slumbered and slept." The wise as well as foolish died, for dust we all are and to dust we must return. It's no reflection at all upon the divine goodness that believers as well as hypocrites must pass through the valley of the shadow of death, for Christ has taken the sting out of it, so that we need fear no evil. It is to them a passage to everlasting life. Death is only terrible to those that have no hope because they live without faith in the world. Whosoever there are among you that have received the first fruits of the Spirit, I am persuaded you are ready to cry out with holy Job, we would not live here always, we long to be dissolved that we may be with Jesus Christ. And though worms must destroy our bodies as well as others, yet we are content, being assured that our Redeemer lives, that he will stand at the latter days upon the earth, and that in our flesh we shall see God.[37]

But it is not so with hypocrites and unbelievers beyond the grave, for what says our Lord? And, at midnight—observe, at midnight—when all was hushed and quiet and no one dreaming of any such thing, a cry was made. The voice of the archangel and the trumpet of God was heard sounding this general alarm: "To things in heaven, to things in earth, and to things in the waters under the earth, behold—." Mark how this awful summons is ushered in with the word *behold* to engage our attention: behold the Bridegroom comes, even Jesus Christ, the desire of nations, the Bridegroom of his spouse the church. Because he tarried for a while to exercise the faith of saints and give sinners space to repent, scoffers were apt to cry out, where is the promise of his coming, but the Lord is not slack concerning his promise, as these men account slackness.[38]

For, behold, he that was to come now comes and will not tarry any longer. He comes to be glorified in his saints and to take vengeance on them that know not God and have not obeyed his gospel. He comes not as a poor, despised Galilean; not to be stabled in a stinking manger; not to be despised and rejected of men; not to be blindfolded, spit upon, and buffeted; not to be nailed to an accursed tree; not as the Son of Man, but as he really was— the eternal Son of an eternal God. He comes riding in the wings of the wind, in the glory of the Father and his holy angels, and to be had in everlasting reverence of all that shall be round about him. . . .

But how may we imagine the foolish virgins were surprised when, notwithstanding their high thoughts and proud imaginations of their security, they now find themselves wholly naked and void of that inward holiness and purity of heart without which no man living at that day shall comfortably meet the Lord. I doubt not but many of these foolish virgins while in this world were clothed in purple and fine linen, [dined] sumptuously every day, and would disdain to set the wise virgins, some of which might be as poor as Lazarus, even with the dogs of their flock.[39] These were looked upon by them as enthusiasts and madmen, as persons that were righteous overmuch, and who intended to turn the world upside down.[40] But now death has opened their eyes and convinced them, to their eternal sorrow, that he is not a Christian who is only one outwardly. Now they find (though, alas, too late) they, and not the wise virgins, had been beside themselves.

Now their proud hearts are made to stoop, their lofty looks are brought low, and as Dives entreated that Lazarus might dip the tip of his finger in water and be sent to cool his tongue,[41] so these foolish virgins, these formal hypocrites, are obliged to turn beggars to those whom they once despised: "Give us of your oil." Oh, impart to us a little of that grace and Holy Spirit for the insisting on which we fools accounted your lives madness. For, alas, our lamps are gone out. We had only the form of godliness, we were whited sepulchers, we were heart hypocrites, we contented ourselves with desiring to be good, and though confident of salvation while we lived, yet our hope is entirely gone now God has taken away our souls. Give us, therefore, oh, give us, though we once despised you. Give us of your oil, for our lamps of an outward profession, transient convictions, are quite gone out.

"Comfort ye, comfort ye, my people," says the Lord with this.[42] My brethren in Christ, hear what the foolish say to the wise virgins and learn in patience to possess your souls if you are true followers of the lowly Jesus. I am persuaded you have your names cast out and all manner of evil spoken against you for his name's sake, for no one ever did or will live godly in Christ Jesus without suffering persecution.[43] Nay, I doubt not but your chief foes are those of your own household.[44] Tell me, do not your carnal relations and friends vex your tender souls day by day in bidding you spare yourselves and take heed lest you go too far? And as you passed along to come and hear the word of God, have you not heard many a Pharisee cry out, "Here comes another troop of his followers?" Brethren, be not surprised. Christ's servants were always the world's fools.

You know it hated him before it hated you; rejoice and be exceeding glad, yet a little while and behold the Bridegroom comes, and then shall you hear these formal, scoffing Pharisees saying unto you, "Give us of your oil, for our lamps are gone out." When you are reviled, revile not again; when you suffer, threaten not; commit your souls into the hands of him that judges righteously. For, behold, the day comes when the children of God shall speak for themselves.

The wise virgins in the parable no doubt endured the same cruel mockings as you may do, but as the lamb before the shearers is [silent], so in this life opened they not their mouths,[45] but now we find they can give their enemies an answer: "Not so, lest there be not enough for us and you, but go ye rather to them that sell and buy for yourselves." These words are not to be understood as though they were spoken in an insulting manner, for true charity teaches us to [treat] the worst of sinners and our most bitter enemies with the meekness and gentleness of Christ. Though Dives was in hell, yet Abraham does not say, "Thou, villain," but only, "Son, remember." And I am persuaded had it been in the power of these wise virgins, they would have dealt with the foolish virgins as God knows I would willingly deal with my most inveterate enemies—not only give them of their oil, but also exalt them to the right hand of God.

It was not then for [lack] of love, but for fear of [lacking] a sufficiency for themselves that made them return this answer: "Not so, lest there be not enough for us and you." For they that have most grace have none to spare; none but self-righteous, foolish virgins think they are good enough or have already attained [salvation]. These who are truly wise are always most distrustful of themselves, pressing forward to the things that are before, and think it well if after they have done all, they can make their calling and election sure. "Not so, lest there be not enough for us and you; but go ye, rather, to them that sell and buy for yourselves. . . ."

We do not hear any reply the foolish virgins make. No, their consciences condemned them; like the person in the parable without a wedding garment, they are struck [silent] and are now filled with anxious thoughts how they shall buy oil that they may lift up their heads before the Bridegroom. "But while they went to buy," verse 10 (i.e., while they were thinking what they should do), the Bridegroom, the Lord Jesus, the Head, the King, the Husband of his spouse the church, comes, attended with thousands and twenty times ten-thousands of saints and angels publicly to count up his jewels, and they that were ready, the wise virgins who had oil in their lamps and were sealed by his Spirit to the day of redemption, these having on a wedding garment of an imputed righteousness and a new nature, went in with him to the marriage.

But who can express the transports that these wise virgins felt when they were thus admitted in a holy triumph into the presence and full enjoyment of him whom their souls hungered and thirsted after! No doubt they had tasted of his love and by faith had often fed on him in their hearts when sitting down to commemorate his last supper here on earth, but how full may we think their hearts and tongues were of his praises when they see themselves sit down together to eat bread in his heavenly kingdom. . . .

Judgment of the Bridegroom

But I even tremble to tell you, oh nominal Christians, that the door will be shut. I mean the door of mercy, never, never to be opened to give you admission, though you should continue knocking to all eternity. For thus speaks our Lord, verse 11, "Afterwards" (i.e., after those that were ready had gone in and the door was shut, after they had to their sorrow found that no oil was to be bought, no grace be procured), "came also the other virgins," and, as Esau after Jacob had got the blessing, cried with an exceeding bitter cry, bless me, even me also, oh my father, so they come saying, "Lord, Lord, open unto us. . . ."[46]

But what answer did Jesus make? He answered and said, verse 12, "Verily, I say unto you." He puts the word *verily* to assure them he was in earnest. "I say unto you"—I am Truth itself, I whom you have owned in words but in works denied—"Verily, I say unto you, I know you not." These words must not be understood literally, for whatever Arians and Socinians may say to the contrary, yet we affirm that Jesus Christ is God, God blessed forever, and therefore knows all things. He saw Nathaniel when under the fig trees; he sees and is now looking down from heaven, his dwelling place, upon us to see how we behave in these fields.[47]

Brethren, I know nothing of the thoughts and intents of your hearts in coming hither, but Jesus Christ, he knows who come like newborn babes desirous to be fed with the sincere milk of the word, and he knows who come to hear what the babbler says and to run away with part of a broken sentence that they may hereof accuse him.[48] This expression, then, *I know you not*, must not be understood literally. No, it implies a knowledge of approbation as though Christ had said, "You call me *Lord, Lord,* but you have not done the things that I have said. You desire me to open the door, but how can you come in hither not having on a wedding garment? Alas, you are naked as you came into the world; where is my outward righteousness imputed to you? Where is my inherent righteousness wrought in you? Where is my divine image stamped upon your souls? How dare you call me *Lord, Lord,* when you have not received the Holy Ghost, whereby I seal all that are truly mine. Verily, I know you not; depart from me, ye cursed, into everlasting fire, prepared for the devil and his angels."

And now he that has ears to hear, let him hear what manner of persons these were whom Jesus Christ dismissed with this answer. Remember, I entreat you, remember they are not sent away for being fornicators, swearers, Sabbath breakers, or prodigals. No, in all probability, as I observed before, they were, touching the outward observances of the moral law, blameless. They were constant as to the form of religion, and if they did no good, yet no one could say they did anyone any harm. The only thing for which they were condemned and eternally banished from the presence of the Lord (for so much is implied in that sentence *I know you not*) was this—they had no oil in their lamps, no principle of a true living faith and holiness in their hearts.

And, good God! If persons may go to church, receive the sacrament, lead honest moral lives, and yet be sent to hell at the last day, as they certainly will be if they advance no further, where will you [be sent], oh drunkard? Where will you, oh swearer? Where will you, oh Sabbath breaker? Where will you that denies divine revelation and even the form of godliness, where will you and such like sinners appear? I know very well where. You must appear before the dreadful tribunal of Jesus Christ.

For however you may, like Felix, put off the prosecution of your convictions, yet you as well as others must arise after death and appear in judgment.[49] You will then find to your eternal sorrow what I just hinted at in the beginning of this discourse; namely, that your damnation slumbers not. Sin has blinded your hearts and hardened your foreheads now, but yet a little while and our Lord will ease him of his adversaries. Methinks already by faith I see the heavens opened and the holy Jesus coming with his face brighter than ten thousand suns, darting fury upon you from his eyes. Methinks I see you rising from your graves, trembling and astonished, and crying out, "Who can abide this day of his coming?"[50]

Encouragement to Watch and Pray

And now, what inference shall I draw from what has been delivered? Our Lord, in the words of the text, has drawn one for me: "Watch, therefore, for ye know neither the day nor the hour wherein the Son of Man comes."

Watch, that is, be upon your guard and keep your graces in continual exercises. For as when we are commanded to watch unto prayer, it signifies that we should continue [urgently] in that duty, so when we are required to watch, in general it means that we should put on the whole armor of God and live every day as though it was our last.[51]

And, oh, that the Lord may now enable me to lift up my voice like a trumpet! For had I a thousand tongues, or could I speak so loudly that the whole world might hear me, I could not sound a more useful alarm than that which is contained in the words of the text—watch, therefore, my brethren, I beseech you by the mercies of God in Christ Jesus. Watch, be upon your guard, awake ye that sleep in the dust, for ye know neither the day nor the hour wherein the Son of Man comes. Perhaps today, perhaps this midnight, the cry may be made. For in a moment, in a twinkling of an eye, the trumpet is to sound.

However, supposing the final day of judgment may yet be a great way off, yet the day of death is certainly near at hand. For what is our life? It is but a vapor, it is but a span long, so soon passes it away and we are gone. Blessed be God, we are all here well, but who out of this great multitude dares say, "I shall go home to my house in safety?" Who knows but while I am speaking, God may commission his ministering spirits immediately to call some of you away by a sudden stroke to give an account with what attention you have heard this sermon. You know, my brethren, some such instances we have lately had given us. And what angel or spirit has assured us that some of you shall not be the next? "Watch, therefore, for ye know neither the day nor the hour wherein the Son of Man will come." And it is chiefly for this reason that God has hid the day of our deaths from us. For since I know not but I may die tomorrow, why, oh my soul, may each of us say, will you not watch today? Since I know not but I may die the next moment, why will you not prepare for dying?

Many such reflections as these, my brethren, crowd in upon my mind. At present, blessed be the Lord who delights to magnify his strength in a poor worm's weakness, I am at a stand, not so much about what shall I say, as what I shall leave unsaid. My belly, like Elihu's, is, as it were, full of new wines, out of the abundance of my heart my mouth speaks.[52] The seeing so great a multitude standing before me, a sense of the infinite majesty of that God in whose name I preach and before whom I as well as you must appear to give an account of, and the uncertainty there is whether I shall live another day to speak to you any more—these considerations, I say, especially the presence of God which I now feel upon my soul, furnishes me with so much matter that I scarce know where to begin or where to end my application. . . .

What I say unto you, I say unto all: watch, high and low, rich and poor, young and old, one with another. I beseech you by the mercies of Jesus, whom I am now preaching, be upon your guard. Fly, fly, to Jesus Christ, that heavenly Bridegroom. Behold, he desires to take you to himself, miserable, poor, blind, and naked as you are, yet he is willing to clothe you with his everlasting righteousness and make you partakers of that glory which he enjoyed with the Father before the world began.

Oh, do not turn a deaf ear to me, do not reject the message on account of the [humbleness] of the messenger. I am a child, a youth of uncircumcised lips, but the Lord has chosen me that the glory might be all his own. Had he sent to invite you by a learned rabbi, you might have been tempted to think the man had done something, but now God has sent a child that cannot speak that the excellency of the power may be seen not to be of man but of God. Let the learned Pharisees, then, despise my youth. I care not how vile I appear in the sight of such men, I glory in it. And I am persuaded if any of you should be married to Christ by this preaching, you will have no reason to repent when you come to heaven that God sent a child to cry, "Behold the Bridegroom comes." Oh, my brethren, the thought of being instrumental in bringing one of you to glory fills me with fresh zeal.

My brethren, once more I entreat you, watch, watch, and pray, for the Lord Jesus will receive all that call upon him faithfully. Let that cry *Behold the Bridegroom comes* be continually sounding in your ears, and begin now to live as though you were assured this night you were to go forth to meet him.

I could say more, but the other business and duties of the day oblige me to stop. May the Lord give you all a hearing ear and obedient heart and so closely unite you to himself by one Spirit that when he shall come in a terrible majesty to judge mankind, you may be found having on a wedding garment and ready to go in with him to the marriage.

CHAPTER VI

Facing Opposition

One of the blessings of pursuing the Lord fervently is that our zeal for God unites us with like-minded Christians who become our companions on the journey of spiritual passion. Yet, we may find at times, often to our surprise, that not everyone in the body of Christ appreciates or shares our passion for Jesus.

Have you ever been told you worship too enthusiastically? Been asked to wrap up a lengthy prayer time? Had your lifestyle choices deemed too "holy" or too "unrealistic?" Received criticism that you are excessively "emotional" when it comes to God? Been censured as "judgmental" because of a moral position you hold?

A sad reality of life in the church is that most of us who desire to pursue the Lord deeply and passionately will at times encounter believers who look askance at our spiritual zeal, question our authenticity, or simply tell us to tone down our excitement and act more like a "normal" Christian. These criticisms hurt, especially when we are genuinely expressing our love for Jesus, and they also surprise us when they come from those inside the church. We expect pushback for loving God from non-believers, but from other Christians? In these instances, instead of feeling like we belong to a safe and encouraging spiritual family, we may experience hurt or isolation from our fellowship group, begin to doubt our spiritual choices, or even suffer a weakening of our own zeal for God.

I am reminded of the well-known story of William Carey, often called the Father of modern Protestant missions. As a young man in eighteenth-century England, Carey experienced spiritual conversion and left his nominal Anglican faith to join the Baptists, eventually becoming a minister. He felt a call from

God to share the gospel internationally with those who had not yet heard the good news of Jesus, but he was surprised by his fellow believers' lack of interest in overseas mission work. The story is told that when Carey contended for the importance of foreign missions at one Baptist leaders' meeting, an older colleague admonished him, "Young man, sit down! You are an enthusiast! When God pleases to convert the heathen, he'll do it without consulting you or me." Thankfully, Carey tenaciously surmounted this opposition to his passion for God and the unsaved, and in 1792 he organized a mission society, traveling to India with his family as a missionary the next year.[1]

Similarly, in John 2:13–22, the story is told of Jesus confounding the people in the temple in Jerusalem as he verbally rebukes and physically drives the merchants and moneychangers from the temple courts. In that moment, John writes, Jesus' disciples remember the words of David in Psalm 69:9a: "Zeal for your house consumes me." Perhaps the disciples also recalled the criticism David endured from the people of Israel for his own spiritual zeal when he welcomed the Ark of the Covenant into Jerusalem with ecstatic dancing in 2 Samuel 6:12–23.[2]

George Whitefield understood opposition from other believers, living as he did in a culture that was a veritable hotbed of religious turmoil and revolution. During the eighteenth century, both disruption and transformation in the spiritual landscape were produced by the rise of new religious sects such as the Moravians and the Methodists, lifestyle-focused movements such as Pietism with its encouragement of rigorous personal devotion and holiness, and evangelicalism's emphases on revivalism and being spiritually born again. Similar to our current time, disagreements in doctrine and practice both among and within Christian sub-groups were, sadly, the order of the day, especially during the years of the First Great Awakening.[3]

Although Whitefield was loved and respected by many for his zeal for the Lord and his passion for sharing the message of spiritual new birth in Jesus, he was not immune to the religious commotion and controversies of the time, especially given his international public image. During his 1739–1741 American preaching tour, Whitefield encountered opposition from those within Church of England parishes as well as Dissenting Protestant churches. Anglican ministers refused to open their pulpits to his preaching, Congregationalists criticized his ministry style, and Presbyterians publicly challenged his theology. Much of the hostility he experienced was intensely personal, occasionally petty, and shockingly vicious.

For example, the front page of the *South Carolina Gazette* for August 8, 1740, boasts a diatribe against Whitefield that scholars suspect may have been written by a fellow clergyman and that alleges Whitefield "seduces people out of the way, misguides them into bogs and fens, and there, bewildering, leaves them."[4] On November 17, 1739, Anglican missionary Jonathan Arnold (1701–1752) published a pamphlet in New York, advising his readers to "treat [Whitefield] as he deserves, i.e., with neglect and contempt as being the most irregular man in doctrine and manners that I ever knew, remarkable for ignorance and confidence."[5] South Carolina Anglican commissary Alexander Garden even brought official ecclesiastical charges against Whitefield, accusing him of breaking his ordination vows by preaching in Dissenting churches and not using the Anglican Book of Common Prayer. Garden's six published letters against Whitefield castigate the evangelist for the "pride and naughtiness" of his heart and insist that Whitefield and his writings will be "sunk into oblivion."[6] These are just a handful of the countless attacks that Whitefield encountered personally and professionally.

Whitefield viewed much of the hostility he faced from believers as persecution for his passionate pursuit of God, often quoting 2 Timothy 3:12: "In fact, everyone who wants to live a godly life in Christ Jesus will be persecuted." However, criticism from those he considered friends hurt him deeply, and his letters are replete with pleas to those close to him to maintain the unity of the Spirit: "Oh, how do I long for heaven! Surely, there will be no divisions, no strife there, [except] who shall sing with most affection to the Lamb that sits upon the throne."[7] Whitefield struggled with his own responses to resistance, over time becoming more adept at managing his relationships with those who opposed him as well as correcting his own faults and mistakes that stirred up resentment. He will be our experienced companion as we seek to understand the sources of resistance from other believers as well as how to respond to opposition in a God-honoring way.

SURPRISED BY OPPOSITION

Whitefield's first encounter with opposition from within the American church during his 1739–1741 preaching tour came from a fellow Anglican minister, William Vesey (1674-1746), commissary of New York.[8] Vesey had become the rector of New York's first Anglican church, Trinity Church, when it opened in 1698. As noted in Chapter 5, Whitefield arrived in New York City after traveling through parts of Pennsylvania and New Jersey, where revival supporter Gilbert Tennent and others joined his entourage. Himself an Anglican clergyman, Whitefield often met first with the commissaries of the larger cities he visited, hoping to preach and conduct services in their churches, and so he connected with Vesey on his second day in New York City, Vesey being away the first day that Whitefield attempted to visit him.

Whitefield's visit with Vesey was not at all what he had hoped for. According to Whitefield's journal, Vesey peremptorily refused Whitefield the use of his church before Whitefield even made the request and then unleashed a barrage of accusations against the young evangelist: preaching without a license, breaking his ecclesiastical oaths, sowing division in the body of Christ, and criticizing his ecclesiastical superiors. According to Whitefield, Vesey "seemed to be full of anger and resentment," which increased even more when Whitefield challenged his elder colleague on his patronizing of taverns. Due to Vesey's resistance, Whitefield had to content himself with preaching in Dissenting churches and fields during his stay in New York City.[9]

Why did Vesey oppose Whitefield, especially since the commissary was a fellow Anglican minister and Whitefield was an ordained Anglican clergyman himself? The answer is difficult to determine, especially from the distance of several centuries. Perhaps Vesey agreed with his English Anglican colleagues who opposed Whitefield's emphasis on the new birth and justification by faith alone for salvation, as well as his field preaching and passionate, extemporaneous sermon delivery. Maybe the commissary was challenged by the young preacher's fame or his ability to draw extraordinarily large crowds and collect equally extraordinarily large donations. Possibly, Vesey was just cantankerous—an earlier governor of New York had accused Vesey of lacking honesty and receiving political bribes as well as being "insolent and wicked."[10] Or perhaps Vesey was suffering from spiritual apathy or ministerial weariness; we all face times when exhaustion, distraction, pride, depression, or other obstacles derail our own passion for God.

The reality is, just as Whitefield probably could not put his finger on exactly why Vesey resisted him when he wished to preach the gospel in New York, we also may face times when we cannot identify why seemingly well-meaning Christians push back against our authentic passion for God. What we can understand and focus on, however, is how to respond in a God-honoring, respectful manner.

Whitefield was only in his mid-twenties when he encountered Vesey's attack in New York City, so perhaps it is not surprising that much of his response to Vesey reveals for us what *not* to do when opposed. From the two full journal pages that Whitefield devotes to describing his conversation with Vesey, we see that Whitefield responded somewhat aggressively to Vesey's questioning of his ministry. In the account, Whitefield not only criticizes his ecclesiastical superior for frequenting taverns, but he pushes back on practically every accusation Vesey levels at him, ending by somewhat brashly assuring the commissary, "I told him I was no respecter of persons—if a bishop committed a fault, I would tell him of it; if a common clergyman did not act aright, I would be free with him also, as well as with a layman."[11]

Whitefield also published his account of the disagreement in his wildly popular journals, a move he knew would make his version of the encounter the only narrative to receive widespread attention and also garner him public sympathy. Even more aggressive are Whitefield's concluding words of the journal entry: "Alas, alas, what manner of spirit are the generality of the clergy possessed with? Is this the Spirit of the meek Lamb of God? Are these the fruits of the Holy Ghost, which they pretend to be moved with when they take Holy Orders? It cannot be. Surely the kingdom of God will be taken from them."[12]

While it is certainly understandable that Whitefield was offended by the slanderous accusations Vesey threw at him, his very public and aggressive counter-attack may not have been the best approach. A few months before Whitefield sailed for America, he professed to a friend, "I always hope well of opposers," but there is little in Whitefield's response to Vesey that suggests he was giving the elder clergyman the benefit of the doubt.[13] In fact, Whitefield's concluding statements in his journal entry seem to convey the opposite senti- ment as he comes dangerously close to prophesying God's judgment on Vesey and others who oppose him.

The apostle James reminds us always to think the best of Christians who challenge us: "Don't speak evil against each other, dear brothers and sisters."[14] Similarly, in Titus 3:2, Paul encourages us to "speak evil of no one, to avoid quarreling, to be gentle, and to show perfect courtesy toward all people" as we pray for and anticipate God's work in their hearts and in our own.[15]

We are empowered to think the best of those who challenge us when we intentionally recognize our own poverty of spirit. In Matthew 5:3, Jesus an- nounces, "Blessed are the poor in spirit, for theirs in the kingdom of heaven." This is the first beatitude, or blessing, stated by Jesus in his Sermon on the Mount and is traditionally understood to mean that those who acknowledge their own spiritual neediness are the most effectively positioned to receive God's salvation and spiritual blessings. Remaining always "poor in spirit" helps us resist the temptation to respond aggressively to sisters and brothers who challenge us and our passion for God.

William Vesey's unexpected and somewhat unaccountable opposition to Whitefield in New York may have caught the young evangelist off guard, which might explain Whitefield's failure to respond to Vesey as graciously as he perhaps should have. Nonetheless, Whitefield got a second chance to react to a challenge to his ministry just six months later, although the reason for the resistance was very different.

GOING TOO FAR

When I was in my twenties, I was part of my church's search committee for a new senior pastor. We were a passionate bunch, and we were deter- mined to find a zealous, fiery minister of God who would come to our church and awaken all those who were spiritually asleep in our congregation. After many months, we selected the man we thought was exactly right. Vigorous, enthusiastic, and uncompromising, he visited our church and preached several sermons, after which a church-wide vote was held to decide if he would be offered the position.

Imagine our surprise and consternation when the vote came out against our candidate! How could this be? Why did our church not appreciate the hard work we had done? How could they not recognize the value of this candidate? Why were they so opposed to us and our passion for God in bringing the perfect minister to them?

Thankfully, some of the older members of the search committee helped diffuse our indignation and led us in reevaluating our process. Had we really allowed the priorities, history, and culture of our congregation to guide our search, or had we zealously pursued the person *we* believed would best fill our pulpit? Assessing our work more objectively, we realized that many of the attributes we loved about our candidate were in almost direct opposition to what our congregation valued. Although our motives were pure in bringing forward the individual we thought would bless our church, if we had acted just a bit more thoughtfully and humbly, we might have recognized that our candidate, while appealing to us, was probably not the best person for the job. That insight helped us acknowledge that the vote against our candidate was not really opposition to our passionate work for God, but instead a sign that we had gotten a bit off track in our sincere desire to serve and bless our brothers and sisters. Thankfully, our next choice was unanimously elected and had a fruitful ministry at the church.

As I discovered through my work on the pastoral search committee, we may experience times when, despite our zeal for God or perhaps even because of it, we make missteps that hurt fellow believers. When this happens and we encounter the inevitable pushback, we may be tempted to view the resistance as "opposition," when it is actually just a normal response to our mistake. These times can be challenging—it's difficult to see your own sin when you are reeling from what looks like hostility against you, as Whitefield's next encounter with resistance reveals.

In the spring of 1740, about halfway through his preaching tour as he returned to the mid-Atlantic region from visiting the southern colonies and his orphanage in Georgia, Whitefield published three letters in Philadelphia. Two of these letters offer Whitefield's opinion on the famous English Anglican archbishop John Tillotson (1630–1694).[16] At the time of the publication, Tillotson was a revered Anglican clergyman whose writings were still very popular and who emphasized rationality in matters of faith and the equality of many different theological belief systems.[17] In his published letters, Whitefield expresses doubt regarding Tillotson's knowledge of the gospel, writing blatantly, "Any spiritual man that reads [Tillotson's writings] may easily see that the archbishop knew of no other than a bare historical faith. And as to the method of our acceptance with God through Jesus Christ and our justification by faith alone, which is the doctrine of the scripture and the Church of England, he certainly was as ignorant thereof as Mahomet himself."[18]

Whitefield's motivation for printing such an inflammatory accusation against a revered minister of the Church of England was probably pure. Like many evangelical revivalists of the time, Whitefield zealously preached and believed in justification by faith alone. Tillotson's writings, on the other hand, did not present such a clear message of salvation by faith, and Whitefield worried that readers of the archbishop would be dangerously misled. However, labeling the respected Tillotson unconverted and, even worse, comparing him to the Muslim prophet Muhammad, the founder of Islam, was certainly uncharitable and perhaps even slanderous, and can be viewed as an unfortunate misstep by Whitefield.

Many people, particularly Anglicans, reacted against Whitefield's denunciation of Tillotson. One Church of England colleague who took great offense was the Rev. Archibald Cummings (d. 1741), commissary of Philadelphia and minister of Christ Church in that city. Whitefield had worked amicably with Cummings when he first visited Philadelphia in the fall of 1739, but when Whitefield returned to Philadelphia after the publication of his letters, the relationship was not the same. Cummings banned Whitefield from preaching in his church and himself preached twice against the evangelist while Whitefield was in the congregation. Cummings also published his sermons against Whitefield, noting in the preface, "My conscience bears me witness that I am doing my duty, that my designs are fair and honest. I am not so much concerned for my own vindication as for the credit of our holy and reasonable religion and for the reputation of our mother church under God, the bulwark of the Reformation, and of her ablest champions industriously abused and defamed of late."[19]

Whitefield did not take Cummings' correction kindly. Adopting the same strategy he had used against William Vesey in New York, Whitefield describes in his published journal how Cummings preached against him using Romans 10:2: "For I bear them record that they have a zeal of God, but not according to knowledge."[20] Whitefield bites back in his entry by declaring, "I bear him record that experience will soon convince him that whatever mine be, his own zeal is by no means according to knowledge."[21]

Even though Cummings was probably correct to challenge Whitefield on his printed defamation of Tillotson, we understand Whitefield's struggle to receive Cummings' rebuke gracefully. Not only is it difficult to remember that "wounds from a friend can be trusted" when we are face-to-face with the reality of our own sin, but doing so feels even more impossible when the one pointing out our misstep does so in a public, clumsy, or mean-spirited way, as Cummings appears to have done.[22] In a letter to his spiritual mentor John Wesley approximately five months before he embarked for his 1739–1741 tour of the colonies, Whitefield recognizes the value of godly reproof, writing, "I thank you most heartily for your kind rebuke; I can only say it was too tender. I beseech you, by the mercies of God in Christ Jesus, whenever you see me do wrong, rebuke me sharply."[23] Perhaps the aggressiveness of Cummings' reprimand or his lack of an intimate relationship with Whitefield simply made it too difficult for the young evangelist to recognize his own mistake in the situation.

In reality, any correction we receive from a sincere believer is an opportunity for the Holy Spirit to teach us, even if the rebuke comes in an inappropriate manner or even if the believer has blind spots of their own. We can trust that if we receive the correction with a humble heart, the Holy Spirit will reveal to us which parts of the message to apply to ourselves and which parts to respectfully discard. It is unfortunate that Whitefield was not able to receive Cummings' correction at this time because publicly identifying living and deceased ministers as unconverted was a polarizing practice of many revivalists in America during the early years of the First Great Awakening and turned many against the movement.

Thankfully, we serve a God who believes in second chances, and Whitefield got one just six months later when he visited the home of Jonathan Edwards in Northampton, Massachusetts, a visit highlighted in Chapter 4. Despite his staunch support for both the Awakening and Whitefield, Edwards also had concerns about the inclination of many revivalists to publicly question the salvation of fellow church members and ministers. According to Edwards, he personally cautioned Whitefield about "judging other persons to be unconverted."[24]

We can speculate that Edwards' reproof was more private and tender than was Cummings' because Edwards seems to have empathy for Whitefield's perspective and position. Edwards recognized that many inside the church were maliciously and inappropriately slandering and outright attacking Whitefield, sadly remarking in a letter to a fellow minister:

> It seems to me worthy greatly to be lamented by all true lovers of the Christian religion, which consists so much in love and forgiveness, that Mr. Whitefield should be pursued with so much violence and appearance of inveterate opposition and indefatigable endeavors to blacken him to the utmost, and with such artifices as it would be mean to use with respect to the basest miscreant . . . when there seems to be so little appearance of obstinacy and incorrigibleness in him and so much of the contrary, and when so little can be found by his most watchful enemies, now, to blame him for.[25]

Edwards appears to have taken the time to consider how painful attacks from professed believers were for Whitefield, and so we may assume that he offered his correction in a way that was easier for the beleaguered young evangelist to receive.

While Whitefield does not offer in his own writings an indication of his response to Edwards' admonition, we do see that just six months after visiting Edwards, Whitefield writes to his friend the Rev. Howell Harris, leader of the Awakening in Wales, "I am less positive than once I was [about judging others], lest [by accident] I should condemn some of God's dear children. The farther we go in the spiritual life, the more cool and rational shall we be, and yet more truly zealous. I speak this by experience."[26] Like Whitefield, most other revivalists eventually repented of condemning fellow church members as unconverted and stopped the practice.

Whitefield's experiences with Cummings and Edwards reveal two important points for us. First, when we do feel called to challenge a fellow Christian in an area of personal holiness, we should do so according to Paul's recommendation in Galatians 6:1a: "Brothers and sisters, if someone is caught in a sin, you who live by the Spirit should restore that person gently." Second, while it can be tempting to label any challenge to our passion for God as "opposition," a more mature and God-honoring response is to recognize godly rebuke and learn from it, regardless of the form in which it comes to us. As Proverbs 15:32 reminds us, "Those who disregard discipline despise themselves, but the one who heeds correction gains understanding." We can trust the Holy Spirit to help us discern and learn from godly correction.

Choosing to Bless

Opposition from those inside the church dogged Whitefield throughout the rest of his 1739–1741 preaching tour of America, and indeed the entirety of his professional ministry, but we do see some evidence as the tour closed that Whitefield had matured in his understanding of how to handle such challenges.

Just two months before he left America, Whitefield began to experience disagreements with a group of Christians with whom he had formerly enjoyed ardent support and fellowship—the Moravians. The Moravians were a pre-Reformation Protestant denomination founded in the early fifteenth century by reformer Jan Hus (c. 1370–1415) in what is now the Czech Republic, united and revitalized in the eighteenth century in Saxony, Germany, under the leadership of Count Nikolas Ludwig von Zinzendorf. Moravians were very involved in the First Great Awakening, sending missionaries to the American colonies and initially working closely with many leading English and American evangelicals, although they differed somewhat in theological beliefs.

In the fall of 1740, as Whitefield's American tour neared its end, James Hutton, Whitefield's friend and London publisher, joined the Moravians and subsequently refused to publish two of Whitefield's writings because his new theological beliefs now differed from Whitefield's Calvinism. This time, instead of striking back publicly or privately, Whitefield wrote to Hutton from Maryland in November: "I desire you to print nothing against your conscience, only do not immediately censure everything that may not seem clear to you. Our Lord may guide me even into things which as yet you may not see into. The day of judgment will discover all."[27]

Around the same time, Whitefield's friendship with German Moravian missionary to America Peter Böhler (1712–1775) became strained, also because of theological differences. Whitefield had connected with Böhler when they were both ministering in Pennsylvania and had worked with him to purchase land for a possible school for African Americans in Nazareth, Pennsylvania, but their frank discussions now began to reveal a growing theological impasse. However, in the same letter to Hutton, Whitefield declares, "I have lately conversed closely with P[eter] B[öhler]. Alas, we differ widely in many respects; therefore, to avoid disputation and jealousies on both sides, it is best to carry on the work of God apart. The divisions among the brethren sometimes grieve, but do not surprise me. . . . God grant that we may keep up a cordial undissembled love towards each other, notwithstanding our different opinions."[28] Almost one year later, Whitefield reiterated his desire for Christian unity with the Moravians, exclaiming in a letter to Böhler from Scotland, "I wish there may be no dissension between us for the time to come. May God preserve us from falling out in our way to heaven!"[29]

Whitefield's decision to pursue his own ministry separately from the Moravians in a spirit of love and blessing reminds me of Paul and Barnabas' disagreement over the suitability for ministry of the disciple John Mark as recorded in Acts 15:36–40:

> Some time later Paul said to Barnabas, "Let us go back and visit the
> believers in all the towns where we preached the word of the Lord and
> see how they are doing." Barnabas wanted to take John, also called
> Mark, with them, but Paul did not think it wise to take him, because
> he had deserted them in Pamphylia and had not continued with them
> in the work. They had such a sharp disagreement that they parted
> company. Barnabas took Mark and sailed for Cyprus, but Paul chose

Silas and left, commended by the believers to the grace of the Lord.

In this case, Paul and Barnabas disagree so strongly over the commitment of John Mark to the cause that they decide to separate. However, we can assume that these two men remained brothers in the unity of the Spirit because later, in 2 Timothy 4:11 and Colossians 4:10, we see that Paul is ministering with John Mark, calling him "useful" and asking the believers at Colossae to "welcome" him.[30] Similarly, in 1 Corinthians 9:6, Paul publicly links himself with Barnabas as two men who both are called by God as apostles and thus are worthy of financial support.

Whitefield's response to his Moravian brethren and their challenges to him at the close of his 1739–1741 preaching tour are strikingly different from his earlier responses to opposition and offer us additional wise advice for responding to criticism from inside the church. First, we should always choose kindness when interacting with believers who are opposing us, as the gentle tone of Whitefield's letter highlights. Remember Paul's exhortation to his disciple Timothy in 2 Timothy 2:24–25: "And the Lord's servant must not be quarrelsome but must be kind to everyone, able to teach, not resentful. Opponents must be gently instructed, in the hope that God will grant them repentance leading them to a knowledge of the truth."

Second, if possible, it is best to communicate directly to Christians who are challenging us instead of complaining or censuring them behind their backs. As Jesus teaches in Matthew 18:15, "If your brother or sister sins, go and point out their fault, just between the two of you. If they listen to you, you have won them over." Whitefield's private letters to Hutton and Böhler appear more in line with Jesus' teaching than does his public denunciations of earlier opponents in his published journals. Addressing disagreements in private with those who oppose us is always preferable so each person has the chance to consider and pray without the pressure of a public debate.

Third, as believers, we are free to bless and pray for those we disagree with, trusting that God will continue to work in their lives and ministries as well as in our own. As the apostle Paul assures us in 2 Corinthians 5:10, we are each ultimately responsible only for ourselves and our own actions: "For we must all appear before the judgment seat of Christ, so that each of us may receive what is due us for the things done while in the body, whether good or bad." We can focus on our own growth in love and godliness and wish the best for others, trusting that God loves them and will work as he wishes in their lives. As Whitefield prayed in a letter to his spiritual mentor John Wesley in 1735, "Oh, heavenly Father, for your dear Son's sake, keep me from climbing. Let me hate preferment! For your infinite mercies' sake, let me love a low, contemptible life and never think to compound matters between the happiness of this world and the next!"[31] Attending to our own hearts during our time on earth will empower us to pray for others, even those who oppose us, that God may bless them and their ministry.

Ultimately, we cannot control all aspects of opposition to our passion for the Lord, but we can pray and hope to honor God and bless our brothers and sisters in Christ. As Paul reminds us in Ephesians 4:1–6:

> As a prisoner for the Lord, then, I urge you to live a life worthy of the calling you have received. Be completely humble and gentle; be patient, bearing with one another in love. Make every effort to keep the unity of the Spirit through the bond of peace. There is one body and one Spirit, just as you were called to one hope when you were called; one Lord, one faith, one baptism; one God and Father of all, who is over all and through all and in all.

By the power of the Holy Spirit, we can maintain the "unity of the Spirit through the bond of peace" as far as it depends upon us as we pursue Jesus with zeal.

I would add one final thought on the topic of handling challenges from fellow believers. Opposition is painful, whatever its source. Criticism, resistance, conflict, and hostility hurt, and our hearts are wounded when those inside the church oppose our passion for God. We can rest in the reality that God is our comfort and strength during these difficult times, and he understands how challenging and complicated it is to deal with opposition in a godly manner. We must consciously and intentionally prioritize time in the Lord's presence during these seasons, so our heart can heal, our mind can be renewed, and we can receive the comfort and wisdom of the Holy Spirit. Ignoring our feelings and responding to opposition without allowing God to heal our spirit can lead to bitterness, anger, discouragement, and resentment.

Recall the story of Elijah, an Old Testament prophet to the northern king-dom of Israel during the reign of the King Ahab and Queen Jezebel. In 1 Kings 18:1–40, Elijah defeats 850 prophets of the false gods Baal and Asherah on Mount Carmel, turning the hearts of the Israelites back to God. But Jezebel is angered by Elijah's actions, vowing to kill him the next day, and her opposition sends the prophet fleeing into the wilderness and spiraling into such a deep depression that he asks God to end his life. Thankfully, God ministers to Elijah during his time in the wilderness, speaking to him in a "gentle whisper," com-forting him, identifying Elisha as his successor, and assuring Elijah that 7,000 Israelites are still faithful followers of Yahweh. Like Elijah, when suffering the pain of opposition, we can press into "the Father of compassion and the God of all comfort, who comforts us in all our troubles."[32] God himself will heal us, guide us, and strengthen us as only he can.

OPPOSITION FROM AMERICAN PRESBYTERIANS

We will conclude this chapter with a deeper look into one of the more hurtful experiences of opposition that Whitefield encountered during his 1739–1741 American preaching tour—a public challenge to his ministry and theology from Presbyterian Dissenters in the mid-Atlantic. Presbyterian min-isters and laypeople were some of Whitefield's most supportive and intimate friends during his visit to the colonies, as evidenced by his close relationship with the Presbyterian clergyman Gilbert Tennent discussed in Chapter 5, but some Presbyterians opposed both Whitefield and the Awakening. In the fall of 1740, as Whitefield neared the end of his preaching tour, a group of anti-reviv-alist laymen from the New Castle Presbytery in what is now Delaware took to the press to publicly dissect and disagree with a cluster of the Grand Itinerant's written sentiments.

Painstakingly scouring Whitefield's printed journals and sermons for po-tentially controversial remarks, the Querists, as the authors styled themselves, produced a thirty-two-page document that offers readers "some paragraphs out of Mr. Whitefield's printed writings" along with the authors' "queries upon such paragraphs."[33] In the document, the Querists accuse Whitefield of a mul-titude of varying and, in some cases, contradictory theological missteps, such as claiming righteous actions help earn salvation; proposing that Christians do not need to follow God's laws; and advocating "popish [Catholic] doctrine," "Antinomian error," and "Arminianism," all damning theological accusations for the Presbyterians, the majority of whom were Calvinist in doctrine.[34]

The attack hurt Whitefield, but he records in his journal that although it was a "bitter pamphlet," God gave him "freedom" to respond in print and "enabled [him] to write it in the spirit of meekness."[35] In his response, Whitefield admits errors in some of the phrases highlighted by the Querists, mentions several additional statements of his in printed sermons that he now believes are also incorrect, and defends his commitment to Calvinism as well as extemporaneous preaching. The tone of Whitefield's response is remarkably gracious, but one also detects some sadness.[36]

Whitefield was in New York for his third visit to that city when *The Querists* appeared in Philadelphia, and although the publication deeply grieved him, he experienced significant professional and personal fruit in the days following the attack. Two days after reading *The Querists*, Whitefield writes in his journal of a powerful Sabbath evening service:

> For near half an hour before I left Mr. Noble's house [to preach], I could only lie before the Lord and say, "I was a poor sinner and wonder that Christ would be gracious to such a wretch." As I went to meeting, I grew weaker and weaker, and when I came into the pulpit, I could have chosen to be silent rather than speak. But after I had begun, the Spirit of the Lord gave me freedom, till at length it came down like a mighty rushing wind and carried all before it. Immediately, the whole congregation was alarmed. Shrieking, crying, weeping, and wailing were to be heard in every corner, men's hearts failing them for fear and many falling into the arms of their friends. My soul was carried out till I could scarce speak anymore. A sense of God's goodness overwhelmed me.[37]

That evening in his room, Whitefield encountered God's presence and a deep spirit of intercession, recording, "Divine manifestations flowed in so fast that my frail tabernacle [his body] was scarce able to sustain them. My dear friends sat round me on the bedsides. I prayed for each of them alternately with strong cries and pierced by the eye of faith, even within the veil."[38]

Whitefield attributed this fruitfulness to the opposition he had just faced. He exults in his journal, "Oh, how am I obliged to my enemies! God has remarkably revealed himself to my soul ever since I have seen the pamphlet published by the Presbyterians against me. Oh, how faithful is he that has promised, 'It shall bruise your heel, and you shall bruise his head!' Lord, enable me to lay hold on this during the time of my sojourning here on earth."[39]

Whitefield faced opposition from fellow Christians his entire life and ministry, but his growth in responding to difficult encounters during his 1739–1741 preaching tour encourages us that we too can learn to handle resistance with grace and kindness. In a letter sent from Edinburgh to a friend in Pennsylvania in 1742, eighteen months after he had returned from America, Whitefield displays remarkable maturity and wisdom:

Though, as you know, I am clear in the truths of the gospel, yet I find that principles of themselves, without the Spirit of God, will not unite any set of men whatever, and where the Spirit of God is in any great degree, there will be union of heart, though there may be difference in sentiments. This I have learned, my dear brother, by happy experience, and find great freedom and peace in my soul thereby. This makes me to love many, though I cannot agree with them in some of their principles. I dare not look upon them as willful deceivers, but as persons who hazard their lives for the sake of the gospel. Mr. W., I think, is wrong in some things, and Mr. L. wrong also, yet I believe that both Mr. L. and Mr. W., and others with whom we do not agree in all things, will shine bright in glory.[40]

What follows are portions of *The Querists* and related excerpts of Whitefield's published response. I hope these extracts provide a window into Whitefield's experience with opposition and how God enabled him to continue to pursue Jesus and ministry with passion and faith.

PAMPHLET

The Querists, or, An Extract of Sundry Passages Taken Out of Mr. Whitefield's Printed Sermons, Journals, and Letters[41]

To the Readers.

Christian friends,

The following queries and remarks seem to us to concern matters of the utmost importance. We are represented in the scripture as pilgrims and travelers [to] a better country, and as a wrong choice of the road may ruin us eternally, we ought to examine every step we tread and take notice that our guides be not blind nor mistaken, lest they lead us astray.[42] None can blame us when our souls are in danger of eternal ruin to look to ourselves and to secure the one thing needful. Nor dare we allow ourselves to follow the multitude if we fear they go astray, nor regard any man further than he follows Christ.

And we hope this will justify us in what we have done in the following pages, for if all our Christian brethren who may think it worthwhile to read our remarks have such superior attainments as to see clearly that all that Mr. Whitefield has printed is sound and agreeable to the holy scriptures, yet we hope that their Christian charity is so great that they will not condemn us for applying as we have done to our teachers and, by their advice, to Mr. Whitefield himself, to remove some unhappy stumbling blocks out of our way. We cannot help thinking for ourselves and judging of things according to the light they appear in, and we promise that when that gentleman satisfies us in these things, we will believe him, and we cannot do it sooner.

But when we reflect that he is but a man, that great and good men have been mistaken, and that infallibility (as far as we know) is entailed neither on him nor his followers, we hope that both he and they are better Christians than to blame us if we can be the instruments of pointing out their mistakes, if there be any. We believe that they regard their souls and will look on it as the most eminent service [that] can be done them if by our means they receive a kindness that will turn to their account through a boundless eternity.

We confess that we are at a loss to know what to make of some of his expressions. If they have any meaning at all, we fear that it is a bad one and will rejoice to find ourselves disappointed if he shows us that they are sound and good. But if he pretends hurry or [lack] of time and does not either justify or condemn them or give us some satisfaction, he will constrain us to think that he has his own glory in view more than the glory of God or the good of his church.

He has such high conceptions of man or such low conceptions of God that we fear he has just conceptions of neither. To say, "That man was adorned with all the perfections of the Deity, that he was the perfection of the moral and material world," as he does, page 17, vol. 2 of *Sermons*, is what we can neither believe nor find ground from reason nor revelation to support it.[43] When our [ministers] prove the divinity of our blessed Lord, they sometimes do it (we think to good purpose) by proving that the scriptures attribute to him all the perfections of the Deity, and, of consequence, that he is the eternal God, equal with the Father and Holy Spirit. But if a mere man may be adorned with all these perfections, we know not what to make of this argument until he give us better light. . . .

When we hear him tell us, "That the regenerate washes away the guilt of sin by the tears of a sincere repentance, joined with faith in the blood of Christ," p. 22, 23, vol. 2, we think that it favors of popery and Arminianism to join anything with the blood of Christ to wash away sin, and hope it will offend none that we cannot believe this on his bare word contrary to many scripture texts, for we abhor an implicit faith. Is not that expression of the same stamp?

Vol. 1, p. 79, where he says, "That a single aim at God's glory alone can render our actions acceptable in God's sight." If a single aim at God's glory alone can render our actions acceptable in his sight, what need is there for the blood of Christ? We hope none of our brethren will be offended that we cannot believe this popish doctrine till he explain or prove it from scripture....

Mr. Whitefield, in his journal, p. 127, says, "I find I gain greater light and knowledge by preaching extemporaneously so that I fear I should quench the Spirit did I not go on to speak as he gives me utterance."

If by preaching extemporaneously be meant preaching without pre-meditation or studying, we would ask whether any since the days of Moses that were found in the faith have said that they gained more scripture light and knowledge by not reading and meditating on God's word than by so doing.... Is there any grounds of fear of quenching God's Spirit, whether in his ordinary or extraordinary gifts, by performing the plain duties of reading of and meditating on God's word? Is not here a plain insinuation of imme-diate impulses and dependence thereupon? If Mr. Whitefield will allow us to try the spirits, what spirit is [it] that Mr. Whitefield fears to quench by reading the scriptures or meditating on them, or by reading and studying other good books, or by writing his sermons and making moderate use of his notes to help his memory....

Is it not evident by comparing Mr. Whitefield's printed sermons with other good sermon books that some of our old Scottish [ministers] have more matter in one page than he has in several pages? And is it not true that though Mr. Whitefield speaks many sound truths on some common heads of divinity, yet we desire to know, what point in divinity is that which some other divines of our own have not more than trebled him in distinctness, exactness, and explicitness? And will any tell us what is the reason that many [recent] sermons preached by Mr. Whitefield's warm adherents are (if we mistake not) more barren of matter and method than some of their former sermons, as being more hung on a common string, if this proceed not from [lack] of studying. . . .

These remarks and queries were considered maturely by the Presbytery of New Castle, and it was thus agreed upon that Mr. Whitefield, being expected soon to come again into these parts, therefore, as he best understands his own intentions in these expressions that seem to us to have a bad aspect, we leave it to the people to print their remarks and Mr. Whitefield himself to answer them.

LETTER

A Letter From the Rev. Mr. Whitefield, to Some Church-Members of the Presbyterian Persuasion, in Answer to Certain Scruples Lately Proposed in Proper Queries Raised on Each Remark[44]

My Dear Friends,

Last night and this morning, I have read your queries and scruples. Whether they were compiled by church members or ministers of the Presbyterian persuasion, I shall not take upon me to determine. I think I may say with David on another occasion, "Joab's hand is in this."[45] If your ministers were really the authors and you only their representatives, they have not acted simply. They had better have spoken out. I should as readily have answered them as you. Solomon says, "He that hates reproof is brutish," and if I know anything of my own heart, I should think myself obliged to anyone that convinces me of any error, either in principle or practice.[46]

I therefore assure you that I do not find the least resentment stirring in my soul against those (whoever they be) that proposed the queries or against the reverend presbytery that advised you to send them to me in a public manner. No, I rejoice in it because it gives me an opportunity of doing what my friends know I have for some time proposed—namely, to correct some passages in my printed sermons. I think it no dishonor to retract some expressions that have formerly dropped from my pen before God was pleased to give me a more clear knowledge of the doctrines of grace. Saint Augustine, I think, did so before me.

The Lord's dealing with me was somewhat out of the common way. I can say, to the honor of rich, free, distinguishing grace, that I received the spirit of adoption before I had conversed with one man or read a single book on the subject of free justification by the imputed righteousness of Jesus Christ. No wonder then that I was not so clear in some points at my first setting out in the ministry. Our Lord was pleased to enlighten me by degrees, and I desire your prayers that his grace may shine more and more in my heart till it breaks forth into perfect day.

But to come to the exceptionable passages in my sermons. You blame me for saying, page 17, vol. 2, "That Adam was adorned with all the perfections of the Deity." It's a wrong expression. I would correct it thus, "All the moral communicable perfections of the Deity." Again, "Man was the perfection of the moral and material world." Let it stand thus, "The perfection of all the visible world."

Pages 22 & 23, vol. 2, "Washes the guilt of sin away by the tears of a sincere repentance, joined with faith in the blood of Jesus Christ." This is false divinity. I would now alter it thus, "Recovers his former peace by renewing his acts of faith on the perfect righteousness of Jesus Christ."

Page 79, vol. 1, "And which alone can render any of our actions acceptable in God's sight." It should be, "And without which, any of our actions cannot be acceptable in God's sight. . . ."

These, if I mistake not, are all the passages in my sermons which you object against. And now, to convince you that I am not ashamed to own my faults, I can inform you of other passages as justly exceptionable. In my sermon on justification, I seem to assert universal redemption, which I now absolutely deny. In my *Almost Christian* [sermon], I talk of works procuring us so high a crown. In my sermon on the *Marks of the New Birth*, I say, "We shall endure to the end if we continue so."[47]

These, and perhaps some other passages, though capable of a candid interpretation, I now dislike, and in the next edition of my sermons, God willing, I propose to alter them. In the meanwhile, I shall be thankful to any that will point out my errors, and I promise, by divine assistance, they shall have no reason to say that I am one who hates to be reformed. "Let the righteous smite me, it shall be a kindness, and let him reprove me, and it shall be an excellent oil, which shall not break my head, for yet my prayer also shall be in their calamities. . . ."[48]

Do not condemn me for preaching extemporaneously and saying I am helped often immediately in that exercise when thousands can prove, as well as myself, that it has been so. Neither should you censure me as one that would lay aside reading. I am of Bishop Sanderson's mind: study without prayer is atheism; prayer without study, presumption.[49] Blame me not for the warmth of some of my adherents, as you call them. One of your ministers knows how sharply I rebuked one of them for his warmth at Fagg's Manor.[50] I am for loving as brethren and wish all would copy after the lowly Jesus. But then I cannot [disparage] those (supposing they do it in the spirit of meekness) who exclaim against dry, sapless, unconverted ministers. Such surely are the bane of the Christian church. But my other affairs will not permit me to enlarge.

Some of the latter part of your queries, for your own and not my sake, I shall not mention. I hope I can say with more sincerity than Hazael, "Is your servant a dog that he should do what you suggest?"[51] But I pray God forgive you. He knows my heart. My one design is to bring poor souls to Jesus Christ. I desire to avoid extremes so as not to be a bigot on the one hand or confound order and decency on the other.

And I could heartily wish the reverend presbytery, when they advised you to publish your queries, had also cautioned you against dipping your pen in so much gall. Surely your insinuations are contrary to that charity that hopes and believes all things for the best. And I appeal to your own hearts whether it was right, especially since you heard the constant tenor of my preaching in America has been Calvinistic, to censure me as a papist or Arminian because a few unguarded expressions dropped from my pen just as I came out of the University of Oxford. Could Archbishop Tillotson or the author of *The Whole Duty of Man* say so?[52] But I have done. The Lord be with you. I am a poor, frail creature, and, as such, I beseech you to pray for, Your affectionate friend and servant,

George Whitefield

N. Hone pinx.   Carington Bowles excudit.   J. Greenwood fecit.

The Reverend M^r*. George Whitefield. A.M.*

Chaplain to the Countess of Huntingdon.

LONDON, Published as the Act directs, July 1st 1769.   Printed for CARINGTON BOWLES, N.º 69 St Pauls Church Yard.

CHAPTER VII

Responding to Culture

Sharing the journey of spiritual passion and facing opposition in a godly manner are important aspects of life as a fiery lover of God within the body of Christ. But every follower of Jesus also exists within larger communities—schools, workplaces, neighborhoods, cities, and the broader society. Thus, our life of spiritual passion unfolds organically and inescapably within the wider culture in which we live and demands that we respond to the environment around us. How do we live out our passion for God within our culture in ways that are authentic and satisfying, honoring to Jesus, and a blessing to others?

The foundation of our interaction with society as a Christian is our identity as a beloved child of God the Father, fervent disciple of Jesus Christ, and overflowing vessel of the Holy Spirit. As such, we are true citizens of heaven, present on earth to testify to the One who saved us and to bring his perfect light and love to a lost and hurting world. As the apostle Peter so beautifully writes in 1 Peter 2:9, "But you are a chosen race, a royal priesthood, a holy nation, a people for his own possession, that you may proclaim the excellencies of him who called you out of darkness into his marvelous light." Similarly, Paul exhorts his readers to be "blameless and innocent, children of God without blemish in the midst of a crooked and twisted generation, among whom you shine as lights in the world."[1] And, lest we forget the words of the Author and Finisher of our faith, Jesus himself declares our mission in his Sermon on the Mount:

> You are the light of the world. A town built on a hill cannot be hidden.
> Neither do people light a lamp and put it under a bowl. Instead they
> put it on its stand, and it gives light to everyone in the house. In the

same way, let your light shine before others, that they may see your
good deeds and glorify your Father in heaven.[2]
As the church of Jesus Christ, we are called to minister God's love and light to
our lost and needy world.

Which is always super easy and fun, right? Wrong. Living as God's eternal
light in a "crooked and twisted generation" is anything but easy and often not
very fun, given that most of the communities in which we live and minister
are not oriented toward the pursuit or reverence of God. Living a life of spiritual passion in a world saturated with sin often means our obedience to God
is challenged, our love for him derided, our witness to him ignored, and our
good-intentioned ministry rejected.

In addition, responding to the culture around us in a godly way is complicated, thanks to the never-ending fluctuations of modern society and our own
struggles with sin. Do I challenge my friend's unbiblical ideas about God or simply share my own experiences with Jesus? Should I pull my kids out of health
class at the local elementary school because I disagree with some of their teachings or help my children think and talk through the class material at home? How
much time does God want me to spend interacting with my friends on social
media, which political candidate should I support, what's the best way to show
Jesus' love to my unfriendly neighbors, how can I work as an advocate for social
justice in the most biblically consistent way? The list goes on and on.

As a college professor, I have seen youth culture change over the decades,
requiring me to adjust my responses to the needs of students. The increased
prevalence of anxiety and depression among undergraduates, for example, has
forced me to rethink my attendance policies, grade penalties for missed dead-
lines, and assignments. Recently, a student informed me that a group project
was causing her extreme stress and asked if she could do the assignment individually. As a Christian educator, how should I respond?

Allowing her to complete the assignment by herself might alleviate her
stress and thus be an act of kindness, but would it be fair to the other students
in the class? Was her unhappiness negatively impacting the learning experience of her fellow group members and should I allow her to work alone to

protect them? Would she learn more by doing the project herself? Was working with the group an opportunity I could provide for the student to grow as a person and a scholar?

After receiving input from several helpful people on campus and asking the Holy Spirit for guidance, I decided to require the student to remain with the group. I met with the student and the group to help them develop a game plan for how to proceed, and the team's final project was excellent, receiving the highest grade in the class. Later, the student thanked me for requiring her to complete the project with the group, sharing that she believed the experience had helped her grow in trusting and working with others. While not every situation ends this favorably, I was thankful that God helped me respond in a way that blessed one of my students.

The challenge and complexity of living and ministering in a fallen world can produce two inappropriate responses in Christians. First, we may consciously or unconsciously retreat from the culture, deeming it too ungodly to be worthy or receptive of our ministry. Second, we may react against society, contenting ourselves with simply condemning or criticizing those around us. Neither response is reflective of the heart of God, who loves and pursues all of his created ones passionately, always trusting, always hoping, always persevering, never failing to love.[3] As his children, we want to respond to the world in which we live as God would, drawing others to Jesus and blessing them.

What are some effective ways we can respond to our culture as zealous disciples of God? How can we bring the light and love of Jesus to our generation? Despite living in a time when most people didn't stray more than a few miles from the place of their birth, globe-trotting George Whitefield encountered more diverse and challenging sub-cultures than probably even most twenty-first-century believers. During his early preaching tours of the American colonies, he interacted with Indigenous peoples, enslaved and free blacks, married and single women and men, children and teenagers, university students and orphans, prisoners and servants, the wealthy and the poor, ministers and lay people, and Christians and non-Christians.

In this chapter, we follow Whitefield on his 1739–1741 preaching tour as he interacts with the highest-ranking government official in Massachusetts, ministers personally to often-overlooked individuals in Philadelphia, and publicly challenges a central component of the culture of the American South. His encounters with these radically diverse communities reveal for us several helpful hints on how to respond to our culture with the passion and love of God.

Stand for Truth

The concept of absolute truth is not much in vogue these days, if it truly ever is. Our natural propensity as humans is to manipulate any given situation, idea, detail, narrative, or tradition to suit our own goals and needs. Historical accounts are contested, eyewitness testimonies differ, and he said-she said encounters resist resolution. Everyone has the inalienable right to their own "truth," and woe to the individual who is so foolhardy as to challenge it.

In contrast to this perspective, the Bible assures us that God believes in, values, and personally defines absolute truth that exists outside of time-dependent circumstances. Paul assures believers in Romans 1:18 that "the wrath of God is revealed from heaven against all ungodliness and unrighteousness of men, who by their unrighteousness suppress the truth."[4] Jesus himself advocated for truth and spoke of it often during his time on earth. He claims he is "the truth" in John 14:6, assures the Jews who follow him that "the truth will set you free" in John 8:32, retorts when questioned by Pontius Pilate that he came to earth "to testify to the truth" in John 18:37, and promises his followers he will send the "Spirit of truth" to live inside them in John 14:17.

As children of God and passionate lovers of Jesus, then, we also must acknowledge the reality of God's absolute truth, despite its rejection by our culture. Living according to God's eternal truth will flavor our lives with a timelessness that reflects God's unchanging nature and perfect veracity, irrespective of our environments. As Paul writes in Ephesians 1:13–14, "In him you also, when you heard the word of truth, the gospel of your salvation, and believed in him, were sealed with the promised Holy Spirit, who is the guarantee of our inheritance until we acquire possession of it, to the praise of his glory."[5] Our passion for an eternal God of truth will inevitably result in responses to culture that preserve and testify to the absolute truth of God.

But standing for God's truth in a culture that prizes relativity and individuality isn't easy. We are tempted daily to massage what we know to be true to protect our own interests, fit in, or simply enjoy the benefits of going along with the crowd. How can we learn to channel our passion for God into standing for truth in a culture that vehemently resists it?

George Whitefield was, beyond all doubt, a man who stood for truth in his generation. Completely convinced of the veracity of the gospel of Jesus Christ and the necessity of being spiritually born again by God's grace and justified by faith alone, Whitefield preached tirelessly and fervently the message of salvation to all who would listen, never softening or denying the truth of God, regardless of his audience. His passion for God's truth was noted by one listener in New York during his visit there in 1739: "He is as meek as a lamb in his own cause, but in the cause of God he is as bold as a lion. His courage seems always to rise in proportion to the opposition he meets with. . . . He seems to be raised up by God for great designs."[6] During Whitefield's 1739–1741 American preaching tour, one high-ranking Bostonian encountered Whitefield and the truth he championed in a very personal and transformative way.

Jonathan Belcher was born in Boston and raised in a wealthy merchant family. Educated at Harvard, Belcher enjoyed his own personal version of the Grand Tour of Europe, meeting the future King George II of England (1660–1727; reign 1714–1727) when in Hanover. When the governor of Massachusetts died suddenly in 1729, Belcher, working in London at the time, was appointed governor of both Massachusetts and New Hampshire and returned to the colonies.

Religiously, Belcher was a staunch supporter of the established Congregational churches in New England, having been a member of the legendary Old South Church in Boston since his childhood. Biographer Michael C. Batinski notes that Belcher was intrigued by the First Great Awakening, excitedly anticipating Whitefield's arrival in Boston in the fall of 1740.[7] But how would Belcher respond to Whitefield's uncompromising message of the necessity of being spiritual born again?

Perhaps even more importantly, how would Whitefield respond to Belcher, the highest-ranking government official in the colony? Whitefield had shared his message of the new birth fearlessly with crowds throughout America, battled in print and in public with those who opposed him, and aligned himself unashamedly with the oft-maligned revivalists. Would he have the courage to maintain his passion for God's truth when confronted with a man as powerful and well-connected as Belcher?

That Whitefield chose to visit Belcher on his very first day in Boston gives us an idea of how the evangelist intended to interact with the governor. Whitefield writes in his journal that Belcher "received me with the utmost respect." Their conversation must have shifted to spiritual topics even during this first meeting because Whitefield also records that the governor "seemed to savor the things which were of God and desired me to see him as often as I could."[8] From Whitefield's journal, we learn that the evangelist maintained his commitment to God's truth in his interactions with the governor during his three-week stay in and around Boston, preaching sermons on the new birth when Belcher was in the audience, dining with Belcher in his home, and sharing many private emotional conversations and prayer times with Belcher.[9]

That Belcher was affected by Whitefield and the truth he shared is revealed by the fact that the day after he left Boston, Whitefield was surprised to see Belcher at the church where he was preaching in Marlborough, Massachusetts, approximately thirty miles away. After the sermon, Belcher traveled with Whitefield and his group to Worcester, Massachusetts, another fifteen miles further, pulling Whitefield aside privately the next morning and exhorting him to "not spare rulers any more than ministers, no, not the chief of them" in his preaching. Upon hearing Whitefield preach at Worcester, Belcher, with tears in his eyes, left Whitefield to return to Boston with these words: "I pray God, I may apply what has been said to my own heart. Pray, Mr. Whitefield, that I may hunger and thirst after righteousness." Whitefield was moved by the governor's eagerness for God, commenting in his journal that he enjoyed "greater power than ordinary whenever the governor has been at public worship. A sign, this, I hope, that the Most High intends to set him at his right hand."[10]

What can account for Whitefield's success in reaching Governor Belcher with the truth of God with passion and without compromise? I would suggest that the evangelist potently combined an unwavering declaration of God's truth during his public sermons with personalized and tender care for Belcher during private meetings. Lest we forget, Jesus himself was "full of grace *and* truth."[11] Whitefield records in his journal more than half a dozen private meetings with the governor to talk and pray. During many of those encounters, Whitefield writes of how "affected" Belcher is, sometimes even crying. During Whitefield's last day in Boston, for example, the evangelist records that Belcher visited him privately in his quarters and, "weeping, most earnestly desired my prayers."[12]

Whitefield was able to overcome any fears he may have had in light of Belcher's position and influence to reach the governor with the truth of his message. And the message stuck. According to his biographer, Belcher became a "champion" of the revival, supporting the "evangelical cause" until his death.[13]

We will close this section with a short letter Whitefield wrote to Belcher just three weeks after he left Boston and preached his way south to Philadelphia. In the letter, Whitefield updates Belcher on his ministry and reinforces his encouragement to Belcher to "follow the simplicity of the blessed Jesus."[14] Whether in person or at a distance, Whitefield never stifled his passion for proclaiming God's life-changing truth.

LETTER

Whitefield to his Excellency Jonathan Belcher, Esq., in Boston, Philadelphia, November 9, 1740[15]

To his Excellency Jonathan Belcher, Esq., in Boston
Philadelphia, Nov. 9, 1740

Though late, I now snatch a few moments to send your excellency my acknowledgments for all honors received at Boston—they are much upon my heart. I pray God to reward your excellency a thousand-fold.

Great things has the glorious Emmanuel done for me and his people on the way: the word has been attended with much power. Surely our Lord intends to set America in a flame. This week, Mr. G[ilbert] T[ennent] purposes to set out for Boston, in order to blow up the divine fire lately kindled there. I recommend him to your excellency as a solid, judicious, and zealous minister of the Lord Jesus Christ. He will be ready to preach daily; I suppose his brethren will readily open their doors. May the Lord at the same time open the people's hearts that they may diligently attend to the things that shall be spoken.

Dear Mr. R. grows in grace.[16] I left him at Brunswick, full of gratitude for his [recent] journey. I am persuaded it was of God. I hope he will be instrumental in quickening both ministers and people. He is worthy of your excellency's particular regard; under God, he may need it. I expect he will soon be reviled and persecuted for his blessed Master's sake. May the Lord enable him to rejoice and be exceeding glad.

Dear sir, the welfare of dear Boston people, especially the welfare of your own soul, lies upon me night and day. I remember your tears. I remember your excellency's words, "Mr. Whitefield, pray that I may hunger and thirst after righteousness." Oh, how did these words rejoice me, for I thought your excellency [needed] a more clear view of your own vileness and of the all-sufficiency of Jesus Christ. I mean a more clear, [experiential] view. For what is all head knowledge without that of the heart? It only settles people more upon [a false assurance]. May God give you to see and to follow the simplicity of the blessed Jesus. While you are in the world, may you not be of it. May you be dead to magnificence and alive to nothing but what leads you directly to your God.

Honored sir, I make no apology for this freedom. Your excellency bid me not spare rulers, no, not the chief of them. Indeed, I long after your salvation. Oh, that I could do anything to promote it! If my prayers or anything within my power may be instrumental thereunto, your excellency may command, honored sir,

Your Excellency's obliged, humble servant,

G.W.

LOVE THE OVERLOOKED

Loving others is one of the two greatest commandments for Christians as well as a second impactful way to respond to culture.[17] As we allow the unceasing, overwhelming, all-consuming, eternal love of God to flow through us and into our communities, we transform those we meet and fulfill Jesus' charge in John 15:12b: "Love each other as I have loved you."

Loving people well is a topic that is beyond the scope of this chapter, but I would like to focus this section on one idea related to investing love into our culture—noticing and loving the overlooked. It's easy for people to go unnoticed. Our human tendency toward ambition, materialism, and self-aggrandizement means that many people feel unseen, and that experience is deeply and profoundly hurtful. As zealous lovers of God, we are uniquely positioned to see and bless those who have been disregarded by our culture because we know that in God's eyes, every individual alive on this earth bears his image and is of infinite worth. We also know that, regardless of our position in the culture, our struggles and hope are identical—we each suffer from original sin and desperately need salvation through Jesus, and we each can become part of the family of God by his grace and indwelt by God's Holy Spirit.

Loving those the culture ignores will look different for each follower of Jesus because people can feel invisible for many reasons. For some, personal realities such as physical disabilities, age, personality traits, or mental health challenges push them to the sidelines of their communities. For others, societal views of race, gender, ethnicity, socioeconomic status, or religion can make them feel unseen. Even practical issues such as busyness, financial stress, or trauma can mean some individuals suffer neglect by those who should love and care for them. Passionate Christians can step into these spaces of need and invest the love of Jesus in a way that truly transforms lives.

For a popular and lauded international celebrity, Whitefield had an astonishing commitment to notice the overlooked. From beginning his professional ministry by reading to prisoners to founding an orphanage in the developing colony of Georgia as his legacy ministry, Whitefield consistently valued the ones society ignored. John Wesley, in a sermon he preached at Whitefield's funeral, celebrates his friend's generosity and kindness to all:

If it be inquired, what was the foundation of his integrity, or of his sincerity, courage, patience, and every other valuable and amiable quality, it is easy to give the answer. It was not the excellence of his natural temper, not the strength of his understanding. It was not the force of education, no, nor the advice of his friends. . . . It was the love of God shed abroad in his heart by the Holy Ghost, which was given unto him, filling his soul with tender, disinterested love to every child of man.[18]

Whitefield's ability to value and care for every one of God's children enabled him to invest God's love into all the spaces in his culture, even the oft-forgotten fringes. As his personal assistant from his mature years insists, Whitefield "was much disposed to be conversant with life, from the lowest mechanic to the first characters in the land."[19]

Whitefield also led the way for the entire First Great Awakening to become arguably the most egalitarian movement in the American colonies before the Revolution, as those outside traditional positions of power not only received ministry, but also participated themselves. As historian Thomas S. Kidd writes, "[Revivalists], on the other hand, believed that outpourings of the Holy Spirit generated the revivals, and that the Spirit did not distinguish between male and female, slave and free, or educated and uneducated. . . . Almost nowhere else in pre-Revolutionary America would white, college-educated ministers listen to the public exhortations of women, children, Native Americans, African Americans, and the poor."[20] Historian Frank Lambert observes that African Americans specifically were involved in the revival in "significant numbers," publishing poems and personal narratives, conducting missionary work, and preaching.[21] Women also played important roles in the movement. Anne Dutton, wife of an English Calvinist Baptist minister, and Selina Hastings, Countess of Huntingdon, were key supporters of Whitefield and true associates in his ministry, with Hastings supporting Whitefield financially and Dutton providing theological and devotional input and direction.[22]

Whitefield's journals from his 1739–1741 American preaching tour reveal the Grand Itinerant's desire to see and minister to those on the edges of society, connecting them with the revival he so passionately promoted. Page after page is filled with reports of his preaching to overflow crowds, but also with descriptions of consistent and frequent interpersonal ministry to those who might have felt unseen by the culture at large—women, African Americans, the enslaved, Native Americans, and the poor, among others. Whitefield's commitment to minister God's love impartially to everyone who crossed his path flowed from his conviction that, at the most foundational level, all humans are equal. We each are created in the image of God and thus are of infinite worth, we each suffer from original sin and desperately need salvation through Jesus, and we each can be spiritually saved and filled with the Holy Spirit. This belief ensured ontological equality for everyone and motivated Whitefield to preach and minister to all people in all places regardless of race, gender, age, nationality, religion, education, or class.

Below is an excerpt from Whitefield's journal for his five-day stay in Philadelphia in May 1740. Despite speaking to tens of thousands of people during his visit to the city, Whitefield also takes the time to record his interactions with individuals. May we be encouraged by Whitefield's passion to share God's blessings with everyone, even those on the outskirts of a culture desperate for love.

JOURNAL

A Continuation of the Reverend Mr. Whitefield's Journal, After his Arrival at Georgia, To a Few Days after his Second Return Thither from Philadelphia[23]

Philadelphia.

THURSDAY, MAY 8. Had what my body much wanted, a thorough night's repose. Was much refreshed in spirit and was called up very early in the morning, as I am always, to speak to poor[24] souls under convictions. The first, I think, was an Indian trader whom God was pleased to bring home by my preaching when here last. The account he gave of God's dealings with him was very satisfactory. He is just come from the Indian nation where he has been praying with and exhorting all he met that were willing to hear. Some of the Indians he had hopes of, but his fellow traders endeavored to prejudice them against him. However, by my advice, he proposes visiting them again at the fall, and I humbly hope the Lord will open a door among the poor heathen. The conversion of one of their traders I take to be one great step towards it. Lord, carry on the work begun. Fulfill your ancient promises, and let your Son have the heathen for his inheritance and the utmost parts of the earth for his possession.²⁵ Come, Lord Jesus, come quickly!

Conversed also with a poor negro woman who has been visited in a very remarkable manner. God was pleased to convert her by my preaching the last fall, but being under dejections on Sunday morning, she prayed that salvation might come to her heart and that the Lord would be pleased to manifest himself to her soul that day. While she was at meeting, hearing one Mr. M—n, a Baptist preacher whom the Lord has been pleased lately to send forth, the word came with such power upon her heart that at last she was obliged to cry out, and such a great concern also fell upon many in the congregation that several betook themselves to secret prayer.

The minister stopped and several persuaded her to hold her peace, but the glory of the Lord shone so brightly round about her that she could not help praising and blessing God and telling how God was revealing himself to her soul. After some time, she was taken out of the meetinghouse, but she fell upon her knees, praising and blessing God. She continued in an agony for some considerable time, and afterwards came in and heard the remainder of the sermon. Many since this have called her mad and said she was full of new wine, but the account she gave me was rational and solid, and I believe in that hour the Lord Jesus took a great possession of her soul. Such cases indeed have not been very common, but when an extraordinary work is carrying on, God generally manifests himself to some souls in this extraordinary manner. And I doubt not, but when the poor negroes are to be called, God will highly favor them, to wipe off their reproach and to show that he is no respecter of persons, but that whoever believes in him shall be saved. . . .

SATURDAY, MAY 10. Though God has shown me great things already in this place, yet today I have seen greater. I preached twice with power and to larger congregations than ever, and in the evening went to settle a society of young women, who I hope will prove wise virgins.²⁶ As soon as I entered the room and heard them singing, my soul was uncommonly delighted.

When the hymn was over, I desired to pray before I began to converse, but, contrary to my expectations, my soul was so carried out that I had not time to talk at all. A wonderful power was in the room, and with one accord, they began to cry out and weep most bitterly for the space of half an hour. They seemed to be under the strongest convictions and did indeed seek Jesus sorrowing. Their cries might be heard a great way off. When I had done, I thought proper to leave them at their devotions. They continued in prayer (as I was informed by one of them afterwards) for above an hour, confessing their most secret faults, and, at length, the agonies of some were so strong that five of them seemed affected as those that are in fits. . . .

SUNDAY, MAY 11. I preached my farewell sermon to, I believe, near 20,000 hearers. . . . The poor people were much concerned at my bidding them farewell, and after I had taken my leave, oh, how many came to my lodgings, sorrowing most of all that they were likely to see my face no more for a long season. I believe near 50 negroes came to give me thanks, under God, for what had been done for their souls. Oh, how heartily did those poor creatures throw in their mites for my poor orphans! Some of them have been effectually wrought upon and in an uncommon manner. Many of them have now begun to learn to read, and one that was free said she would give me her two children whenever I settle my school. . . . I intended, had time permitted, to have settled a society for negro men and negro women, but that must be deferred till it shall please God to bring me to Philadelphia again. I have been much drawn out in prayer for them and have seen them exceedingly wrought upon under the word preached.

CHALLENGE WRONGS

Along with standing for truth and offering love, passionate followers of Jesus must also respond to their culture by challenging the wrongs they witness. As God's representatives on earth, we reveal to a lost world the loving, just, and compassionate heart of our Father, and so we are called to stand against ideologies, practices, and assumptions in our culture that produce hurt, injustice, inequity, and hopelessness. As Paul advises in Romans 12:9, "Love must be sincere. Hate what is evil; cling to what is good." Standing against the wrongs of society is part of the responsive lifestyle of a zealous Christian.

The Old Testament prophet Micah hailed from a small village in Judea and prophesied during years of great prosperity in Judah. Despite his culture's affluence, Micah obeys the commands of God to challenge several wrongs in his society, one of which is fraudulent economic practices:

Woe to those who plan iniquity,
> to those who plot evil on their beds!
At morning's light they carry it out
> because it is in their power to do it.
They covet fields and seize them,
> and houses, and take them.
They defraud people of their homes,
> they rob them of their inheritance.[27]

Micah responds to the dishonesty present in his culture by prophesying God's displeasure and warning of God's impending judgment, and his words have an impact. Upon his ascension to the throne of Judah, King Hezekiah (reign c. 715–686 BC), one of the kings alive during Micah's ministry, returns Judah to following God by purging the land of idols, restoring the priesthood, and resuming proper worship in the temple.[28] Micah's willingness to challenge corruption in his community reveals for us the responsibility and power we have as passionate believers to confront the wrongs in our own culture.

As he toured the American colonies, Whitefield had his own opportunities to challenge injustices in eighteenth-century America. After spending the first month of his tour in the mid-Atlantic colonies of New York, Pennsylvania, and New Jersey, Whitefield left the region on December 3, 1739, and began traveling south through Maryland, Virginia, North Carolina, and South Carolina, preaching as he went.[29] Five weeks later, he arrived in Savannah, Georgia, where he was building his orphanage Bethesda.[30]

According to his journal, Whitefield was underwhelmed by the religious culture of the South. In Annapolis, Maryland, he laments that "a false politeness and the pomps and vanities of the world eat out the vitals of religion." In Virginia, Whitefield worries that the inhabitants "seem more dead to God, but far less prejudiced, than in the northern parts." In North Carolina, Whitefield complains, "It grieves me to find that in every little town there is a

settled dancing master, but scarce anywhere a settled minister to be met with."
Arriving in South Carolina on New Year's Day, Whitefield argues in a local
tavern with those intent upon drinking and dancing in an attempt to convince
them of the "folly of such entertainments," but loses the battle. Only upon
arriving in Savannah does Whitefield experience a "joyful meeting" with his
Christian friends who had arrived before him and is "much refreshed" with
letters from the northern colonies as well as England.[31]

The lack of religious interest in the southern colonies at the time of
Whitefield's visit can be attributed to several factors. Colonists in the settle-
ments were scattered, making it difficult to settle permanent churches and
clergy. Wealth was concentrated in the hands of a few who endeavored to
imitate the lifestyles of the English nobility with a focus on pastimes such as
dancing and fashion, and fewer Dissenting believers and pastors who held to
the importance of being spiritually born again resided there.

Despite his concern about the religious atmosphere of the American South,
it was the mistreatment of the enslaved population that troubled Whitefield
the most. Whitefield interacted with enslaved Africans during his time in the
South in much the same ways he did with everyone: visiting them in their lodgings, teaching their children, preaching to them the need for spiritual rebirth,
and praying with them.[32] In North Carolina, for example, Whitefield records
in his journal, "Afterwards I went, as my usual custom is, among the negroes
belonging to the house. One man was sick in bed, and two of his children said
their prayers after me very well. This more and more convinces me that the
negro children, if early brought up in the nurture and admonition of the Lord,
would make as great a proficiency as any white people's children whatsoever."[33] In South Carolina, Whitefield notes a time of prayer he and his companions shared with the five enslaved black men who were employed in rowing
their canoe.[34]

His interactions with enslaved Africans in the South, his concerns about
the refusal of many slaveowners to introduce Christianity to those they held
in bondage, and reports he received from others of cruelty and abuse within the institution led Whitefield to challenge the treatment of the enslaved

population in the South.[35] On January 23, 1740, less than two weeks after he arrived in Savannah, he penned an open letter to the inhabitants of the southern colonies expressing his concerns and sent the epistle to Benjamin Franklin in Philadelphia to publish it.[36]

At the time, public criticism of slavery in the British-American empire was fairly rare. As historian Katharine Gerbner writes, "Protestants, like Catholics, accepted slavery as part of the natural order."[37] Historian George M. Marsden similarly observes, "Before [the American Revolution], most British-Americans simply absorbed African slavery into their hierarchical views of society, where it was assumed that the higher orders of society would have servants to perform domestic and farm labor."[38] Although sparks of resistance to the slave trade appeared in the colonies as early as Rhode Island's anti-slavery law of 1652 and Samuel Sewall's anti-slavery tract *The Selling of Joseph* in 1700, an effectual shift across the colonies toward abolition did not begin until several decades after Whitefield's 1739–1741 visit to America.[39]

Thus, Whitefield's candid and strongly-worded challenge to southern slaveowners was unique and caused immediate backlash in the South when it appeared two months later in April 1740. The most virulent public counter-attack came from the South Carolina Anglican commissary Alexander Garden, with whom Whitefield had tangled just a month or so earlier in Charleston over ecclesiastical and theological issues.[40] In his *Six Letters to the Rev. Mr. Whitefield,* Garden devotes the majority of his sixth letter to Whitefield's accusations against southern slaveowners, responding,

> But, pray, sir, on what grounds do you bring this charge against the generality of those inhabitants who own negroes of using them as bad, nay, worse, than as though they were brutes? Do you know this charge to be just and honest? Or have you sufficient evidence to support it? No, you only think it to be so, and fear it, and believe it. But, on the contrary, I shall presume—and on much better grounds—to think, fear, and believe that your charge is false and injurious and that the very reverse of it is true .... And that in a certain country I know, you would be indicted for meddling, as you have done in this matter, which may endanger the peace and safety of the community.[41]

Garden did, however, agree with Whitefield's charge that those who owned enslaved laborers in the South refused to teach them the tenets of Christianity, calling it a "sore evil," but attributing the neglect to the lack of "one certain uniform method of teaching them."[42]

Whitefield's letter rebuking southerners for their mistreatment of the enslaved men and women among them is an encouraging example of a passionate lover of God challenging something he believes is sinful in his culture. I hope this letter motivates us to step out in faith and identify wrongs in our own societies and communities.

LETTER

"To the Inhabitants of Maryland, Virginia, North and South Carolina"[43]

As I lately passed through your provinces in my way hither, I was sensibly touched with a fellow-feeling of the miseries of the poor negroes. Could I have preached more frequently among you, I should have delivered my thoughts in my public discourses, but as my business here required me to stop as little as possible on the road, I have no other way to discharge the concern which at present lies upon my heart than by sending you this letter. How you will receive it, I know not; whether you will accept it in love or be offended with me, as the master of the damsel was with Paul for casting the evil spirit out of her when he saw the hope of his [financial] gain was gone, I am uncertain.[44]

Whatever be the event, I must inform you, in the meekness and gentleness of Christ, that I think God has a quarrel with you for your abuse of and cruelty to the poor negroes. Whether it be lawful for Christians to buy slaves and thereby encourage the nations from whom they are bought to be at perpetual war with each other, I shall not take upon me to determine. Sure I am, it is sinful, when bought, to use them as bad, nay, worse, than as though they were brutes. And whatever particular exceptions there may be (as I would charitably hope there are some), I fear the generality of you that own negroes are liable to such a charge, for your slaves, I believe, work as hard if not harder than the horses whereon you ride.

These [horses], after they have done their work, are fed and taken proper care of, but many negroes, when wearied with labor in your plantations, have been obliged to grind their own corn after they return home. Your dogs are caressed and fondled at your tables, but your slaves, who are frequently styled dogs or beasts, have not an equal privilege. They are scarce permitted to pick up the crumbs which fall from their masters' tables.[45] Nay, some, as I have been informed by an eyewitness, have been, upon the most trifling provocation, cut with knives and had forks thrown into their flesh. Not to mention what numbers have been given up to the inhuman usage of cruel taskmasters, who by their unrelenting scourges have ploughed upon their backs and made long furrows, and at length brought them even to death itself.

It's true, I hope, there are few such monsters of barbarity [allowed] to subsist among you. Some, I hear, have been lately executed in Virginia for killing slaves, and the laws are very severe against such who at any time murder them. And perhaps it might be better for the poor creatures themselves to be hurried out of life than to be made so miserable as they generally are in it. And, indeed, considering what usage they commonly meet with, I have wondered that we have not more instances of self-murder among the negroes, or that they have not more frequently rose up in arms against their owners. Virginia has once, and Charleston more than once, been threatened in this way.

And though I heartily pray God they may never be permitted to get the upper hand, yet should such a thing be permitted by providence, all good men must acknowledge the judgment would be just. For is it not the highest ingratitude, as well as cruelty, not to let your poor slaves enjoy some fruits of their labor?

When, passing along, I have viewed your plantations cleared and culti-
vated, many spacious houses built, and the owners of them faring sumptuously every day, my blood has frequently almost run cold within me to consider how many of your slaves had neither convenient food to eat or proper
raiment to put on, notwithstanding most of the comforts you enjoy were
solely owing to their indefatigable labors. The scripture says, "You shall not
muzzle the ox that treads out the corn."⁴⁶ Does God take care of oxen? And
will he not take care of the negroes also? Undoubtedly, he will.

Go to now, you rich men, weep and howl for your miseries that shall
come upon you! Behold the provision of the poor negroes which have
reaped down your fields, which is by you denied them, cries, and the cries
of them which reaped are entered into the ears of the Lord of Sabaoth. . . .

But this is not all. Enslaving or misusing their bodies would, comparatively speaking, be an inconsiderable evil, was proper care taken of their
souls. But I have great reason to believe that most of you, on purpose, keep
your negroes ignorant of Christianity, or, otherwise, why are they permitted
through your provinces openly to profane the Lord's Day by their dancing,
piping, and such like? I know the general pretense for this neglect of their
souls is that teaching them Christianity would make them proud and consequently unwilling to submit to slavery.

But what a dreadful reflection is this on your holy religion? What blasphe-
mous notions must those that make such an objection have of the precepts
of Christianity? Do you find any one command in the gospel that has the least
tendency to make people forget their relative duties? Do you not read that
servants, and as many as are under the yoke of bondage, are required to be
subject, in all lawful things, to their masters, and that not only to the good
and gentle, but also to the [harsh]?⁴⁷ Nay, may I not appeal to your own hearts
whether deviating from the laws of Jesus Christ is not the cause of all the evils
and miseries mankind now universally groans under and of all the vices we
find both in ourselves and others? Certainly, it is. And, therefore, the reason
why servants generally prove so bad is because so little care is taken to breed
them up in the nurture and admonition of the Lord. . . .

But, farther, if teaching slaves Christianity has such a bad influence upon their lives, why are you generally desirous of having your children taught? Think you they are any way better by nature than the poor negroes? No, in no wise. Blacks are just as much, and no more, conceived and born in sin as white men are. Both, if born and bred up here, I am persuaded, are naturally capable of the same improvement. . . .

But I know all arguments to prove the necessity of taking care of your negroes' souls, though never so conclusive, will prove ineffectual till you are convinced of the necessity of securing the salvation of your own. That you yourselves are not effectually convinced of this, I think is too notorious to [need] evidence. A general deadness as to divine things, and not to say a general prophaneness, is discernible both in pastors and people.

Most of you are without any teaching priest, and whatever quantity of rum there may be, yet I fear but very few Bibles are annually imported into your different provinces. God has already begun to visit for this as well as other wicked things. . . . Nothing will more provoke God . . . than impenitence and unbelief. Let these be removed, and the sons of violence shall not be able to hurt you.

No, your oxen shall be strong to labor, there shall be no decay of your people by epidemical sickness, no leading away into captivity from abroad, and no complaining in your streets at home. Your sons shall grow up as young plants, and your daughters be as the polished corners of the temple.[48] And to sum up all blessings in one, then shall the Lord be your God. That you may be the people who are in such a happy case is the earnest prayer of,

Your sincere well-wisher and servant in Christ,

G. Whitefield

Savannah, Jan. 23, 1740

THINK OUTSIDE THE BOX

Standing for truth, loving the overlooked, and challenging wrongs are all important ways that passionate followers of Jesus can respond to culture and share God's blessings and love with their communities. George Whitefield preached God's truth to Governor Jonathan Belcher in Boston, loved the unseen in Philadelphia, and challenged the mistreatment of the enslaved in the American South. One final response we can make to our society as zealous believers is to think outside the box. What do I mean by that?

As Christians, we know that our world is fallen and corrupt, hopelessly mired in sin and the suffering it inevitably produces. Jesus' declared purpose in coming to earth was to offer humankind the love and blessings of his Father's kingdom and to "destroy the devil's work,"[49] and so we as his followers are called to do the same. To accomplish this, we must think outside the box of our current culture, challenging society's prevailing principles and customs that do not align with God's kingdom values and pioneering changes that society does not even recognize are needed. Thankfully, because we live by the standards of the kingdom of heaven and are indwelt by the Holy Spirit, we are uniquely positioned and empowered to work to redirect the harmful and unhelpful conventions and traditions of our communities.

In the first three chapters of the Old Testament book of Daniel, we read of four young men of Israel who are taken as captives to Babylon when Jerusalem falls in battle, there to learn the history and traditions of the Babylonian empire and to serve King Nebuchadnezzar (642–562 BC; reign 605–562 BC). The young men refuse to comply with certain customs and laws of the foreign land, such as eating the royal food which conflicts with God's dietary commands and worshipping a pagan image. For this defiance, three of the men, Shadrach, Meshach, and Abednego, are cast into a burning furnace. Miraculously, they are unharmed by the fire, and their loyalty to the God of Israel convinces King Nebuchadnezzar to declare protections for the worship of Yahweh throughout his empire.

The young men of Israel know the God of all nations, and by remaining true to his commands and promises, they challenge the pagan laws of their culture and initiate a significant shift in their society toward respect for Yahweh that no one else even realizes is needed. In the same way, as zealous disciples of Jesus, we can think outside the box of our own society and pioneer changes that can lead our communities into a closer alignment with God's kingdom values. Aligning with God's principles brings blessing to all and is an act of true service to our culture.

Whitefield thought outside the box of his culture in two important ways we have already discussed, the first being his commitment to preaching the opportunity for spiritual rebirth through the grace of God. He recognized the need for the gospel message to be declared to his generation against the opposition and derision of the vast majority of society, both inside and outside the church. His passion for God drove him to almost single-handedly bring the good news of God's salvation into the public consciousness.

We also have seen how Whitefield defied convention and elevated his culture's understanding of individual human worth. He preached acceptance of all Christians regardless of religious tradition or denomination, the responsibility of believers to minister to all individuals impartially and with equity, the infinite value of every person as created in God's image, and the need of all people both great and small to receive God's saving grace. His ministry was defined by its unique inclusiveness and effectiveness within many diverse communities. Thus, in declaring the gospel and valuing all people, Whitefield's life and ministry are testaments to the power of an individual Christian to think outside the box and respond to culture with unconventional approaches that shift it significantly toward the values of the kingdom of God.

Thinking outside the box of our own culture, however, is difficult for finite humans, bound as we are in so many ways to our own time and place. Whitefield experienced his own missteps in questioning cultural assumptions in one specific area: the international slave trade.

On the one hand, we have seen that Whitefield was unique for his time in treating enslaved blacks in America equitably, preaching to them, praying with them, and encouraging them to pursue spiritual rebirth. He publicly challenged the treatment of the enslaved with his 1740 letter to the southern colonies. He spearheaded his own charitable projects, attempting to build a

school for African Americans in three separate locations in the colonies, one
of which was in South Carolina. In one venture, he purchased 5,000 acres of
land in Pennsylvania.[50] He evidenced a true tenderness and care for African
Americans, eternally impacting many with his ministry, as testified to by contemporaneous black writers such as Phillis Wheatley (1753–1784), Olaudah
Equiano (c. 1745–1797), and John Marrant (1755–1791).[51]

But, on the other hand, Whitefield accepted his culture's general approv-
al, tacit or explicit, of the legality of slavery and never publicly condemned
the practice. In fact, the historical record reveals that in an effort to keep his
orphanage Bethesda in Savannah, Georgia, financially solvent, Whitefield
favored the legalization of slavery in Georgia as early as 1741, purchased a
South Carolina plantation with an enslaved workforce in 1747 as a source
of income for Bethesda, and obtained enslaved laborers for the orphanage
upon legalization of the institution in the colony in 1751.[52]

As modern readers, we struggle to understand how Whitefield could lead
the way in valuing and ministering to African Americans, even challenging
the mistreatment of those in bondage in the South, yet still participate in the
institution of slavery. Why couldn't Whitefield think outside the box and
use his international platform to work for a shift in the culture toward God's
kingdom values of freedom and dignity for all?

Most of Whitefield's modern biographers attempt to answer this question,
and their analyses highlight similar points: passages in the Bible that appear to
accept slavery, the belief that the opportunity for Africans to hear and receive the
gospel by living in America outweighed the hardships of being enslaved, and a
steadfast commitment to God's providence even when his ways are mysterious.[53]
For Whitefield personally, his lifelong commitment to the success of Bethesda as
well as his single-minded focus on the ministry of evangelism to the exclusion of
most earthly concerns offer additional motives for his actions.[54]

That Whitefield accepted the assumptions held by many eighteenth-
century Christians regarding slavery is made clear by a letter he wrote to a
friend soon after the legalization of slavery in Georgia:

I think now is the season for us to exert our utmost for the good of the poor Ethiopians. We are told that even they are soon to stretch out their hands unto God.[55] And who knows but their being settled in Georgia may be overruled for this great end? As for the lawfulness of keeping slaves, I have no doubt, since I hear of some that were bought with Abraham's money and some that were born in his house, and I cannot help thinking that some of those servants mentioned by the apostles in their epistles were or had been slaves. . . .[56] And though it is true that they are brought in a wrong way from their own country and it is a trade not to be approved of, yet as it will be carried on whether we will or not, I should think myself highly favored if I could purchase a good number of them, in order to make their lives comfortable and lay a foundation for breeding up their posterity in the nurture and admonition of the Lord. . . . It rejoiced my soul to hear that one of my poor negroes in Carolina was made a brother in Christ. How know we but we may have many such instances in Georgia ere it be long? By mixing with your people, I trust many of them will be brought to Jesus, and this consideration, as to us, swallows up all temporal inconveniences whatsoever.[57]

For all these reasons, Whitefield participated in the slave trade, missing an opportunity to lead his society toward aligning with God's kingdom values of freedom and honor for all.

As Christians who hope to think outside the box and shift our culture toward greater agreement with God's principles, what are some practical actions we can adopt? First, from Whitefield's failure to defy convention in the area of slavery, we learn that all of us, regardless of spiritual passion, maturity, or gifting, have blind spots. Cultivating a practice of asking ourselves where we might be missing an opportunity to stand for God's values against societal conventions can help us recognize occasions to help shift our culture closer to God's priorities.

Second, refusing to allow the ends to justify the means can enable us to think outside the box of culture. Whitefield's ministry of sharing the gospel message and helping the needy, including the enslaved, were noble endeavors, as was his kind and fair treatment of the enslaved Africans on his own properties.[58]

However, by utilizing enslaved laborers, despite the cultural acceptance of the practice and his own altruistic goals, Whitefield denied the basic human right of freedom to the enslaved and missed a chance to influence his society toward God's values of justice and liberty.

Third, intentionally connecting with communities of people with different perspectives and life experiences than our own can help us see new ways to push our culture to align with God's principles. Joining a local group focused on a social justice issue with which you are personally unfamiliar, cultivating a friendship with an individual from a contrasting economic background, serving in a ministry to folks who differ from you in age, or creating a book or podcast list to learn about a historical event that impacted social groups other than your own are all ways to gain new perspectives and innovative ideas that might help you shift the communities you are a part of closer to the kingdom of God.

Fourth, trust the guidance and wisdom of the Holy Spirit. He is the source of all truth and will guide us into insights we do not expect and could never discover for ourselves. The Rev. Johann Martin Boltzius (1703–1765), a German Lutheran pastor in Georgia whose orphanage in Ebenezer, Georgia, was one of the models for Whitefield's orphanage in Savannah, was a rare vocal opponent of slavery at the time of Whitefield's ministry.[59] In fact, Boltzius unsuccessfully challenged Whitefield on the topic more than once.[60] Boltzius and his attempts to convince Whitefield of the wrongness of enslaving fellow humans reveals for us that the Holy Spirit can lead us to see spiritual realities that others miss and can use us to attempt to influence our culture toward Christian values.

CULTURE IS PEOPLE

As we conclude our discussion of how to respond to culture as passionate lovers of Jesus, perhaps the most essential reminder is that "culture," after all, is really just people. People alive within the margins of a particular time and place, but still just people. God loves people, all people, so as we consider how God may be calling us to respond to our generation with spiritual passion, we can rest in the assurance that the most important response we can make is simply to love and care for people as God does.

Perhaps Whitefield's greatest strength in responding to culture was his true and deep love for people. The Grand Itinerant did not establish a denomination, spark a political movement, or found an enduring charitable or educational institution. Instead, he touched people and changed their lives. As the African American poet Phillis Wheatley wrote in her published elegy for Whitefield:

Thy sermons in unequall'd accents flow'd,

And ev'ry bosom with devotion glow'd;

Thou didst in strains of eloquence refin'd

Inflame the heart, and captivate the mind.[61]

Whitefield's passionate love for God drove him to respond to the society around him by blessing and loving anyone and everyone he encountered.

Whitefield's story also should encourage us that responding to culture as passionate followers of Jesus does not require special spiritual giftings, inexhaustible resources, a towering intellect, or flawless personal holiness. All we need is God's love, flowing through us to the people we meet. Whitefield's loving heart was what his friend John Wesley admired the most about the evangelist:

Mention has already been made of his unparalleled zeal, his indefatigable activity, his tenderheartedness to the afflicted, and charitableness toward the poor.... Should we not mention that he had a heart susceptible of the most generous and the most tender friendship? I have frequently thought that this, of all others, was the distinguishing part of his character. How few have we known of so kind a temper, of such large and flowing affections? Was it not principally by this that the hearts of others were so strangely drawn and knit to him? Can anything but love beget love? This shone in his very countenance and continually breathed in all his words, whether in public or private. Was it not this, which, quick and penetrating as lightning, flew from heart to heart? Which gave that life to his sermons, his conversations, his letters? Ye are witnesses.[62]

God can empower each of us to respond to our society in ways that transform it. May we commit our lives to bringing the life-changing blessings and love of heaven to our own culture and communities.

CHAPTER VIII

Sustaining the Fire

Passionate love for God, once ignited in our hearts by God's grace, empowers us to embrace purpose, establish a resilient foundation and zealous lifestyle, experience joyful relationships with others on our life journey, and respond to both opposition and culture with compassion and effectiveness. Over a lifetime, these traits produce in us a divine fruitfulness that spills over into all areas of our lives and enables us to share God's love with everyone we encounter.

But maintaining a fiery spiritual passion throughout the entirety of our lives is not as simple or as effortless as we might imagine when we begin our relationship with God. Obstacles, anxieties, suffering, doubts, trauma, confusion, resistance, and fatigue push against our zeal for the Lord, making it easy to get off track. Sustaining a robust, authentic passion for our Beloved until the Father calls us home is not for the faint of heart.

We have seen George Whitefield's inspiring passion for God during our journey through the life events and writings of his early years and his 1739–1741 First Great Awakening preaching tour of America. But the young evangelist was still only twenty-six years old with three decades of life and ministry ahead of him when he boarded the *Minerva* at Charleston, South Carolina, in January 1741 for his return trip to England after almost fifteen months in the colonies. He had enjoyed tremendous success in America, but, sailing across the Atlantic, Whitefield knew stressful circumstances awaited him in London.

His publisher, James Hutton, had become a Moravian and refused to continue printing Whitefield's writings.[1] John Wesley, Whitefield's spiritual father and friend, had separated from Whitefield over doctrinal differences, although the two men would later reconcile. The parents of the woman Whitefield had hoped to marry had rejected his proposal. William Seward, one of Whitefield's financial backers and intended manager of Whitefield's orphanage Bethesda in Savannah, Georgia, had been killed by an angry mob while preaching in Wales, and Whitefield's outstanding debts for the operation of Bethesda had to be paid or the evangelist would end up in jail.[2] Little wonder that upon his arrival in London two months after leaving the colonies, Whitefield writes to a friend, "It has been a trying time with me."[3]

Beyond Whitefield's immediate circumstances, the next thirty years would bring the usual litany of earthly trials and triumphs: professional successes and challenges, marriage, collaborations and disagreements with friends and colleagues, failed pregnancies and the loss of his only child, nonstop international travel and work, personal health concerns, and the demands of leading the burgeoning evangelical movement. Could Whitefield sustain his passion for God through all that life would throw at him?

As history reveals, Whitefield *did* maintain his zeal for Jesus amidst the sorrows and joys of the next three decades and is remembered to the present day as a hero of the Christian faith. In his funeral sermon for Whitefield, John Wesley encourages his listeners to "cry to him that works all in all for a measure of the same precious faith, of the same zeal and activity, the same tenderheartedness, charitableness, bowels of mercies" as Whitefield evidenced in his life.[4] In the nineteenth century, the Rev. Charles Spurgeon (1834–1892), a popular English Baptist preacher called "the modern Whitefield" in his day, recalls Whitefield in glowing terms and identifies the evangelist as one whose "reliance was wholly on the Lord and that God was within him."[5] As I note in the introduction to this book, scholars, clergy, and laypersons gathered virtually in 2020 for a symposium dedicated to the evangelist on the 250th anniversary of his death, hosted by the Old South Presbyterian Church in Newburyport, Massachusetts, the site of Whitefield's grave.[6] Whitefield persevered in his love for God, fulfilled his earthly calling, and received his chief desire, recorded in his journal when he was just twenty-four years of age: "I was full of joy and longed to be dissolved and to be with Jesus Christ, but I have a baptism first to be baptized with. Father, your will be done."[7]

As we close this study of Whitefield's life and writings, I believe the Grand Itinerant has one last lesson to teach us in our pursuit of a life of spiritual passion: how to sustain fervent zeal for God over the span of a lifetime. To learn from Whitefield, we will first examine the concluding event of his 1739–1741 preaching tour of America—his six weeks on board the *Minerva* as he returned to England. Second, we will jump forward in time almost three decades to Whitefield's final words and thoughts through letters and a sermon written during his last year of life. Through these two lenses, we will discover three helpful hints for maintaining the fire of passion for the One we love.

HEAVENLY LONGING

I hope your encounters with Whitefield's life and writings in this book have convinced you of one truth—Whitefield had a deep personal relationship with Jesus. Whitefield knew Jesus not only as his Teacher, his Savior, and his Master, but also his Friend. Perhaps *chiefly* as his Friend, and that is the first important factor in the perseverance of his spiritual zeal.

One specific aspect of Whitefield's friendship with Jesus that stands out to me as I read his personal writings is his longing for Jesus. The connection between longing for Jesus and perseverance in the faith is rarely discussed, but I believe it is important to consider, and I believe Whitefield's life embodied it. The apostle Paul recognized the connection; note his words to his spiritual son Timothy near the end of his own life: "I have fought the good fight, I have finished the race, I have kept the faith. Now there is in store for me the crown of righteousness, which the Lord, the righteous Judge, will award to me on that day—and not only to me, but also to all who have longed for his appearing."[8]

We long for the ones we truly love, not the ones we admire, the ones we serve, the ones we fear, or the ones we work alongside. Longing is birthed from love. Paul knew, as did Whitefield, that those who long for Jesus are the ones who highly value, carefully cultivate, and painstakingly pursue a profound, deep-rooted, personal intimacy with the Lover of their souls that enables them to fight the good fight, finish the race, and keep the faith.

King David also knew this truth. In fact, there is perhaps no better description of longing for God than Psalm 63, which opens with David's heartfelt cry, "You, God, are my God, earnestly I seek you; my whole being longs for you, in a dry and parched land where there is no water." In the psalm, David sings of how he has pursued God publicly in the sanctuary as well as privately on his bed at night: "I have seen you in the sanctuary and beheld your power and your glory. . . . On my bed I remember you; I think of you through the watches of the night." His profound desire for God produces a friendship that is startling in its simplicity and strength: "I cling to you; your right hand upholds me."[9]

On board the *Minerva*, headed back to England and the challenges that awaited him there, Whitefield writes of his longing for Jesus, as he often does, in a letter to a recipient back in Charleston, South Carolina. Reading his words, we can feel the passion with which Whitefield desires full union with his divine Friend:

> I long for that happy time when we shall be swallowed up in the vision and full fruition of the glorious Godhead. The bunch of grapes makes me long to eat of the full clusters in the heavenly Canaan. The first fruits make me pant after the full harvest. Perhaps you may go and partake of it first and drink new wine before me in the kingdom of our Father. I hope I shall not stay long after you, if not called before. My soul is sick [with] love. Nothing can satisfy it but the full sight and enjoyment of Christ. He now visits my soul and causes it mightily to rejoice in his salvation.[10]

Whitefield's longing ushered him into times of deep fellowship with Jesus. He rejoices on the same day in another letter, "The Lord gives me a feeling possession of himself."[11]

How do we increase our longing for Jesus and full union with him in heaven? One way is to intentionally focus our heart and mind on the beauty of Jesus. Meditating on the beauty and loveliness of our divine Friend never fails to activate our desire for him, as Whitefield knew well. In the same letter in which he admits the "trying time" he is facing in England, he declares, "But, through infinite mercy, I am enabled to strengthen myself in the Lord my God. . . . Jesus, the ever-loving, altogether lovely Jesus, pities and comforts me."[12]

Whitefield references the Old Testament book Song of Songs when he notes that the "altogether lovely Jesus" helps "strengthen" him to persevere. Whitefield quotes often from Song of Songs in his writings, a book that is interpreted on one level as a picture of the eternal love story between Jesus Christ and his bride the church. Here, Whitefield quotes Song of Songs 5:16, the final verse in a lengthy passage in which the bride extols the spectacular qualities of her beloved, ending her tribute with the words, "His mouth is sweetness itself; he is altogether lovely. This is my beloved, this is my friend, daughters of Jerusalem."

Psalms is another biblical book that can be used fruitfully to meditate on the beauty of Jesus. For example, Psalm 45 includes an eight-verse exaltation of "the most excellent of men," while Psalm 24:7–10 offers loving praise to the "King of glory." Similarly, Revelation has many powerful passages that exalt our winsome Savior. Let the words of Revelation 1:12b–16 provoke longing for Jesus in your heart:

And when I turned I saw seven golden lampstands, and among the lampstands was someone like a son of man, dressed in a robe reaching down to his feet and with a golden sash around his chest. The hair on his head was white like wool, as white as snow, and his eyes were like blazing fire. His feet were like bronze glowing in a furnace, and his voice was like the sound of rushing waters. In his right hand he held seven stars, and coming out of his mouth was a sharp, double-edged sword. His face was like the sun shining in all its brilliance.

Revelation 19:11–16 is another awe-inspiring description of our stunning "Faithful and True" King who will return at the end of time on a white horse to establish his perfect kingdom of justice and love. Biblical passages such as these turn our hearts toward our beautiful Savior and spark a fire of divine longing for him.

It is perhaps paradoxical that the more we pursue Jesus, the more we long for him, and the more we long for him, the more we are drawn to pursue him. As Whitefield expresses above, "The first fruits make me pant after the full harvest." Turning our minds and hearts toward the beauty of Jesus deepens our intimacy with him and strengthens us to persevere in passionate love for God.

ETERNAL TRUTH

Whitefield's globe-trotting lifestyle and innovative ministry ensured that he would encounter many unique and varied circumstances in his fifty-five years of life. Perhaps, then, it is not surprising that the second feature of Whitefield's spirituality that enabled him to persevere in his passion for God over a lifetime was his intentional focus on God's timeless words and promises found in the Bible.

Like it or not, we are creatures of the moment. Trapped in time and space, our physical condition, current mindset, immediate situation, and even present company are almost foolproof determiners of how we think and feel at any point in our lives. I can awaken in the morning feeling supremely confident about the world and my place in it and dissolve into tears of fear and discouragement before I've even finished brushing my teeth. And I know I'm not alone.

Basing my zeal for God and his eternal kingdom on my present mood is a surefire recipe for disaster. I need something outside myself to anchor me if I have any hope at all of pursuing Jesus zealously over a lifetime. Thankfully, the Bible, God's divine word to humankind, is just such an infallible anchor.

Paul's instructions to Timothy are helpful again: "All Scripture is God-breathed and is useful for teaching, rebuking, correcting and training in righteousness, so that the servant of God may be thoroughly equipped for every good work."[13] In Psalm 119:105, the psalmist reaches a similar conclusion: "Your word is a lamp for my feet, a light for my path." Accessing the eternal promises, wisdom, and comfort of the Bible through reading, meditation, study, memorization, and song provides for us a timeless foundation for a lifetime of passion for God. Our zeal for the Lord is stoked and supported by the unchanging power and truth of God's word, and we are freed from depending on our constantly fluctuating heart, mind, and circumstances to maintain our fervency for God.

Whitefield valued the Bible greatly; in fact, his commitment to the foundational role of the Bible in the Christian life began at his conversion. During the months he spent at home in Gloucester, England, after his new birth experience at Pembroke College, Whitefield sought to absorb every nuance of God's word. In his autobiography, he recalls, "I got more true knowledge from reading the book of God in one month than I could ever have acquired from all the writings of men. In one word, I found it profitable for reproof, for correction, for instruction in righteousness, every way sufficient to make the man of God perfect, thoroughly furnished unto every good word and work."[14] The language and truths of the Bible flavor Whitefield's every thought and word in his writings, from his journals to his letters to his sermons to his autobiographical texts. In the truest sense, Whitefield was a man of the Book.

Whitefield spent much of his time on board the *Minerva* reading the Bible and receiving encouragement from its stories and promises. In fact, in his seventh and final published journal, he records very little of the events of his return voyage to England, but he does elaborate on four biblical passages that fortified his spirit during the weeks at sea:

> These words came one day with great power upon my heart, "Arise, go
> into Nineveh, the great city, and preach unto it the preaching that I bid
> you." At another time, the Lord spoke to me by these words, "Take the fox-
> es, the little foxes that spoil the vines, for our vines have tender grapes."
> This part of Joseph's blessing was one night brought home to me with a
> sweet power: "The archers have sorely grieved him, and shot at him, and
> hated him. But his bow abode in strength, and the arms of his hands
> were made strong by the hands of the mighty God of Jacob." And, at an-
> other time, when my soul was dejected at a sense of my own weaknesses
> and the number and greatness of my impending trials, the Lord raised
> and comforted me with this promise: "Fear not, for I am with you. Be not
> dismayed, for I am your God. I will strengthen you, yea, I will help you;
> yea, I will uphold you with the right hand of my righteousness."[15]

Whitefield adds that the Old Testament books of Genesis and Exodus "were much blessed to my spiritual comfort" when he preached from them on board.[16] In a letter from the *Minerva* to his friend William Cooper (1694–1743), an associate minister at Boston's Brattle Street Church, Whitefield writes, "God has blessed the reading of the prophecy of the prophet Jeremiah to my soul, as also the history of Joseph."[17]

We notice from Whitefield's experiences on the *Minerva* that he was impacted by the Bible not only in an intellectual way, but also was strengthened, comforted, and encouraged by the word of God in his spirit. How can we connect with the Bible in a similar manner? One answer is through the spiritual practice of meditation.

Meditation on the Bible is a historic Christian tradition that helps us shift the power and truth of God's word from our minds to our hearts. The practice is recommended in the very first sentence of the very first Old Testament psalm: "Blessed is the one . . . whose delight is in the law of the Lord, and who meditates on his law day and night."[18] Meditation is a form of prayer in which we intentionally focus on a spiritual truth or scriptural passage in an unhurried way, allowing ourselves to reflect and ponder rather than dissect and study. As Christian writer Richard Foster phrases it, "We bring the mind into the heart so that we can listen with the whole being."[19]

Recently, I have been meditating on the presence of Jesus in the Old Testament book of Psalms. I read one psalm in the morning during my devotional time, usually in several different translations, and a two-page chapter in a book that identifies messianic references within the psalm. Then I sit in silence for about fifteen minutes, asking the Holy Spirit to reveal and apply to my heart and mind the import of what I have read. The results of my time of meditation vary. My spirit may be struck by the power of one verse in the psalm, my affection for Jesus may be stirred up by the revelation of one of his attributes, or I may experience conviction for a thought pattern or habit that I need to repent of and change in light of what I have read. Beyond any specific outcome I may experience, my spirit is strengthened and reset by lingering in God's presence, allowing his word to sweep over my heart with his peace and love.

Whitefield records his practice of meditation in his autobiography, recalling, "The lively oracles of God were my soul's delight. The book of the divine laws was seldom out of my hands; I meditated therein day and night."[20] He also notes the profound impact of approaching God's word in an attitude of meditative prayer: "I began to read the holy scriptures (upon my knees), laying aside all other books and praying over, if possible, every line and word. This proved meat, indeed, and drink, indeed, to my soul. I daily received fresh life, light, and power from above."[21] Meditation on God's eternal truth was an important source of spiritual sustenance and encouragement for Whitefield as he navigated life's never-ending challenges and changes.

Meditation is fruitful because it is powered by the Holy Spirit inside us. As Paul affirms in 1 Corinthians 2:10b–12:

> The Spirit searches all things, even the deep things of God. For who knows a person's thoughts except their own spirit within them? In the same way no one knows the thoughts of God except the Spirit of God. What we have received is not the spirit of the world, but the Spirit who is from God, so that we may understand what God has freely given us.

The Holy Spirit guides our times of meditation, revealing to our hearts the "deep things of God." Thus, the living and powerful word of God strengthens and inspires us as we seek to maintain our zeal for the Lord over a lifetime.

INTIMATE ENCOUNTERS

Lastly, Whitefield knew that persevering in spiritual passion requires times of spiritual refreshing through intimate encounters with God. As he writes from the *Minerva,* "The present season is a time of refreshing to my soul."[22]

Living in a fallen and painful world, we need times of "refreshing" when God's eternal and perfect love pours into our inmost being, healing our hearts, restoring our strength, and reigniting our zeal. We were never meant to maintain our spiritual passion over the decades by sheer grit and willpower. Receiving God's love in the deepest parts of our spirit sustains and supports us as nothing else can in our journey of faith.

Recall the last time you felt a profound touch from God—during a corporate worship service, while meditating on a Bible passage, in prayer with a fellow Christian, while in a private time of devotion. I'm sure you also recall how your own passion for God intensified as a result of that encounter.

A glimpse into the life of the New Testament apostle John reveals the importance of loving encounters with God to sustain our spiritual passion. Traditionally believed to have been the last of Jesus' original twelve disciples to die, John is credited with writing five New Testament books, serving as a leader of the early Christian church, and receiving the revelation of Jesus Christ while in exile on the island of Patmos which he recorded as the New Testament book of Revelation. John maintained his zeal for God through brutal Roman persecution, internal challenges to the fledgling Christian church, and a long and varied life.

One reason for John's perseverance in passion can be found in how he identifies himself in his gospel: "the disciple whom Jesus loved."[23] This brief appellation points to John's understanding of the crucial importance of experiencing the love of God in our lives. He expands on this idea in 1 John 4:15–16a, declaring, "If anyone acknowledges that Jesus is the Son of God, God lives in them and they in God. And so we know and rely on the love God has for us. God is love." According to John, God's love sustains us.

Whitefield's "time of refreshing" aboard the *Minerva* included many intimate encounters with God and powerful effusions of his love. On February 8, 1741, he exclaims in a letter, "Oh, the love of Christ! I feel it, I feel it. God now sheds it abroad in my heart."[24] On February 17, Whitefield writes to several friends in Charleston about his profound encounters with God. To one he observes, "My body waxes stronger, and last night the great God in a glorious manner filled and overshadowed my soul."[25] To another he relates, "Since I have been on board, the Lord has heard the voice of my weeping, and now fills my soul with all peace and joy in believing."[26] To a third he remarks, "My soul is now in a heavenly frame, swallowed up in God and melted down by the love of my dear Lord Jesus. It is almost too big to speak."[27]

For Whitefield, these are not just hyper-emotional experiences or melodramatic words, but authentic encounters with the One who loves him. During his 1739–1741 preaching tour, he writes often of experiencing God's love in deeply affecting ways. In a letter from Philadelphia dated November 9, 1740, he declares to John Wesley, "I think few enjoy such continued manifestations of God's presence as I do, and have done, for some years.... Oh, I am a poor sinner, but our Lord frequently manifests himself in such a manner that it throws me into an agony which my body is almost too weak to bear."[28] On May 14, 1740, while in Nottingham, Pennsylvania, with other Christians and revivalists, Whitefield records in his journal, "Oh, how sweetly did I lie at the feet of my Jesus! With what power did a sense of his all-constraining, free, and everlasting love flow in upon my soul! It almost took away my life."[29] Whitefield's intimate experiences of God's powerful and abiding love are an integral part of his sustained spiritual zeal.

But we can't make profound encounters with God happen on demand. How can we genuinely and consistently "know and rely on the love God has for us" in a way that helps us persevere in spiritual passion?

Whitefield's letters from the *Minerva* offer a simple answer to this question: availability. Whitefield was available for intimate encounters with God through two decisions he made both during his ocean voyage and consistently throughout his life. First, he chose faith. Whitefield took God at his word that God loved him and wanted to share profound, tender encounters with him, relying on the promise in James 4:8a to "come near to God and he will come near to you." From the *Minerva,* Whitefield exhorts a female friend in Charleston to "trust and hang on God, even when he hides himself from you. He will be your guide unto death.... God is love; we cannot think too highly of him. We cannot expect too great [of] things to be done by him."[30]

Second, Whitefield prioritized time with God, individually and corporately. Note his simple yet ardent encouragement during his voyage to a letter recipient in Edisto, South Carolina: "Let nothing intercept or interrupt your communion with the Bridegroom of the church."[31] To another he references Psalm 84:10b by asserting, "To be a doorkeeper in the house of God is a glorious post."[32] It is perhaps little wonder that he writes to another friend, "I want to leap my seventy years and fly away to God."[33]

Prioritizing being available to God with an attitude of faith fulfills the admonition in Hebrews 11:6: "And without faith it is impossible to please God, because anyone who comes to him must believe that he exists and that he rewards those who earnestly seek him." Our trust in God to meet us with his love is based on the unchanging character of the One "who is able to do immeasurably more than all we ask or imagine" and who longs to encounter us and fully pour out his affection upon us by his grace. As Whitefield writes in a letter about seven months after he landed in London, "And in the night, my soul was carried out in a most unusual manner towards God. I scarce felt that I had a body. Oh, free grace! I have more reason to admire it than all the men in the world."[34] May we seek always to be available to God and expect his radiant love to refresh our souls and strengthen our spiritual zeal.

FINISHING WELL

If we disembark from the *Minerva* and time-travel almost thirty years to the fall of 1769, the beginning of the last year of Whitefield's life, we find the Grand Itinerant in his mid-fifties and a widower. By God's grace, he has sustained three decades of living and ministering as a passionate lover of God—supporting his orphanage Bethesda, growing an international network of like-minded evangelical believers, maintaining an itinerant preaching ministry including four additional trips to America, and navigating challenging political and personal circumstances both at home and abroad.

Whitefield is preparing to embark upon one final trip to America. The world is very different from the one he had entered as a newly-ordained minister of the Church of England thirty years earlier. The First Great Awakening is a distant memory, Americans are marching toward independence from England, evangelical Christianity has taken firm root in the West, and Britain's overseas empire and the concomitant consumer culture has exploded.

Yet Whitefield's passion for God and insatiable drive to share the message of spiritual rebirth remain the same. On the day he embarks upon the *Friendship* in September 1769 for his final voyage to America, he writes to a friend,

> Just now, we have taken up the anchor, and I trust my anchor is cast within the veil, where the ground will never give way. Otherwise, how should I have withstood the shock of parting and put to sea at this time, or rather, this decline of life? But our God can and our God does renew both bodily and spiritual strength. I have not been in better spirits for some years, and I am persuaded this voyage will be for the Redeemer's glory and the welfare of precious and immortal souls.[35]

In a comment reminiscent of his return voyage to England aboard the *Minerva* three decades earlier, Whitefield proclaims in another letter written aboard the *Friendship,* "Oh, amazing love! Jesus, a never-failing, ever-loving, altogether lovely Jesus, cares for and comforts [me] on every side. Hitherto it seems like my first voyage."[36]

Whitefield landed in Charleston, South Carolina, about two months later and passed the winter ministering in and around his orphanage Bethesda in Savannah, Georgia. His gift of preaching was as formidable as ever. In Charleston, South Carolina, a young African American musician and carpentry apprentice named John Marrant, a self-reported prisoner to "every vice suited to my nature and to my years," joined one of Whitefield's sermons with the intent to disturb the meeting by blowing his French horn. Note Marrant's description of what happened next:

> I was pushing the people to make room to get the horn off my shoulder
> to blow it, just as Mr. Whitefield was naming his text. And looking
> round, and, as I thought, directly upon me, and pointing with his
> finger, he uttered these words, "Prepare to meet thy God, O Israel." The
> Lord accompanied the word with such power that I was struck to the
> ground and lay both speechless and senseless for twenty-four minutes.
> When I was come a little to, I found two men attending me and a
> woman throwing water in my face and holding a smelling bottle to my
> nose; and when something more recovered, every word I heard from
> the minister was like a parcel of swords thrust into me.[37]

Marrant spends the next three days overcome with a sense of his sin, finally breaking through to salvation with a local minister who prays with him. Marrant would go on to abandon both professional music and his trade and receive ordination as a clergyman, serving in Nova Scotia and publishing in 1785 his popular account of his dramatic conversion under the preaching of Whitefield.

In April 1770, Whitefield traveled north to the mid-Atlantic region and preached throughout those colonies through the end of the summer. He informed a friend in England of his overwhelmingly positive reception in the area, remarking from New York, "Oh, what a new scene of usefulness is opening in various parts of this new world! All fresh work where I have been. The divine influence has been as at the first. Invitations crowd upon me both from ministers and people from many, many quarters."[38] From Philadelphia, Whitefield exults to the same friend, "Pulpits, hearts, and affections seem to be as open and enlarged towards me as ever." Even the demands of itinerant preaching did not faze him as he announces in the same letter, "Through infinite mercy, I still continue in good health and more and more in love every day with a pilgrim life."[39]

Whitefield left the mid-Atlantic region in August to travel further north to New England and, sadly, began to experience a decline in his health the next month. He was unable to minister at a scheduled event in Boston on September 21, yet preached his way to York, Maine, after recovering. On September 29, he delivered sermons in the New Hampshire towns of Portsmouth and Exeter on his way south to the home and church of his friend the Rev. Jonathan Parsons (1705–1776) in Newburyport, Massachusetts, where he arrived that evening. Begged by crowds in the street to preach from Parson's home, Whitefield shared a short message and retired for the evening. That night, Whitefield experienced difficulty breathing and died early in the morning of September 30. He was buried under the pulpit of Parson's Old South Church, the burial site that Whitefield had reportedly personally requested.

The colonies were convulsed with mourning for the revered evangelist. In Boston, *The Massachusetts Gazette* reported Whitefield's death the next day, praising his passion and ministry:

Filled with the spirit of grace, he spoke from the heart and with a
fervency of zeal perhaps unequalled since the days of the apostles....
It were to be wished that the good impressions of his ministry may be
long retained and that the rising generation, like their pious ancestors,
may catch a spark of that ethereal flame which burned with such distinguished luster in the sentiment and practice of this faithful servant
of the Most High God.[40]

Whitefield had finally achieved his greatest desire—to complete his earthly mission and be fully united with his God. In the final surviving letter we have, written from Portsmouth, New Hampshire, one week before his death, Whitefield declares, "The day of release will shortly come.... Oh, for a warm heart! Oh, to stand fast in the faith, to [conduct] ourselves like men and be strong!"[41]

FINAL WORDS

As modern readers who will never hear Whitefield deliver a sermon in person, we can rejoice that we have perhaps the next best thing: the Grand Itinerant's final sermon delivered in England during his lifetime, taken down in shorthand by a member of the audience. On August 30, 1769, just days before he boarded the *Friendship* for his last voyage to America and just one year before he died, Whitefield preached an exposition of Jesus' words in John 10:27–28: "My sheep listen to my voice; I know them, and they follow me. I give them eternal life, and they shall never perish; no one will snatch them out of my hand."[42]

The main themes of the sermon reveal Whitefield's lifelong commitment to his calling to preach God's offer of spiritual rebirth to all who would listen. He asserts that "there are but two sorts of people," those who are disciples of Jesus and those who are not. He extends an urgent call to follow Jesus in "every word and every good work, out of one climate into another, by sea or by land." He exhorts his listeners to "inquire whether we belong to Christ's sheep or no."[43] Through thirty years of international preaching, Whitefield's message does not change.

However, the sermon is unique in two respects. First, it is very personal. Whitefield shares with his listeners his struggles with feeling unprepared to receive ordination and begin his professional ministry, the temptation to accept worldly advancement, his continued hope for the future of Bethesda, and his profound sadness over parting from his friends for what he suspects will be the final time. He closes with a heartfelt exhortation that his Christian brothers and sisters remain steadfast in Christ.

Whitefield's disclosure of how deeply he cherishes his fellow travelers on the road of Christian discipleship is moving: "My friends, spare your tears! I cannot bear your tears! I should have been glad to have been spared this parting; it cuts me to the heart! But, by and by, partings will be all over, and all tears shall be wiped away from our eyes!"[44] Whitefield reminds us that brothers and sisters in Christ help us persevere in the spiritual life until we all enjoy the fullness of union with God and each other in God's eternal kingdom.

A second unique aspect of the sermon is what today we might call its unfiltered nature, not being revised for publication as his sermons typically were. In fact, Whitefield complained that the published version of his message was "wretchedly unconnected," although he rejoiced that "if any one sentence is blessed to the conviction of one sinner or the edification of any individual saint, I care not what becomes of my character."[45] Just as Whitefield's original audience expressed an "earnest desire" to preserve the candid words of his final discourse, as the title page notes, we too cherish the opportunity to hear Whitefield's last thoughts as he says farewell to his lifelong friends and contemplates his imminent departure from this world.

As we conclude this intimate look at George Whitefield's life and writings, I hope you have been as blessed as I have been by the Grand Itinerant. Although his years were lived out in a time and place very different from our own, the force and vividness of his encounters with God, the joy of his ministry successes, the honesty of his personal challenges, and the relentlessness of his pursuit of God can still stoke and inform our own desire to follow Jesus fervently. My prayer for each of us echoes Whitefield's in a letter to a friend from August 19, 1769: "That God may make you flame more and more, till you are called to be a flaming seraph in yonder heaven, earnestly prays ... G.W."[46]

SERMON

A Sermon by the Reverend Mr. George Whitefield, Being his Last Farewell to his Friends[47]

Preface
Reader,

The publication of the following sermon, being the last Mr. Whitefield preached in England and which was delivered to a crowded audience, cannot but be highly acceptable to those of his hearers who are willing to retain in their memories the substance of that solemn and affectionate discourse.

I need not say that those who are acquainted with Mr. Whitefield's preaching will not expect to find this sermon (though taken verbatim) in every respect answerable to its delivery from the pulpit, as it is impossible for the press to convey an idea of that [emotional], moving manner which is peculiarly his own.

A great many of Mr. Whitefield's friends, who came with a desire to hear this sermon, were disappointed on account of the place being filled so soon, and many were obliged to retire through the heat of the place.

On these accounts it is published, together with a hearty and sincere desire that the Great Shepherd of the sheep, the Lord Jesus Christ, may accompany the reading of it with divine success to every unrenewed heart.

John 10:27, 28
My sheep hear my voice, and I know them, and they follow me. And I give unto them eternal life, and they shall never perish, neither shall any man pluck them out of my hand. . . .

Jesus the Great Shepherd

We need go no farther than this chapter to find that Christ is the great shepherd that laid down his life for his sheep. . . . Says he, whether you believe or no, some will believe, shall believe. *My sheep hear my voice, and follow me.*

It is very remarkable, there are but two sorts of people. Christ does not say, are you an Independent, or Baptist, or Presbyterian, or are you a Church of England man? Nor did he ask, are you a Methodist? All these things are of our own silly invention. But the whole world the Lord divides into two classes of people—sheep and goats. The Lord give us to see this morning to which class we belong. . . .

But, my brethren, with what propriety Christ speaks, *my sheep.* O blessed be God for that little, dear, great word, *my.*

How are they Christ's sheep? They are by his eternal election—*those which you have given me.* They are given by the Father in a covenant passed from eternity, and they that cannot see this, I wish them better heads, though I believe some have better hearts. They are his by purchase. Oh, sinners, you are come to hear a poor creature take his last farewell, but I want you to forget the creature and his preaching. I want to lead you farther than the tabernacle, to Mount Calvary, to see with what an expense of blood Jesus Christ purchased his own.

He bought them with his own blood, so that they are his by eternal election and by actual redemption in time. They were given him by the Father on condition, that he should purchase them with his own heart's blood. And though it was a hard bargain, yet Jesus Christ was willing to strike it to save you and I from eternal damnation. So they are his because in the day of his power, they are willing to give themselves up to him, to act as his sheep, to hear his voice and follow him. . . .

We hear his voice—that bespeaks the habitual temper of the soul. The wicked hear the voice of the devil. This is what Christ's people did before their conversion, but when they are born of God, they hear Christ's voice, the voice of his providence, the voice of his word, the voice of his blessed will, and the consequence of hearing this voice and a proof of it is [that] they will be willing to follow him. "If any man," says Christ, "comes after me, let him deny himself, take up his cross and follow me," and it is said, "they followed the Lamb whithersoever he went."[48] Wherever the shepherd turns his crook, they follow him.

Following Christ represents following him in life and death, following him in self-denial, in humility and heavenly-mindedness, following him in every word and every good work, out of one climate into another, by sea or by land.

"Bid me come to you on the waters," said Peter,[49] and if we are bid to cross the water, God Almighty enable us to go. We must be sure of our call, we must be sure that he turns his crook this way. And this is the character of a true servant of Christ, that he endeavors to follow Christ in thought, word, and work.

Now, before I go any further, will you be so good, before the world gets into your hearts (sure it did not get into your hearts before you rose from your beds, and I suppose many of you were up sooner than usual; I hope the world has not got into your hearts before nine o'clock in the morning), now we are here, let us enquire whether we belong to Christ's sheep or no?

Man! Woman! Sinner! Whoever you are, put your hand to your heart and say, did you ever hear Christ's voice so as to follow him? I verily believe from my inward soul that I am now preaching to a vast body of good people, though there is a mixed multitude.

Oh, blessed be free grace, sovereign electing love, that God chose you and me! And if he has been pleased to let you hear his voice through the ministry of a poor miserable sinner, a poor, but happy pilgrim, may the Lord Jesus Christ have all the glory! And if you belong to Christ's sheep, here is good news for you: I know he knows their number, their names. Christ knows every one for whom he died, and if there was but one missing for whom he died, God the Father would send him down again.

Of all that you have given me have I lost none. Christ knows his sheep, but the words speak a peculiar knowledge he takes of them. I know them, and I take as much care of them as if there was but a single sheep in the world. I know all their sorrows, I know all their temptations; I take notice of every tear, and I have a bottle to receive their tears in. I know their deepest trials, I know their corruptions, I know their peculiar infirmities, and I know all their wanderings. . . .

Jesus Gives Eternal Life

Some are ready to think God has forgotten to be gracious and what a mercy is it that God knows us. But, mind, my brethren, here is something still better. I have got to part from you with good news in my mouth. *I give them eternal life.* Oh, that these words may come with as much warmth to your hearts as they did to mine near five-and-thirty years ago!

I am sure I never prayed so much against my infirmities as against going into holy orders so soon. However some may come and preach here and there, I don't know how much it may concern them, but I am sure it concerned me greatly indeed. I have prayed hundreds of times that God would not let me go so soon.[50]

I remember once at Gloucester (I know the room, and I cannot help looking up at the window whenever I am there and go by; I know the bed-side, I know the floor on which I have prostrated for weeks together), and I remember once I was crying, "I cannot go! I am a novice! I shall fall into the condemnation of the devil!" I wanted to be at Oxford; I wanted to stay there three or four more years that I might make one hundred and fifty sermons at least, for I thought I would set up with a good stock in trade however. I remember wrestling, praying, groaning, striving with God, and said, "I am undone, unfit to speak in your name, my God, send me not yet!"

After I had written to all my friends in town to pray against the bishop's solicitations [for ordination], at last these words came into my mind, *My sheep hear my voice, etc., and none shall pluck them out of my hand.* Then I said, "Lord, I will go, send me when you will." And you have often heard me tell that story.

[Later], I was at a place called Dover Island in America, I had a hundred and fifty in family to maintain and not a farthing to maintain them with, and in the [most expensive] part of the coast. I remember I told a minister of Christ (now with God), "I remember once I had these words strongly impressed upon my mind, 'I will never leave you, nor forsake you.'" "Oh," says he, "you may be sure God will be as good as his word, if he never tells you so again."

I will give them eternal life. Here is a free, blessed promise to dejected, disconsolate souls. They think they shall perish, they think they shall fall by the hand of Saul, by the hand of their corruptions, but Christ says, *They shall not perish.*

I give them eternal life. Not, I will give it, but I give it now. There are some talk of being justified at the day of judgment, but if we are not justified here, we shall not there.

Jesus Keeps Us Safe in Him

He gives the Spirit of God here as a [deposit] of glory hereafter. *None shall pluck them out of my hands.* It implies that always there is somebody plucking at Christ's sheep. The lust of the flesh is plucking, the lust of the eye is plucking, and the devil is continually plucking at Christ's sheep. But nothing shall pluck them out of my hands. I have bought them, and I am gone to heaven to prepare a place for them.

Nothing, my brethren! If it was not for keeping you too long, I would call you to leap for joy. There is not a more glorious text that stands by the perseverance of the saints than this. I wonder how some good people can talk of perseverance as a doctrine not contained in our Bibles.

But, my brethren, with this text I can leave you, and all my cares, and all my friends, and all Christ's sheep to the protection of Jesus Christ, the never-failing, the good shepherd.

I thought this morning when I came here riding from the other end of town, it was just like a person coming to be executed publicly. And when the carriage turned away into the walk, and I saw you running here, I thought it was like a person now coming to the place where he is to be executed. And when I got up and put on my gown, I thought it was just like dressing myself to be a public spectacle.

I call heaven to witness, and earth to witness, and God to witness, and his holy angels to witness, that though I had preferment enough offered me, though I was offered two parishes before I was two-and-twenty, though the late bishop of Gloucester was my friend and used always to invite me to his table before the sacrament, God knows I cared for no other preferment than to suffer for the Lamb of God.

In this spirit, I came [into ministry], in this spirit, I came up to this metropolis [London]. I was thinking, Jacob went over the brook with a staff, but I could not say I had so much as a staff. I had no friend, no servant, not a single person to introduce me. Supported by this spirit, through the divine grace, I continue to this day. Yet I feel my affections and my passions strong, though in the decline of life one would think they should be somewhat weakened. Yet I feel my affections as strong as ever towards the people of the living God.

The congregations at both ends of the town are dear to me.[51] God has honored me to build this and the other place, and yet, blessed be his name, I shall leave everything complete and easy. God called me to Georgia first, when I had all the churches in London open to me, when five or six constables were obliged to be placed at the doors to prevent the people from crowding too much. I might have settled in London, I was offered hundreds then, yet I gave it all up to turn pilgrim for God, to go over into a foreign clime, out of a love for immortal souls, and I go, I hope, with that single intention now.

When I came from America last, I thought I had no other river to cross but the river Jordan, and as the orphan house was going to be placed in other hands and as my body was in such a weak condition, I thought of nothing but retiring into some little corner that I might pray though I could not preach. But God has been pleased to renew my strength. God has been pleased in some measure to bring back my spirits, and as I find my spirits return, I find my heart willing to be a pilgrim preacher for the blessed God. . . .

Whitefield's Final Farewell

And now, my friends, I must take my last farewell, and it is the hardest part I have to act. I was afraid when I came out [today], I could not bear the shock, but I hope the Lord Jesus will help me to bear it and you to give me up to his blessed hands to do with me as he will. This is the thirteenth time of my crossing the water, and I find it a little difficult at this time of life.[52] But I am willing to go. I am clear as light in my call.

May God bless me with that peace which is unutterable! And this is what sustains me and keeps up my spirits. And I beg that when I am gone from you, this may be your language—"Lord Jesus! Let nothing pluck him out of your hands."

I expect many trials when I am on board, but I assure you, I humbly hope and believe that the God who has kept me will keep me. And my prayers for you shall be, "Lord! Let nothing pluck them out of your hands. . . ."

Some of you are certainly hearing my dying sermon; some of you are certainly hearing your last sermon. I shall hear of many of you being gone. But, my brethren, however that may be, we shall part but to meet again forever! I dare not meet you now! My friends, spare your tears! I cannot bear your tears! I should have been glad to have been spared this parting; it cuts me to the heart! But, by and by, partings will be all over, and all tears shall be wiped away from our eyes! Oh God, grant that none who weep now may weep at our parting on the great day! Take care, take care, if you never were among Christ's sheep, may you be brought into the number now.

Come, come, see what it is to have eternal life! Haste, haste, haste away to the great, the glorious shepherd! He calls you, he holds up his crook, and if you never heard his voice before, God grant this may be the happy time, that I may have the same comfort now I had the last time of my leaving you, to be the means of converting one soul to God!

Oh, may it prove a farewell sermon indeed to some, to make them bid a farewell to the world and the devil. *Come, come, come, come,* said the Lord Jesus, *nothing shall pluck you out of my hand!* With this, I leave you, you dear sheep!

God keep you from wandering! I don't care where you go, so [long] as you are kept under the conduct of the great Shepherd and Bishop of souls. May the Lord Jesus bless his preaching to you! My brethren, I cannot leave you in better hands than Christ's. Be steadfast and unmovable, always abounding in the work of the Lord.[53]

For the present, farewell! May you be kept in God's way from going astray from him! The Lord Jesus have mercy upon you! The Lord bless you and keep you! The Lord make his face shine upon you and be gracious unto you! The Lord lift up his countenance upon you and give you peace![54]

STUDY QUESTIONS

Chapter I

1. What do you remember the most strongly about your conversion process and decision to follow Jesus? Can you identify some of the ways God worked in your life prior to conversion to awaken your heart to his existence and love?

2. Why do you think it is so tempting for humans to believe they can save themselves spiritually, as Whitefield did?

3. Can you recall a time you went to unhealthy extremes in your life, either spiritually, emotionally, financially, relationally, etc.? How did you return to balance?

4. What truths might we learn about ourselves and God when we admit our need and ask him for help?

5. Describe a time after conversion when God deepened or reignited his spark of spiritual passion in you. How did the experience change you?

6. What part of Whitefield's conversion story resonated the most with you and why?

CHAPTER II

1. Describe a time you felt a strong sense of purpose. How did this feeling of purpose affect what you were able to accomplish?

2. Have you been able to identify some specific purposes God has for your life? Share them.

3. In what ways do you think having a sense of purpose deepens our intimacy with God?

4. Whitefield believed choosing to spend time in acts of service helped him discover God's purposes for his life. What areas of service have impacted how you see your purpose?

5. Which parts of Whitefield's sermon did you enjoy the most? Which parts surprised you?

6. Can you identify and share one or two points in Whitefield's sermon that you think are applicable to today's secular society? To today's church?

CHAPTER III

1. Have you ever kept a spiritual journal? How did that experience enhance your relationship with God?

2. What did you enjoy the most about reading Whitefield's journal excerpts?

3. Can you describe a time you were let down or disappointed in your pursuit of God by something you trusted—for example, a Christian community, an established spiritual discipline, ministry success, personal reputation?

4. Share two or three words that best describe your relationship with God at this point in your life. What words do you *wish* described your relationship with him?

5. Which of the three elements of Whitefield's relationship with God—cherished, honest, and affectionate—do you most desire to grow in? How might you begin that process?

6. What outward-facing activities help you grow the most spiritually—fellowship with other Christians, missions work, corporate worship, acts of service?

CHAPTER IV

1. What are the most important factors for you when making lifestyle decisions?

2. What aspects of your current lifestyle most accurately reflect your passion for God?

3. What has been your experience with dynamic, impactful Christian speakers? Have you been present at religious services in which you or others responded physically to God's presence? Describe that experience.

4. What spiritual practices help you determine the leading of the Holy Spirit? Can you share a time you followed the Spirit's direction in your life?

5. Why do you think it is so difficult for believers to leave the results of our life and ministry in God's hands? What characteristics of God help you trust him?

6. In what ways would you like to see your current lifestyle transformed by God to better reveal your passion for him?

CHAPTER V

1. What do you appreciate the most about sharing the spiritual journey with other believers?

2. Can you describe a time you shared a common God-given purpose with another follower of Jesus? What were you able to accomplish together?

3. Whitefield was moved when he saw the power and passion his friend Gilbert Tennent displayed while preaching. What are some of the unique passions, talents, and ministries of your Christian friends? How have they influenced your thinking, actions, or perspectives?

4. How has God blessed Christian brothers and sisters through you—spiritual counsel, admonition, encouragement, service, comfort, leadership, or other blessings?

5. How do you personally cultivate joy in God? What do you value about celebrating God and his kingdom with other Christians?

6. How do you think listeners in eighteenth-century Philadelphia responded to Whitefield's sermon *The Wise and Foolish Virgins?* How do you think listeners today would respond?

Chapter VI

1. Were you surprised to read that Whitefield encountered significant opposition from fellow Christians because of his life and ministry? Why or why not?

2. Have you ever experienced conflict with another believer because of your passion for God? What were the causes of the opposition? How did it impact you spiritually and emotionally?

3. Can you describe a time a fellow Christian helped you see an area of your own sin? What enabled you to receive their rebuke in a beneficial manner?

4. Maintaining a heart posture of spiritual poverty can help us remain humble and gracious with other believers, even in the face of opposition. Can you describe a Christian you know who recognizes their own spiritual poverty in a modest and healthy way?

5. Describe your response to reading the excerpt from *The Querists.* How do you imagine Whitefield felt upon reading it?

6. Which suggestions for dealing with opposition from the chapter did you find the most helpful?

CHAPTER VII

1. What are some effective and godly responses to culture that Christians have made throughout history or that you have witnessed personally?

2. What are some of your current communities? How are aspects of those groups challenging for you as a Christian? How are you blessing those communities?

3. Which do you think is the more common negative response of Christians today to cultural challenges—retreat or condemnation? Why? Have you struggled with either one?

4. Is there one truth of God that you have felt called to defend recently? How did you do it? What was the outcome?

5. Who would you identify as "overlooked" in our broader culture today? In your own communities? Can you think of ways Christians can invest love into those individuals?

6. What helps you think outside the box in regard to cultural assumptions both inside and outside the church? In which areas of your life is it hardest for you to think and act unconventionally?

Chapter VIII

1. How long have you followed Jesus? What are some challenges you have faced and overcome during your time of discipleship? What are some successes?

2. Are you surprised that Whitefield was able to sustain his zeal for God over thirty years of life and ministry? Why or why not?

3. What role has the Bible played in strengthening you to persevere in the spiritual life? What are some of your most cherished biblical passages and promises? Is there one individual mentioned in the Bible with whom you deeply relate?

4. Can you describe a recent encounter with God that reignited love for him in your heart?

5. In what ways is Whitefield's final sermon in England representative of the evangelist and his ministry?

6. Which part of this study of Whitefield's passion for God has been the most helpful for you? Is there one aspect of your spiritual life that you plan to change after encountering Whitefield's life and writings?

NOTES

A NOTE ON THE TEXTS

[1] Two sources for writings by and about Whitefield are Richard Owen Roberts, *Whitefield in Print: A Bibliographic Record of Works by, for, and against George Whitefield* (Wheaton, IL: R.O. Roberts, 1988) and David Ceri Jones, "'So Much Idolized by Some, and Railed at by Others': Towards Understanding George Whitefield," *Wesley and Methodist Studies* 5 (2013): 3–29.

[2] David Ceri Jones, Reader in Early Modern History at Aberystwyth University in Wales, is working on a six-volume scholarly edition of Whitefield's trans-Atlantic correspondence. See Geordan Hammond, "The Correspondence of George Whitefield Project: A Report and Reflection on the Early Stages," *Wesley Theological Journal* 54, no. 1 (Spring 2019): 57–70.

INTRODUCTION

[1] G[eorge] W[hitefield] to Mr. H[owell] H[arris], Philadelphia, Nov. 9, 1740, in *Letters of George Whitefield for the Period 1734–1742*, ed. S.M. Houghton (Carlisle, PA: Banner of Truth Trust, 1976), 220. This work is a facsimile edition of *The Works of the Reverend George Whitefield*, ed. John Gillies, vol. 1, *A Select Collection of Letters of the Late Reverend George Whitefield* (London, 1771). For all eighteenth-century writings, I have modernized spelling and punctuation, adjusted paragraphing, added subtitles where needed, and expanded some contractions for ease of reading.

[2] Stuart C. Henry, *George Whitefield: Wayfaring Witness* (New York: Abingdon Press, 1957), 7.

[3] Frank Lambert, *"Pedlar in Divinity": George Whitefield and the Transatlantic Revivals, 1737–1770* (Princeton, NJ: Princeton University Press, 1994), 137.

[4] C. Harold King, "God's Dramatist," in *Studies in Speech and Drama in Honor of Alexander M. Drummond*, eds. Donald C. Bryant et al. (Ithaca: Cornell UP, 1944), 369, quoted in Albert M. Lyles, *Methodism Mocked: The Satiric Reaction to Methodism in the Eighteenth Century* (London: Epworth Press, 1960), 127–128.

[5] J.W. Laycock, "Great Britain's Indebtedness Under God to George Whitefield," *Proceedings of the Wesley Historical Society* 10, no. 1 (March 1915): 27, https://www.biblicalstudies.org.uk/pdf/whs/10-1.pdf.

6   B[enjamin] Franklin to Noble Wimberly Jones, March 5, 1771, in *The Papers of Benjamin Franklin*, ed. William B. Wilcox, vol. 18, *January 1 through December 31, 1771* (New Haven, CT: Yale UP, 1974), 53, https://franklinpapers.org/framedVolumes.jsp. For Franklin's comments on Whitefield's unanswered prayers for his conversion, see Franklin's *Autobiography*.

7   G[eorge] W[hitefield] to Mr. J[ames] H[utton], Bohemia, Maryland, Nov. 24, 1740, in *Letters*, 224.

8   G[eorge] W[hitefield] to the Same, Oxon, England, Dec. 4, 1734, in *Letters*, 5. Volume editor S.M. Houghton suggests the recipient is Gabriel Harris Sr., a prominent bookseller in Gloucester, England, who also held several civic positions and whose son Gabriel Harris Jr. was a boyhood friend of Whitefield's (519).

9   George Whitefield, *The Last Will and Testament, of the Late Reverend and Renowned George Whitefield* (London, 1771), vii–viii.

10 Holy Bible, New International Version (Colorado Springs, CO: Biblica, 2011). All quotations are from the New International Version unless otherwise noted.

11 Lisa Smith, *Godly Character(s): Insights for Spiritual Passion from the Lives of 8 Women in the Bible* (Baltimore, MD: Square Halo Books, 2018), 1–2.

12 Harry S. Stout, *The Divine Dramatist: George Whitefield and the Rise of Modern Evangelicalism* (Grand Rapids, MI: Eerdmans, 1991); Lambert, Pedlar; and Peter Y. Choi, *George Whitefield: Evangelist for God and Empire* (Grand Rapids, MI: Eerdmans, 2018) are all modern biographies that view Whitefield in this context.

13 George Whitefield, *A Continuation of the Reverend Mr. Whitefield's Journal, From a few Days after his Return to Georgia to his Arrival at Falmouth, on the 11th of March 1741* (London, 1741), 76. Jerome Dean Mahaffey's two monographs, *Preaching Politics: The Religious Rhetoric of George Whitefield and the Founding of a New Nation* (Waco, TX: Baylor University Press, 2007) and *The Accidental Revolutionary: George Whitefield and the Creation of America* (Waco, TX: Baylor UP, 2011) highlight Whitefield's role in spreading the ideas of liberty and self-government a full quarter century before the Stamp Act and the American Revolution.

14 These four characteristics of evangelicalism are commonly referred to as the Bebbington quadrilateral, first developed by David Bebbington in his 1989 book *Evangelicalism in Modern Britain: A History from the 1730s to the 1980s*.

15 Thomas S. Kidd explores the central role of Whitefield in evangelicalism in his biography *George Whitefield: America's Spiritual Founding Father* (New Haven, CT: Yale UP, 2014). Kidd's biography is my choice for readers who desire an authoritative, informative, and readable modern biography of Whitefield. For a book-length treatment of Whitefield's orphanage Bethesda in Savannah, Georgia, see Edward J. Cashin, *Beloved Bethesda: A History of George Whitefield's Home for Boys, 1740–2000* (Macon, GA: Mercer University Press, 2001). For Whitefield's writings and other contemporaneous documents on Bethesda, see Luke Tyerman, *The Life of the Rev.*

George Whitefield, 2 vols. (London: Hodder and Stoughton, 1876), 1:440–446; John Gillies, *The Works of the Reverend George Whitefield,* 6 vols. (London, 1771–1772), 3:428–509.

16   There are numerous excellent books on the First Great Awakening, but one well-researched recent treatment is Thomas S. Kidd, *The Great Awakening: The Roots of Evangelical Christianity in Colonial America* (New Haven, CT: Yale UP, 2007).

17   Lambert, *Pedlar,* 128.

18   NIV84. The verse is Matthew 11:12 and is in the King James Version on the ticket: "And from the days of John the Baptist until now the kingdom of heaven suffereth violence, and the violent take it by force."

Chapter I: Igniting the Fire

1   Genesis 15:17; Exodus 3:2; Exodus 13:21; Exodus 19:18; Deuteronomy 4:24.

2   Acts 2:3; Hebrews 12:29.

3   George Whitefield, *A Short Account of God's Dealings with the Reverend Mr. George Whitefield* (London, 1740), 73.

4   Whitefield, *Short Account,* 73. Whitefield's last phrase is a reference to Ephesians 1:23.

5   2 Timothy 1:6a.

6   Hosea 11:1, 4a.

7   Whitefield, *Short Account,* 18.

8   Whitefield, *Short Account,* 22.

9   Whitefield, *Short Account,* 22.

10   Whitefield, *Short Account,* 23.

11   Whitefield, *Short Account,* 28.

12   Henry Scougal, *The Life of God in the Soul of Man: Or, The Nature and Excellency of the Christian Religion,* reprint with an introduction by J.I. Packer (London, 1677; Ross-shire, Scotland: Christian Heritage, 2021), 14.

13   Scougal, *Life of God,* 13.

14   Whitefield, *Short Account,* 40. For a letter dated April 1, 1735, from Whitefield at Oxford to John Wesley which details the physical strain Whitefield was under at this time, see Whitefield to John Wesley, Oxford, April 1, 1735, in "Letters of George Whitefield: From the Collection of Mr. George Stampe," *Proceedings of the Wesley Historical Society* 10, no. 1 (March 1915): 17–19, https://www.biblicalstudies.org.uk/pdf/whs/10-1.pdf.

15   Whitefield, *Short Account,* 49.

16   George Whitefield, *The First Two Parts of his Life, with his Journals, Revised, Corrected, and Abridged* (London, 1756), 17. Whitefield uses the phrase "day of my espousals" to refer to his conversion and his new position as a member of God's church, the bride of Christ.

17   See D. Bruce Hindmarsh, *The Evangelical Conversion Narrative: Spiritual Autobiog-
      raphy in Early Modern England* (Oxford: Oxford University Press, 2005), 88–92, for
      more on the early evangelical understanding of conversion.

18   Whitefield to Mrs. [Gabriel] H[arris], [Sr.], Gloucester, June 28, 1736, in *Letters*, 18.

19   Whitefield, *Short Account,* 45.

20   Whitefield, *Short Account,* 33.

21   Whitefield, *Short Account,* 36.

22   Edward B. Pusey, trans., *The Confessions of Saint Augustine* (New York: Simon &
      Schuster, 1997), 200–201.

23   Whitefield, *Short Account,* 36.

24   Whitefield, *Short Account,* 72–73.

25   Selections are from Whitefield, *Short Account,* 26–30, 36–41, 47–49. Complete bib-
      liographic information for all texts cited, excerpted, or reprinted can be found in the
      bibliography.

26   A reference to Isaiah 35:3 and Hebrews 12:12.

27   *Nicodemus: Or, A Treatise Against the Fear of Man* by Augustus Hermannus Franke
      (1663–1727) was first published in London in English translation in 1706; a second
      edition appeared in 1731. *The Country-Parson's Advice to his Parishioners* was first
      published in London in 1701; a second edition appeared in 1737.

28   *The Life of God in the Soul of Man: Or, The Nature and Excellency of the Christian
      Religion* was a popular work by Scottish theologian and minister Henry Scougal
      (1650–1678). By 1733, the book was in its sixth edition, which is probably the edition
      Whitefield read. A modern reprint of the work, with a helpful introduction by J.I.
      Packer, is listed in the bibliography.

29   Whitefield is referring to the Christian sacrament of communion or the Eucharist.

30   A reference to 1 Corinthians 10:31.

31   A reference to Judges 8:1–21.

32   Thomas à Kempis (c. 1380–1471) wrote the devotional work *The Imitation of Christ,* a
      popular Christian text during Whitefield's lifetime.

33   A reference to the story of Job in the Old Testament book titled Job.

34   Probably a reference to 2 Peter 1:19 in the King James Version: "We have also a more
      sure word of prophecy; whereunto ye do well that ye take heed, as unto a light that
      shineth in a dark place, until the day dawn, and the day star arise in your hearts."
      See also the last paragraph of the excerpt.

35   A reference to 2 Corinthians 11:14.

36   Juan de Castaniza's *The Spiritual Combat: Or, The Christian Pilgrim in his Spiritual
      Conflict and Conquest* was in its second English edition by 1710.

37   Lent is the forty-day period of the church liturgical year leading up to Easter in
      which Christians remember and commemorate the suffering of Jesus. It is celebrat-
      ed in varying ways by the different Christian traditions.

38 Passion week refers to the week leading up to Easter.

39 A reference to John 19:28.

40 A reference to Ephesians 4:30b.

CHAPTER II: EMBRACING PURPOSE

1 See Genesis 37, 39–47 for Joseph; the book of Esther for Esther; Acts 9:1–19 for Paul.

2 1 Corinthians 12:18, 27.

3 Romans 8:28; Ephesians 2:10.

4 Whitefield to Mr. [Matthew] S[almon], Gloucester, June 20, 1736, in *Letters,* 15–16.

5 Matthew 22:34–40 and Mark 12:28–31.

6 John Gillies, *Memoirs of the Life of the Reverend George Whitefield* (London, 1772), 290.

7 Whitefield to the Inhabitants of Savannah, Oct. 2, 1738, in *Letters,* 490. "One thing needful" refers to Jesus' visit with Mary and Martha recorded in Luke 10:38–41.

8 Kidd, *Spiritual Founding Father,* 63–65.

9 George Whitefield, *The Nature and Necessity of our New Birth in Christ Jesus, in Order to Salvation* (London, 1737), vii.

10 George Whitefield, *A Journal of a Voyage from London to Savannah in Georgia* (London, 1738), 13.

11 Whitefield, *Short Account,* 57.

12 Whitefield to the Rev. Mr. G[abriel] W[ilson], Edinburgh, Aug. 1, 1741, in *Letters,* 306.

13 Whitefield to [students of Dr. Doddridge's Academy at Northampton], Philadelphia, Nov. 10, 1739, in *Letters,* 81.

14 Whitefield to Mr. Thomas N[oble], Edinburgh, Aug. 8, 1741, in *Letters,* 308.

15 Whitefield, *Short Account,* 59.

16 Whitefield, *Short Account,* 60–64.

17 Whitefield, *Short Account,* 61. At this time, Whitefield was ordained as a deacon of the Church of England, the first official step to being ordained as a priest. Whitefield would go on to receive his final ordination as a priest on January 14, 1739. See George Whitefield, *A Continuation of the Reverend Mr. Whitefield's Journal, From his Arrival at London, to his Departure from thence on his Way to Georgia* (London, 1739), 9.

18 George Whitefield, *A Further Account of God's Dealings with the Reverend Mr. George Whitefield* (London, 1747), 5.

19 Whitefield, *Further Account,* 8.

20 Whitefield, *Further Account,* 10–11.

21 Whitefield to Mr. —, Kilrush, Ireland, Nov. 16, 1738, in *Letters,* 45.

22 Whitefield to Mr. [Gabriel] H[arris], London, Dec. 30, 1738, in *Letters,* 46.

23 Whitefield to the Rev. Mr. R.D., Philadelphia, Nov. 10, 1739, in *Letters,* 105.

24 Kidd, *Spiritual Founding Father,* 71.

25 Whitefield to Mr. [Gabriel] H[arris], London, April 27, 1739, in *Letters,* 49. Islington

and Moorfields are both in the greater London area.

26   Whitefield to Mr. [James] H[utton], Margate, Jan. 9, 1738, in *Letters*, 33.

27   Whitefield, *Short Account*, 54–55. Whitefield may be referencing Jeremiah 33:6.

28   Whitefield, *Short Account*, 55.

29   Whitefield, *Short Account*, 57–58.

30   Whitefield to the Rev. Mr. R.D., Philadelphia, Nov. 10, 1739, in *Letters*, 105.

31   Whitefield, *Short Account*, 58–59.

32   For example, see Whitefield, *Short Account*, 70.

33   Whitefield, *Short Account*, 59.

34   Whitefield, *Further Account*, 15–16.

35   Whitefield to the Rev. Mr. Charles Wesley, Oxon, Dec. 30, 1736, in *Letters*, 488.

36   Whitefield, *Further Account*, 16.

37   Whitefield, *Further Account*, 8.

38   Whitefield, *Short Account*, 66–67.

39   Whitefield, *Short Account*, 69. The Bible verse Whitefield references is Acts 18:9.

40   Whitefield, *Short Account*, 71.

41   Whitefield, *Nature and Necessity*, front matter.

42   Whitefield, *Nature and Necessity*, vi–vii.

43   Whitefield, *Nature and Necessity*, 3.

44   Whitefield, *Nature and Necessity*, 27.

45   Whitefield, *Further Account*, 19.

46   Whitefield, *Further Account*, 19.

47   Whitefield, *Nature and Necessity*, viii.

48   Selections are from Whitefield, *Nature and Necessity*, v–viii, 1–10, 12–14, 16–18, 21–22, 25–28. Complete bibliographic information for all texts cited, excerpted, or reprinted can be found in the bibliography.

49   Habakkuk 2:2. Whitefield references numerous biblical texts throughout his sermon; I will identify the primary ones.

50   Acts 19:2.

51   1 Timothy 2:5.

52   Acts 4:12.

53   John 3:9.

54   Acts 17:18.

55   2 Timothy 2:19.

56   John 3:5.

57   Acts 1:5.

58   Romans 9:6.

59   Matthew 7:22–23.

60   1 Peter 4:13.

61   2 Corinthians 12:2; Philippians 3:9.

62 See Romans 2–4.
63 Galatians 5:6.
64 John 3:4.
65 The story of Naaman is told in 2 Kings 5:1–19.
66 1 Corinthians 2:11.
67 John 3:8.
68 2 Peter 3:16.
69 John 3:9.
70 Psalm 51:10.
71 John 3:5.
72 Habakkuk 1:13; Job 15:15; Job 4:18.
73 Psalm 51:5; Romans 7:18; Romans 7:14; Romans 8:7.
74 2 Corinthians 6:14.
75 Belial is a biblical term for the devil or for wickedness.
76 1 Corinthians 2:9.
77 Matthew 20:28 and Mark 10:45 (parallel passages).
78 Micah 6:8.
79 Hebrews 6:9.
80 Revelation 19:6–9.
81 Isaiah 59:1.
82 Matthew 5:29–30; Matthew 18:7–9.
83 Romans 12:2.
84 This reference is to Wisdom of Solomon 5:4, a deuterocanonical book which was included in the 1611 King James Version of the Bible, which included the Apocrypha.
85 Philippians 4:7.

Chapter III: Building a Foundation

1 Whitefield, *Further Account,* 17.
2 Braxton Boren, "Whitefield's Voice," in *George Whitefield: Life, Context, and Legacy,* eds. Geordan Hammond and David Ceri Jones (Oxford: Oxford University Press, 2016). Using contemporary acoustic simulation techniques, Boren estimates that Whitefield could have been heard by a crowd of approximately 50,000 people "under ideal acoustic conditions." Boren, "Whitefield's Voice," 188.
3 John Wesley to James Hutton and the Fetter Lane Society, Bristol, April 2, 1739, in *The Works of John Wesley,* ed. Frank Baker, vol. 25, *Letters I: 1721–1739* (Oxford: Clarendon Press, 1980), 620. For more on Whitefield's preaching style, particularly as it relates to the stage, see Vaughn Scribner, "Transatlantic Actors: The Intertwining Stages of George Whitefield and Lewis Hallam, Sr., 1739–1756," *Journal of Social History* 50, no. 1 (Fall 2016): 1–27, https://doi.org/10.1093/jsh/shw006.

4   Lambert, *Pedlar,* 75.

5   Whitefield to [Gabriel Harris], London, Oct. 25, 1737, in *Letters,* 29.

6   William Seward had a professional background in finance when he became a Christian and an assistant to and promoter of Whitefield. For more on Whitefield's use of the press and the role of Seward, see Lambert, *Pedlar,* 52–69. For more on Whitefield in American colonial newspapers specifically, see Lisa Smith, *The First Great Awakening in Colonial American Newspapers: A Shifting Story* (Lanham, MD: Lexington Books, 2012), 93–120.

7   Edmund Gibson, *The Bishop of London's Pastoral Letter to the People of his Diocese . . . Against Lukewarmness on One Hand, and Enthusiasm on the Other* (London, 1739), 27, 28, 31. Whitefield responded to Gibson's letter with *The Bishop of London's Pastoral Letter Answer'd by the Reverend Mr. George Whitefield* (London, 1739).

8   Whitefield to Mr. —, August 7, 1739, in *Letters,* 60.

9   Whitefield to an unidentified recipient, On board the *Elizabeth,* Gravesend, Aug. 14, 1739, in *Letters,* 60.

10 George Whitefield, *A Continuation of the Reverend Mr. Whitefield's Journal, From his Embarking after the Embargo, To his Arrival at Savannah in Georgia* (London, 1740), 12.

11 2 Chronicles 16:9a (NKJV).

12 Song of Songs 5:16b.

13 Whitefield to Mr. Ebenezer Blackwell, On Board the *Elizabeth,* Aug. 16, 1739, in *Letters,* 503–504.

14 Luke 12:50a (NLT); Hebrews 12:2.

15 Zephaniah 3:17; Romans 8:39b.

16 Song of Songs 4:12.

17 Whitefield to Mr. Howel[l] Harris, London, Dec. 20, 1738, in *Letters,* 491; Whitefield to the Rev. Mr. John Wesley, Bristol, March 22, 1739, in *Letters,* 494; Whitefield to an unidentified recipient, London, July 24, 1739, in *Letters,* 54.

18 Whitefield, *Journal, Embargo to Savannah,* 17.

19 Whitefield, *Journal, Embargo to Savannah,* 24.

20 Revelation 2:4.

21 Whitefield, *Journal, Embargo to Savannah,* 13.

22 Whitefield, *Journal, Embargo to Savannah,* 14.

23 Whitefield, *Journal, Embargo to Savannah,* 15.

24 Whitefield, *Journal, Embargo to Savannah,* 14.

25 Whitefield, *Journal, Embargo to Savannah,* 16.

26 Whitefield, *Journal, Embargo to Savannah,* 21.

27 Whitefield, *Journal, Embargo to Savannah,* 21.

28 Sereno Dwight, ed., *The Works of President Edwards,* vol. 1 (New York, 1830), 178, 173. For both Sarah and Jonathan Edwards' writings, I have modernized spelling and punctuation for ease of reading.

29 Jonathan Edwards, *A Treatise Concerning Religious Affections* (Boston, 1746), 9–10.

30 Edwards' theory of the role of the affections in the spiritual life is much more complex than what I refer to here, as he examines how holy emotions can be triggered by learning about God and thus become catalysts for our will to choose obedience to God and to love the things he loves. For more on the role of the affections in early American religion, see Caroline Wigginton and Abram Van Engen, eds., *Feeling Godly: Religious Affections and Christian Contact in Early North America* (Amherst, MA: University of Massachusetts Press, 2021).

31 Edwards, *Religious Affections*, 9.

32 Whitefield to the Bishop of Gloucester, Bristol, July 9, 1739, in *Letters*, 501. Whitefield's reference to the wind alludes to John 3:8–11.

33 Whitefield to Mr. Ebenezer Blackwell, Cirencester, June 27, 1739, in *Letters*, 498.

34 Whitefield, *Journal, Embargo to Savannah*, 12–13.

35 Whitefield, *Journal, Embargo to Savannah*, 15.

36 Whitefield, *Journal, Embargo to Savannah*, 11.

37 Whitefield, *Journal, Embargo to Savannah*, 20.

38 Whitefield, *Journal, Embargo to Savannah*, 15.

39 Whitefield, *Journal, Embargo to Savannah*, 20.

40 Whitefield, *Journal, Embargo to Savannah*, 21. Whitefield references Isaiah 35:3 and Hebrews 12:12.

41 Whitefield, *Journal, Embargo to Savannah*, 17. See Whitefield, *Journal, Embargo to Savannah*, 19, for a list of several of the books Whitefield was reading at the time.

42 Whitefield, *Journal, Embargo to Savannah*, 17.

43 Selections are from Whitefield, *Journal, Embargo to Savannah*, 7, 10–25. Complete bibliographic information for all texts cited, excerpted, or reprinted can be found in the bibliography.

44 This stanza is from a hymn based on Psalm 139 by Nahum Tate and Nicholas Brady, *A New Version of the Psalms of David*, 2nd ed. (London, 1698), 293–95. Whitefield may have seen the hymn in John Wesley, ed., *A Collection of Psalms and Hymns* (London, 1738), 14–15, which I accessed at https://divinity.duke.edu/sites/divinity.duke.edu/files/documents/cswt/03_Collection_of_Psalms_and_Hymns_%281738%29_mod.pdf.

45 The Bay of Biscay is located along the coasts of France and Spain.

46 Whitefield references the marriage of Jesus the Bridegroom and his bride the church in God's end-time kingdom as noted in Revelation 19:6–9.

47 Whitefield is probably reading August Hermann Francke, *Pietas Hallensis: Being an Historical Narration of the Wonderful Foot-Steps of Divine Providence in Erecting, Carrying on, and Building the Orphan House, and other Charitable Institutions, at Glaucha near Hall in Saxony, Without any Visible Fund to Support It*, trans. Anthony William Boehm (London, 1705). Francke (1663–1727) was a German clergyman

and theologian who founded a school for impoverished children and an orphanage, along with other charitable endeavors, in Halle, Germany, in the late seventeenth century. Whitefield hoped to imitate Francke's success with his orphanage Bethesda in Savannah, Georgia. For more on the influence of Germanic Lutheran Pietism on English Protestants, see Katharine Gerbner, *Christian Slavery: Conversion and Race in the Protestant Atlantic World* (Philadelphia: University of Pennsylvania Press, 2018), 141–143; Daniel L. Brunner, *Halle Pietists in England: Anthony William Boehm and the Society for Promoting Christian Knowledge* (Göttingen: Vandenhoeck & Ruprecht, 1993).

48 For the story of Adam, see Genesis 3; for David, see 2 Samuel 11–12:23; for Peter, see Matthew 26:69–75, Mark 14:66–72, Luke 22:54b–62, and John 18:25–27.

49 See Luke 18:9–14 and Psalm 38:6b for Whitefield's biblical references.

50 John 20:3–10.

51 Exodus 14:25.

52 Psalm 4:6b.

53 Permanent east-to-west winds near the equator.

54 The Feast of Saint Matthew is a holiday in the Anglican church that falls on September 21.

55 Love Feasts were extended times of fellowship, prayer, shared meals, and worship.

56 Martin Luther (1483–1546) was a German theologian and former monk who is best known for his pivotal role in the Protestant Reformation. Whitefield also references 1 Corinthians 11:1.

57 Psalm 145:19a.

58 2 Corinthians 1:3.

59 Psalm 149:14b.

60 Mark 9:24.

61 For the story of Enoch, see Genesis 5:21–24.

62 Psalm 103:5b; Ecclesiastes 9:7.

63 Romans 8:28a.

64 Genesis 28:16.

65 Although Whitefield combines lines from two different stanzas, the hymn he quotes was written by German mystic Gerhardt Tersteegen (1697–1769) and translated by John Wesley, possibly accessed by Whitefield in John Wesley and Charles Wesley, eds., *Hymns and Sacred Poems* (London, 1739), 188–189.

66 The story of Jesus' first recorded miracle at a wedding in Cana can be found in John 2:1–11.

67 Probably a reference to Matthew 26:29, Mark 14:25, and Luke 22:18.

68 Now Lewes, Delaware. At the time of Whitefield's visit, the three counties of Delaware were part of the colony of Pennsylvania.

69 Now Cape Henlopen, Delaware.

70   This stanza is from a hymn by Count Nikolas Ludwig von Zinzendorf (1700–1760), translated by John Wesley. Whitefield may have seen the hymn in John Wesley, ed., *A Collection of Psalms and Hymns* (London, 1738), 55–56, which I accessed at https:// divinity.duke.edu/sites/divinity.duke.edu/files/documents/cswt/03_Collection_of_ Psalms_and_Hymns_%281738%29_mod.pdf.

Chapter IV: Adopting a Lifestyle

1   Peter 2:12.

2   John 13:35.

3   NLT.

4   *God in America*, episode 1, "A New Adam," directed and written by David Belton, aired October 11, 2010, on PBS, http://www.pbs.org/godinamerica/view/.

5   Kidd, *Spiritual Founding Father*, 84, 115, 121, 126, 90; *New England Weekly Journal*, October 14, 1740.

6   George Whitefield, *A Continuation of the Reverend Mr. Whitefield's Journal, After his Arrival at Georgia, To a Few Days after his Second Return Thither from Philadelphia* (London, 1741), 42. Whitefield is referring to the current city of Wilmington, Delaware, and to White Clay Creek Presbyterian Church in Newark, Delaware.

7   William Jay, ed., *Memoirs of the Life and Character of the Late Reverend Cornelius Winter* (Bath, UK, 1808), 24. See also Michał Choinski, *The Rhetoric of the Revival: The Language of the Great Awakening Preachers* (Bristol, CT: Vandenhoeck & Ruprecht, 2016), 117–145, for a study of the rhetorical devices present in several of Whitefield's most famous sermons.

8   Whitefield to Mr. J[ames] H[utton], Bohemia, Maryland, Nov. 24, 1740, in *Letters*, 224.

9   Stout, *Divine Dramatist*, 115.

10   Whitefield, *Journal, Georgia to Falmouth*, 54.

11   Smith, *Colonial American Newspapers*, 82, Figure 2.1.

12   Stout, *Divine Dramatist*, 118–119, 122.

13   Whitefield, *Journal, Georgia to Falmouth*, 30.

14   Whitefield, *Journal, Georgia to Falmouth*, 32, 36–37.

15   Whitefield, *Journal, Georgia to Falmouth*, 55.

16   Selections are from Whitefield, *Journal, Georgia to Falmouth*, 38–39. Complete bibliographic information for all texts cited, excerpted, or reprinted can be found in the bibliography.

17   Joseph Sewall (1688–1769) ministered at the Old South Church from his ordination in 1713 until his death in 1769. He was a supporter of the First Great Awakening and Whitefield, although he spoke against some of the extremes of the Awakening.

18   John 3:10.

19 This reference is to Jonathan Belcher (1682–1757), the governor of Massachusetts and New Hampshire. Belcher's relationship with Whitefield is discussed in Chapter 7.

20 A reference to Leviticus 10 in which Nadab and Abihu, sons of the High Priest Aaron, are killed by the fire of God's presence when they offer in their censers "strange fire" (KJV) to the Lord against his command.

21 An almshouse was a residence for those struggling with poverty. The verse is found in Matthew 11:5 and Luke 7:22.

22 A workhouse provided employment for the needy.

23 John 5:17,19.

24 For Peter, see Acts 10:1–48; for Paul, see Acts 16:6–10; for Philip, see Acts 8:26–40.

25 Whitefield to [Jonathan Edwards], New York, Nov. 16, 1739, in *Letters,* 121.

26 *The Works of Jonathan Edwards,* ed. George S. Claghorn, vol. 16, *Letters and Personal Writings* (New Haven: Yale University Press, 1998), 80.

27 For more detail on Whitefield's visit to Northampton from Jonathan Edwards' perspective, see George M. Marsden, *Jonathan Edwards: A Life* (New Haven, CT: Yale University Press, 2003), 201–213.

28 Whitefield, *Journal, Georgia to Falmouth,* 47.

29 Edwards to the Reverend Thomas Prince, Northampton, December 12, 1743, in Claghorn, *Works of Edwards,* 116.

30 Whitefield, *Journal, Georgia to Falmouth,* 47.

31 Whitefield, *Journal, Georgia to Falmouth,* 46.

32 Whitefield, *Journal, Georgia to Falmouth,* 49. For more on this visit and Whitefield's 1745 visit to Northampton, see Kenneth P. Minkema, "Whitefield, Jonathan Edwards, and Revival," in *George Whitefield: Life, Context, and Legacy,* eds. Geordan Hammond and David Ceri Jones (Oxford: Oxford University Press, 2016).

33 Edwards to [Whitefield], Northampton, December 14, 1740, in Claghorn, *Works of Edwards,* 87. For more on the effects of Whitefield's visit on Edwards' life and ministry, see see Marsden, *Jonathan Edwards,* 214–226. See also Ava Chamberlain, "The Grand Sower of the Seed: Jonathan Edwards' Critique of George Whitefield," *New England Quarterly* 70, no. 3 (Sept. 1997): 368–385, for a discussion of the sermons Edwards preached to his congregation in the month following Whitefield's visit.

34 Selections are from Whitefield, *Journal, Georgia to Falmouth,* 45–47. Complete bibliographic information for all texts cited, excerpted, or reprinted can be found in the bibliography.

35 Solomon Stoddard (1643–1729), Jonathan Edwards' grandfather on his mother's side, was a well-known and respected Congregationalist minister and the previous pastor of Jonathan's church in Northampton. Whitefield refers to Stoddard's *A Guide to Christ. Or, The Way of Directing Souls that are under the Work of Conversion* (Boston, 1714) and *The Safety of Appearing at the Day of Judgement, in the Righteousness of Christ* (Boston, 1687).

36   A reference to John 4:32.

37   Probably a reference to 1 Corinthians 2:3 (KJV).

38   Jesus refers to "new wine" in the parallel passages of Matthew 9:17, Mark 2:22, and Luke 5:37–39.

39   Jesus uses the phrase "daughter of Abraham" in Luke 13:16. Revivalists at the time of Whitefield often used the phrase to designate a woman who was truly converted and following God passionately.

40   The story of the courtship of Rebekah and Isaac is told in Genesis 24. Whitefield married a Welsh Christian widow with one daughter named Elizabeth James (c. 1704–1768) on November 14, 1741. Their union did not produce any surviving children.

41   A reference to the story of Jesus changing water into wine at a wedding in Cana, related in John 2:1–12.

42   A reference to Jesus' words in Revelation 2:4–5 to the church in Ephesus.

43   Esther 4:16.

44   Whitefield, *Journal, Georgia to Falmouth,* 33.

45   Whitefield, *Journal, Georgia to Falmouth,* 45.

46   Whitefield, *Journal, Georgia to Falmouth,* 45.

47   Selections are from Whitefield, *Journal, Georgia to Falmouth,* 33, 35, 44–45. Complete bibliographic information for all texts cited, excerpted, or reprinted can be found in the bibliography.

48   John 3:8a.

49   Psalm 42:5a.

50   William Shurtleff (1689–1747) served churches in Newcastle and Portsmouth, New Hampshire. He was a strong supporter of both the First Great Awakening and Whitefield.

51   Psalm 115:1.

52   Whitefield references Matthew 11:12.

53   Whitefield, *Journal, Georgia to Falmouth,* 82–83.

CHAPTER V: SHARING THE JOURNEY

1   NLT.

2   A churchwarden is a lay official in an Anglican church. Whitefield, *Journal, Embargo to Savannah,* 28.

3   Whitefield, *Journal, Embargo to Savannah,* 28.

4   *Pennsylvania Gazette,* November 15, 1739.

5   Whitefield references Revelation 3:1, Jesus' warning to the church in Sardis: "And to the angel of the church in Sardis write, 'These things says He who has the seven Spirits of God and the seven stars: I know your works, that you have a name that you are alive, but you are dead.' "(NKJV)

6   Whitefield, *Journal, Georgia to Falmouth*, 42. Whitefield references 2 Timothy 3:5a.
7   Whitefield, *Journal, Embargo to Savannah*, 31. For more on the Log College, see Ar-
    chibald Alexander, *Biographical Sketches of the Founder and Principal Alumni of the
    Log College* (Princeton, NJ, 1845), and Thomas C. Pears, *Documentary History of William
    Tennent and the Log College* (Philadelphia: Department of History of the Office of the
    General Assembly of the Presbyterian Church in the USA, 1940). For the preaching of
    Log College graduates, see Archibald Alexander, ed., *Sermons of the Log College: Being
    Sermons and Essays by the Tennents and their Contemporaries* (Presbyterian Board of
    Publication, 1855; repr., Ligonier, PA: Soli Deo Gloria Publications, 1993).
8   Whitefield, *Journal, Embargo to Savannah*, 31. Whitefield is probably referencing the
    story of Elijah and the prophets of Baal in 1 Kings 18:16–46.
9   Whitefield, *Journal, Embargo to Savannah*, 33; see Acts 16:9 for Whitefield's reference
    to Paul. Thomas Noble and his wife were connected with both Presbyterians and
    Moravians in New York and internationally. His papers are held at Lehigh University
    and can be viewed digitally at http://digital.lib.lehigh.edu/hidden/finding.php?id=137.
10 Whitefield, *Journal, Embargo to Savannah*, 34. For a biography of Tennent, see Mil-
    ton J. Coalter Jr., *Gilbert Tennent, Son of Thunder: A Case Study of Continental Pietism's
    Impact on the First Great Awakening in the Middle Colonies* (New York: Greenwood
    Press, 1986).
11 The Wall Street Presbyterian Church was pastored at the time by Ebenezer Pember-
    ton (1704–1779) and had been served for eight months by Jonathan Edwards from
    1722 until April 1723. Pemberton and the church strongly supported Whitefield and
    the Awakening. For a history of the church including a brief mention of Pemberton,
    Whitefield, and the Awakening, see Dorothy Ganfield Fowler and Donna W. Hurley,
    A City Church: The First Presbyterian Church in the City of New York, 2nd ed. (New York:
    The First Presbyterian Church in the City of New York, 2016).
12 Whitefield, *Journal, Embargo to Savannah*, 35. Ezekiel 22:28: "And her prophets have
    daubed them with untempered mortar, seeing vanities, and divining lies unto them,
    saying, Thus saith the Lord God, when the Lord had not spoken" (1599 Geneva Bible).
    See also Ezekiel 13:10–15 for additional references to "untempered mortar," which was
    material that was not sufficiently hardened or constituted to successfully repair a wall.
    See Mark 3:17 for Jesus' nicknaming of James and John, the sons of Zebedee, the "Sons
    of Thunder." Whitefield may also be referencing Jeremiah 1:8 in this entry.
13 Whitefield, *Journal, Embargo to Savannah*, 36. For more on the impact of this
    incident on Whitefield, see Kidd, *Spiritual Founding Father*, 89–90. Following is a
    description of Tennent's preaching: "From his first entrance on the public work of
    the ministry, the preaching of Gilbert Tennent was very popular and attractive, with
    all classes of hearers. He possessed uncommon advantages as a preacher. In person,
    he was taller than the common stature, and well proportioned in every respect.
    His aspect was grave and venerable, and his address prepossessing. His voice was

clear and commanding, and his manner in the pulpit was exceedingly earnest and impressive. His reasoning powers, also, were strong, and his language often nervous, and, indeed, sublime. No one could hear him without being convinced that he was deeply in earnest. His style was copious, and sometimes elegant. Indeed, in the vigour of his age, few preachers could equal him" (Alexander, *Biographical Sketches,* 27).

14 Whitefield, *Journal, Embargo to Savannah,* 37–38.

15 See Whitefield to J[ames] H[utton], Savannah, June 25, 1740, in *Letters,* 190–191, for additional remarks by Whitefield on how the preaching of the Tennents influenced his own. Gilbert Tennent preached the Awakening's most famous, or perhaps infamous, sermon in Nottingham, Pennsylvania, on March 8, 1740, later published as *The Danger of an Unconverted Ministry* (Philadelphia, 1740).

16 Whitefield, *Journal, Georgia to Falmouth,* 62–63, and Whitefield to his Excellency Jonathan Belcher, Esq., in Boston, Philadelphia, Nov. 9, 1740, in *Letters,* 220–221. For Tennent's two preaching tours, see Coalter Jr., *Gilbert Tennent,* 71–76. Daniel Rogers (1707–1785), an itinerant minister at the time, traveled with Tennent on the New England preaching tour.

17 Whitefield, *Journal, Embargo to Savannah,* 40.

18 1 Peter 1:8b.

19 Psalm 45:7b; Hebrews 12:2b.

20 Whitefield, *Journal, Embargo to Savannah,* 41–42.

21 Whitefield, *Journal, Embargo to Savannah,* 41.

22 Whitefield, *Journal, Embargo to Savannah,* 45.

23 *American Weekly Mercury,* November 29, 1739.

24 Whitefield, *Journal, Embargo to Savannah,* 44–45. Whitefield references Revelation 12:7–10 and Genesis 3:15.

25 Whitefield, *Journal, Embargo to Savannah,* 51.

26 *Three Letters to the Reverend Mr. George Whitefield* (Philadelphia, 1739), 13.

27 *Three Letters,* 8.

28 Whitefield to the Rev. Mr. G[ilbert] T[ennent], Williamsburg, Dec. 15, 1739, in *Letters,* 138. Whitefield references Psalm 23:4b.

29 Whitefield to [Gilbert Tennent], Savannah, Jan. 22, 1740, in *Letters,* 141. Whitefield references Deuteronomy 33:25b.

30 In journal entries for November 28 and November 29, 1739, Whitefield notes that he "corrected" two "extempore discourses" to be published (*Journal, Embargo to Savannah,* 52, 53). On November 29, 1739, the day of Whitefield's departure from Philadelphia, the Philadelphia newspaper *The American Weekly Mercury* advertised the following: "There is now in the press two of the Rev. Mr. Whitefield's sermons, which were preached here and never in print before, which he has given to be printed here." See the *American Weekly Mercury,* January 15, 1740, for an additional notice of the printing of the sermon *The Wise and Foolish Virgins* by name.

31 Selections are from George Whitefield, *The Wise and Foolish Virgins: A Sermon Preached at Philadelphia, 1739* (Philadelphia, 1739), 3, 5–21, 26–27. Complete bibliographic information for all texts cited, excerpted, or reprinted can be found in the bibliography.

32 The first edition incorrectly cites the biblical reference as Matthew 25:14. Whitefield's sermon references the parable found in Matthew 25:1–13.

33 Hebrews 9:27.

34 Matthew 5:8.

35 Romans 9:6.

36 1 Corinthians 13:3.

37 Job 19:25–27.

38 2 Peter 3:9a.

39 The New Testament parable of Lazarus and the rich man is found in Luke 16:19–31.

40 Whitefield references Acts 17:6: "And when they found them not, they drew Jason and certain brethren unto the rulers of the city, crying, These that have turned the world upside down are come hither also." (KJV)

41 In the parable of Lazarus and the rich man in Luke 16:19–31, the rich man was traditionally referred to as "Dives," which means "rich man" in Latin.

42 Isaiah 40:1.

43 2 Timothy 3:12.

44 Matthew 10:36.

45 Isaiah 53:7b.

46 The Old Testament story of Jacob and Esau is recorded in Genesis 27.

47 The theological systems of Arianism and Socinianism questioned the orthodox view of the Trinity. See the story of Nathanael in John 1:45–51.

48 Acts 17:18.

49 Antonius Felix (born c. AD 5–10) served as procurator of Judea from AD 52 until AD 60. His interactions with the apostle Paul are described in Acts 24.

50 Malachi 3:2a.

51 See Ephesians 6:10–17 for a description of the "armor of God."

52 For Elihu, see Job 32:19; for Whitefield's second biblical reference, see Matthew 12:34.

Chapter VI: Facing Opposition

1 "William Carey, Father of Modern Protestant Missions," Christian History, *Christianity Today,* October 22, 2022, https://www.christianitytoday.com/history/people/missionaries/william-carey.html.

2 David's story is also related in 1 Chronicles 25–29.

3 See W. R. Ward, *The Protestant Evangelical Awakening* (Cambridge: Cambridge University Press, 1992), for an insightful analysis of this time in European religious history.

4   South Carolina Anglican commissary Alexander Garden (1685–1756) may have
    been the author of this letter.
5   Taken from a reprinting of Jonathan Arnold's "To the Inhabitants of New-York" in
    the *Boston Weekly News-Letter,* November 30, 1739.
6   Alexander Garden, *Six Letters to the Rev. Mr. Whitefield, With Mr. Whitefield's Answer
    to the First Letter,* 2nd ed. (Boston, 1740), 36. Although Garden pursued the case
    against Whitefield in South Carolina, church officials in England chose to take no
    official action, and so Whitefield experienced no real effect on his ministry. For more
    on the case and on Garden and Whitefield's relationship in general, see William
    Howland Kenney, III, "Alexander Garden and George Whitefield: The Significance
    of Revivalism in South Carolina 1738–1741," *The South Carolina Historical Magazine*
    71, no. 1 (Jan. 1970): 1–16, https://www.jstor.org/stable/27566968.
7   Whitefield to Mr. J[ames] H[utton], Bohemia, Maryland, Nov. 24, 1740, in *Letters,*
    224.
8   Because the Church of England in the American colonies did not have resident
    bishops, commissaries were installed by the bishop of London in various colonial
    cities to manage church business.
9   Whitefield, *Journal, Embargo to Savannah,* 36–37.
10 Earl of Bellomont to the Lord Bishop of London, Boston, September 11, 1699, in
    Ecclesiastical Records, State of New York, 7 vols. (Albany, NY: State of New York,
    1901–1916), 2:1334, https://archive.org/details/ecclesiasticalre02newy/page/1334/
    mode/2up?q=vesey.
11 Whitefield, *Journal, Embargo to Savannah,* 37.
12 Whitefield, *Journal, Embargo to Savannah,* 37.
13 Whitefield to Mr. H[abersham], London, April 27, 1739, in *Letters,* 49.
14 James 4:11 a (NLT).
15 ESV.
16 Whitefield's two letters on Tillotson were published first in the *Pennsylvania Gazette*
    on April 10, April 24, and May 1, 1740, and then subsequently printed in Philadel-
    phia as a pamphlet. The third letter contains Whitefield's thoughts on the treatment
    of enslaved blacks in the southern colonies and will be discussed in Chapter 7.
17 For more on the influence of Tillotson's writings in New England, see Norman
    Fiering, "The First American Enlightenment: Tillotson, Leverett, and Philosophical
    Anglicanism," *The New England Quarterly* 54, no. 3 September 1981): 307–344,
    https://www.jstor.org/stable/365467.
18 George Whitefield, *Three Letters from the Reverend Mr. G[eorge] Whitefield* (Philadel-
    phia, 1740), 3.
19 Archibald Cummings, *Faith Absolutely Necessary, But Not Sufficient to Salvation
    Without Good Works* (Philadelphia, 1740), iii.
20 KJV.

21 Whitefield, *Journal, Georgia from Philadelphia,* 39. See Whitefield's entry for Sunday,
    May 11, pages 38–39, for his full description of Cummings' preaching against him.
22 Proverbs 27:6a.
23 Whitefield to John Wesley, Bristol, March 22, 1739, in "Collection of Stampe," 22.
24 Edwards does not give specifics about when and where he spoke to Whitefield
    about judging other ministers as unconverted, but it is likely that it was during this
    1740 visit as this was the first time Whitefield met Edwards. Jonathan Edwards, *Cop-
    ies of the Two Letters Cited by the Rev. Mr. Clap, Rector of the College at New Haven*
    (Boston, 1745), 7.
25 Edwards, *Two Letters,* 13.
26 Whitefield to Mr. H[owell] H[arris], Bristol, April 28, 1741, in *Letters,* 260.
27 Whitefield to Mr. J[ames] H[utton], Bohemia, Maryland, Nov. 24, 1740, in *Letters,*
    224.
28 Whitefield to Mr. J[ames] H[utton], Bohemia, Maryland, Nov. 24, 1740, in *Letters,*
    224.
29 Whitefield to Peter B[öhler], Aberdeen [Scotland], Oct. 10, 1741, in *Letters,* 332. See Col-
    in Podmore, *The Moravian Church in England, 1728–1760* (Oxford: Clarendon Press,
    1998), 80–96 for more on Whitefield and the Moravians. See Aaron Spencer Fogle-
    man, *Jesus is Female: Moravians and Radical Religion in Early America* (Philadelphia:
    University of Pennsylvania Press, 2007), 276n8, for a list of relevant letters written by
    Whitefield. For more on Böhler, see Albert F. Jordan, "The Chronicle of Peter Böehler,
    Who Led John and Charles Wesley to the Full Light of the Gospel," *Transactions of
    the Moravian Historical Society* 22, no. 2 (1971): 100–178, https://www.jstor.org/sta-
    ble/41179802. Whitefield had a more public break with the Moravians in 1753—see
    George Whitefield, *An Expostulatory Letter Addressed to Nicholas Lewis, Count Zinzen-
    dorff, and Lord Advocate of the Unitus Fratrum,* 3rd ed. (Philadelphia, 1753).
30 Second Timothy 4:11b reads, "Get Mark and bring him with you, because he is
    helpful to me in my ministry." Colossians 4:10 reads, "My fellow prisoner Aris-
    tarchus sends you his greetings, as does Mark, the cousin of Barnabas. (You have
    received instructions about him; if he comes to you, welcome him.)"
31 Whitefield to the Rev. Mr. John Wesley, approx. Summer, 1735, in *Letters*, 485.
32 2 Corinthians 1:3b–4a.
33 *The Querists, Or, An Extract of Sundry Passages Taken Out of Mr. Whitefield's Printed
    Sermons, Journals, and Letters* (Philadelphia, 1740), 9.
34 *Querists,* iv–v. "Antinomian error" refers to the belief that Christians, being saved by
    grace, are free from having to obey God's law. "Arminianism" refers to a theological
    belief system that emphasizes human free will as opposed to God's sovereignty,
    particularly in the area of eternal salvation.
35 Whitefield, *Journal, Georgia to Falmouth,* 56–57.
36 In a letter to John Wesley at the time, Whitefield writes, "Here is a close opposition

from some of the Presbyterian clergy. The seed of the serpent is the same in all, of whatever communion. I expect much more opposition every hour." Whitefield to the Rev. Mr. J.W., Bohemia (Maryland), Nov. 24, 1740, in *Letters,* 225.

37 Whitefield, *Journal, Georgia to Falmouth,* 57.

38 Whitefield, *Journal, Georgia to Falmouth,* 58. See also Whitefield to Mr. M. at London, Philadelphia, Nov. 10, 1740, in *Letters,* 222, in which Whitefield writes, "At New York my soul was taken almost out of the body."

39 Whitefield, *Journal, Georgia to Falmouth,* 58. Whitefield references Genesis 3:15b.

40 Whitefield to Mr. F., in Pennsylvania, Edinburgh, Sept. 22, 1742, in *Letters,* 438. Mr. W. is probably John Wesley.

41 Selections are from *Querists,* ii–iv, 26–27, 32. Complete bibliographic information for all texts cited, excerpted, or reprinted can be found in the bibliography.

42 This reference is to Matthew 15:14 and Luke 6:39.

43 The collection of Whitefield's sermons referred to by the Querists is George Whitefield, *Sermons on Various Subjects,* 2 vols. (Philadelphia, 1740).

44 Selections are from George Whitefield, *A Letter From the Rev. Mr. Whitefield, to Some Church Members of the Presbyterian Persuasion, in Answer to Certain Scruples Lately Proposed in Proper Queries Raised on Each Remark* (Philadelphia, 1740), 1–5, 7–8. Complete bibliographic information for all texts cited, excerpted, or reprinted can be found in the bibliography.

45 A reference to 2 Samuel 14:19.

46 A reference to Proverbs 12:1b.

47 Whitefield's sermons appear as follows in Whitefield, *Sermons:* "Of Justification by Christ," 1:22–39; "The Almost Christian," 1:57–75; "The Marks of the New Birth," 2:15–33.

48 Psalm 141:5.

49 Robert Sanderson (1587–1663), Bishop of London, was an English theologian and philosopher.

50 A reference to the Presbyterian church at Fagg's Manor in Chester County, Pennsylvania, pastored by Samuel Blair (1712–1751), a strong supporter of the Awakening and a graduate of the Log College.

51 2 Kings 8:13.

52 *The Whole Duty of Man* was an anonymous text published in England in 1658 that was well-respected by high-church Anglicans.

CHAPTER VII: RESPONDING TO CULTURE

1 Philippians 2:15 (ESV).

2 Matthew 5:14–16.

3 1 Corinthians 13:7b–8a.

4   ESV.

5   ESV.

6   *New York Gazette,* November 26, 1739.

7   Michael C. Batinski, *Jonathan Belcher, Colonial Governor* (Lexington: University
     Press of Kentucky, 1996), 84.

8   Whitefield, *Journal, Georgia to Falmouth,* 24.

9   For Whitefield's record of his interactions with Governor Belcher during his time in
     Boston, see Whitefield, *Journal, Georgia to Falmouth,* 23–43.

10   Whitefield records Belcher's words and his own thoughts in Whitefield, *Journal,
     Georgia to Falmouth,* 44.

11   John 1:14b, emphasis mine.

12   Whitefield, *Journal, Georgia to Falmouth,* 41. For other instances, see Whitefield,
     Journal, Georgia to Falmouth, 29, 38.

13   Batinski, *Jonathan Belcher,* 84, 169.

14   Whitefield to his Excellency Jonathan Belcher, Esq., in Boston, Philadelphia, Nov. 9,
     1740, in *Letters,* 221.

15   Whitefield to his Excellency Jonathan Belcher, Esq., in Boston, Philadelphia, Nov. 9,
     1740, in *Letters,* 220–221.

16   Probably Daniel Rogers, a former tutor at Harvard and an itinerant minister who
     traveled with Whitefield and later pastored a church in Exeter, New Hampshire.

17   See Jesus' teaching on the two greatest commandments in Matthew 22:34–40 and
     Mark 12:28–34.

18   John Wesley, *A Sermon on the Death of the Rev. Mr. George Whitefield* (London, 1770),
     21.

19   Jay, *Memoirs of Winter,* 23.

20   Thomas S. Kidd, "Daniel Rogers' Egalitarian Great Awakening," *The Journal of The
     Historical Society* 7, no. 1 (March 2007): 112, 115.

21   Frank Lambert, "'I Saw the Book Talk': Slave Readings of the First Great Awakening,"
     The Journal of African American History 87 (1992): 16.

22   Kidd, *Spiritual Founding Father,* 143–144. For a detailed, albeit older, account of
     women involved in early Methodism, see Abel Stevens, *The Women of Methodism:
     Its Three Foundresses, Susanna Wesley, the Countess of Huntingdon, and Barbara Heck*
     (New York: Carlton & Porter, 1866).

23   Selections are from Whitefield, *Journal, Georgia from Philadelphia,* 35–40. Complete
     bibliographic information for all texts cited, excerpted, or reprinted can be found in
     the bibliography.

24   Whitefield uses the adjective "poor" often in his writings to refer to those who are
     needy in any way, such as spiritually or materially. Whitefield also refers to himself
     using the adjective to denote his own position of spiritual humility and dependence
     on God.

25 Whitefield references Psalm 2:8.

26 Whitefield references the parable Jesus tells in Matthew 25:1–13.

27 Micah 2:1–2.

28 For Hezekiah's story, see 2 Kings 16:20–20:21; 2 Chronicles 28:27–32:33; Isaiah 36:1–39:8.

29 Whitefield, *Journal, Embargo to Savannah,* 56.

30 Whitefield arrived in Savannah, Georgia, on January 10, 1740 (Whitefield, *Journal, Embargo to Savannah,* 82).

31 Whitefield, *Journal, Embargo to Savannah,* 60, 66, 73, 77, 82.

32 Whitefield, *Journal, Embargo to Savannah,* 74, 82.

33 Whitefield, *Journal, Embargo to Savannah,* 74.

34 Whitefield, *Journal, Embargo to Savannah,* 82.

35 For southern slaveowners' unwillingness to proselytize the enslaved, see Kidd, *Spiritual Founding Father,* 109–110; Gerbner, *Christian Slavery,* 11; Jessica M. Parr, *George Whitefield: Race, Revivalism, and the Making of a Religious Icon* (Jackson, MS: University Press of Mississippi, 2015), 62–64.

36 *The South Carolina Gazette,* February 2, 1740. Whitefield's letter was published first in *The Pennsylvania Gazette* on April 17, 1740, and subsequently as a pamphlet which also included two letters on English Anglican archbishop John Tillotson, discussed in Chapter 6. See Gerbner, *Christian Slavery,* 189–190, for a short discussion of Whitefield's published letter.

37 Gerbner, *Christian Slavery,* 22.

38 Marsden, *Jonathan Edwards,* 256.

39 Marsden, *Jonathan Edwards,* 255–256; Kidd, *Spiritual Founding Father,* 262; Fred E. Witzig, *Sanctifying Slavery and Politics in South Carolina: The Life of the Reverend Alexander Garden, 1685–1756* (Columbia, SC: The University of South Carolina Press, 2018), 151. For a general discussion of colonial African slavery, see Betty Wood, *Slavery in Colonial America, 1619–1776* (Lanham, MD: Rowman and Littlefield, 2005); Peter Kolchin, *American Slavery, 1619–1877,* rev. ed. (New York: Hill and Wang, 2003), 28–62; and the scholarship of Yale historian David Brion Davis.

40 See Whitefield's entries from Charleston, beginning March 14, 1740, for his disagreement with Garden in Whitefield, *Journal, Georgia from Philadelphia,* 10–14. See also Kenney, "Alexander Garden and George Whitefield," and Travis Glasson, *Mastering Christianity: Missionary Anglicanism and Slavery in the Atlantic World* (Oxford: Oxford University Press, 2012), 111–123.

41 Garden, *Six Letters,* 51.

42 Garden, *Six Letters,* 53. See Witzig, *Sanctifying Slavery,* 129–157, for more on Garden, Whitefield, and slavery.

43 Selections are from Whitefield, *Three Letters,* 13–16. Complete bibliographic information for all texts cited, excerpted, or reprinted can be found in the bibliography.

[44] Whitefield references Acts 16:16–24.

[45] Whitefield references the story in Matthew 15:21–28 and Mark 7:24–30.

[46] Deuteronomy 25:4.

[47] 1 Peter 2:18.

[48] Whitefield references Psalm 144:12.

[49] 1 John 3:8b.

[50] Choi, *God and Empire*, 146–148; William A. Sloat II, "George Whitefield, African-Americans, and Slavery," *Methodist History* 33, no. 1 (October 1994): 3.

[51] See Phillis Wheatley, "On the Death of the Rev. Mr. George Whitefield," in *Poems on Various Subjects, Religious and Moral* (London, 1773); Olaudah Equiano, *The Interesting Narrative of the Life of Olaudah Equiano* (London, 1789); John Marrant, *A Narrative of the Lord's Wonderful Dealings with John Marrant*, 2nd ed. (London, 1785).

[52] Choi, *God and Empire*, 129, 143. See Kidd, *Spiritual Founding Father*, 199, for details on the South Carolina plantation.

[53] See Choi, *God and Empire*, 127–168; Kidd, *Spiritual Founding Father*, 261–262; Parr, *Religious Icon*, 61–80; Lambert, *Pedlar*, 204–207; Henry, *Wayfaring Witness*, 115–117; Philippa Koch, "Slavery, Mission, and the Perils of Providence in Eighteenth-Century Christianity: The Writings of Whitefield and the Halle Pietists," *Church History* 84, no. 2 (June 2015): 369–393.

[54] For Whitefield's commitment to Bethesda, see Choi, *God and Empire*, 164–168; Koch, "Perils of Providence," 373; Lambert, *Pedlar*, 207; Whitefield to the Reverend Mr. D., Savannah, August 15, 1740, in *Letters*, 202. For Whitefield's resolute focus on the ministry of evangelism, see Koch, "Perils of Providence," 382; Sloat, "George Whitefield and Slavery," 13.

[55] Whitefield references Psalm 68:31b: "Ethiopia shall soon stretch out her hands unto God" (KJV).

[56] Whitefield may be referencing Onesimus in the New Testament book of Philemon.

[57] Whitefield to Mr. B., Bristol, March 22, 1751, in Gillies, *Works of Whitefield*, 2:404–405.

[58] That the enslaved laborers on Whitefield's properties were treated well, see Arnold A. Dallimore, *George Whitefield: The Life and Times of the Great Evangelist of the Eighteenth-Century Revival*, 2 vols. (London: Banner of Truth Trust, 1970), 1:509, and Cashin, *Beloved Bethesda*, 75.

[59] For Whitefield's inspiration from the Ebenezer orphanage, see Brunner, *Halle Pietists*, 174. For more on Boltzius and slavery, see Koch, "Perils of Providence."

[60] Betty Wood, *Slavery in Colonial Georgia, 1730–1775* (Athens, GA: University of Georgia Press, 1984), 64–67; Kidd, *Spiritual Founding Father*, 189–190.

[61] Phillis Wheatley, *Poems*, 22.

[62] Wesley, *Sermon*, 18–19.

Chapter VIII: Sustaining the Fire

[1] See Chapter 6 for background on the Moravians, a German Protestant group heavily involved in the First Great Awakening in England and America.

[2] See Kidd, *Spiritual Founding Father,* 139–140, for details on the challenges facing Whitefield in England. See also Whitefield to Mr. J[ames] H[abersham], London, March 25, 1741, in *Letters,* 256–257.

[3] Whitefield to Mr. J[ames] H[abersham], London, March 25, 1741, in *Letters,* 256.

[4] Wesley, *Sermon,* 26.

[5] C.H. Spurgeon, *"The Modern Whitfield": Sermons of the Rev. C.H. Spurgeon, of London; with an Introduction and Sketch of his Life by E.L. Magoon* (New York: Sheldon, Blakeman, 1856), 12.

[6] At the time of publication, Whitefield's grave can be visited at the Old South Presbyterian Church in Newburyport, Massachusetts. See https://www.oldsouthnbpt.org for more information.

[7] Whitefield, *Journal, London to Georgia,* 45.

[8] 2 Timothy 4:7–8.

[9] Psalm 63:1, 2, 6, 8.

[10] Whitefield to Mr. J.B., Charles-Town, On board the *Minerva,* Feb. 17, 1741, in *Letters,* 244–245.

[11] Whitefield to Mr. [Jonathan] B[arber] and his wife at Bethesda, On board the *Minerva,* Feb. 17, 1741, in *Letters,* 244.

[12] Whitefield to Mr. J[ames] H[abersham], London, March 25, 1741, in *Letters,* 257. Whitefield references Song of Songs 5:16.

[13] 2 Timothy 3:16–17.

[14] Whitefield, *Short Account,* 52–53. Whitefield references 2 Timothy 3:16–17.

[15] Whitefield, *Journal, Georgia to Falmouth,* 84. Whitefield quotes Jonah 3:2; Song of Songs 2:15; Genesis 49:23–24a; Isaiah 41:10.

[16] Whitefield, *Journal, Georgia to Falmouth,* 84.

[17] Whitefield to the Rev. Mr. [William] C[ooper], in Boston, On board the *Minerva,* Feb. 26, 1741, in *Letters,* 255.

[18] Psalm 1:1–2.

[19] Richard J. Foster, *Meditative Prayer* (Downers Grove, IL: InterVarsity Press, 1983), 21.

[20] Whitefield, *Short Account,* 30. Whitefield references Joshua 1:8.

[21] Whitefield, *Short Account,* 52. See Jesus' words in John 6:55 (KJV) for Whitefield's reference: "For my flesh is meat indeed, and my blood is drink indeed."

[22] Whitefield to Mrs. B., in Charles-Town, On board the *Minerva,* Feb. 17, 1741, in *Letters,* 243.

[23] John 21:20.

[24] Whitefield to Mr. Wm. G., On board the *Minerva,* Feb. 8, 1741, in *Letters,* 234.

25 Whitefield to the Reverend Mr. C., In Charles-Town, On board the *Minerva*, Feb. 17, 1741, in *Letters*, 237.

26 Whitefield to the Rev. Mr. [Josiah] S[mith], Charles-Town, On board the *Minerva*, Feb. 17, 1741, in *Letters*, 246.

27 Whitefield to Mrs. S., in Charles-Town, On board the *Minerva*, Feb. 17, 1741, in *Letters*, 245.

28 Whitefield to Mr. J[ohn] W[esley], Philadelphia, Nov. 9, 1740, in *Letters*, 219.

29 Whitefield, *Journal, Georgia from Philadelphia*, 43.

30 Whitefield to Mrs. S., in Charles-Town, On board the *Minerva*, Feb. 17, 1741, in *Letters*, 245–246.

31 Whitefield to the Rev. Mr. T., at Edisto, On board the *Minerva*, Feb. 17, 1741, in *Letters*, 242.

32 Whitefield to Mr. H., at Port Royal, South Carolina, On board the *Minerva*, Feb. 16, 1741, in *Letters*, 237.

33 Whitefield to Mrs. T., On board the *Minerva*, Feb. 12, 1741, in *Letters*, 236.

34 Whitefield to Howell Harris, Bristol, Oct. 28, 1741, in "Collection of Stampe," 24.

35 Whitefield to Mr. T[homas] A—ms, On board the *Friendship*, Sept. 5, 1769, in Gillies, *Works of Whitefield*, 3:392.

36 Whitefield to Mrs. H—ge, On board the *Friendship*, Sept. 6, 1769, in Gillies, *Works of Whitefield*, 3:393.

37 Marrant, *Wonderful Dealings*, 11. Whitefield's preaching text is Amos 4:12b.

38 Whitefield to Mr. R[obert] K[een], New York, July 29, 1770, in Gillies, *Works of Whitefield*, 3:425.

39 Whitefield to Mr. R[obert] K[ee]n, Philadelphia, May 9, 1770, in Gillies, *Works of Whitefield*, 3:422.

40 *The Massachusetts Gazette, and Boston Post-Boy and the Advertiser,* October 1, 1770.

41 Whitefield to R[obert] K[een], Portsmouth, New Hampshire, Sept. 23, 1770, in Gillies, *Works of Whitefield*, 3:427.

42 George Whitefield, *A Sermon by the Reverend Mr. George Whitefield, Being His Last Farewell to His Friends* (London, 1769), title page.

43 Whitefield, *Last Farewell*, 11, 18, 19.

44 Whitefield, *Last Farewell*, 30.

45 Gillies, *Memoirs of Whitefield*, 261–262.

46 Whitefield to Mr. J—s, London, Aug. 19, 1769, in Gillies, *Works of Whitefield*, 3:392.

47 Selections are from Whitefield, *Last Farewell*, iii–iv, 5–6, 11, 15–32. Complete bibliographic information for all texts cited, excerpted, or reprinted can be found in the bibliography.

48 Matthew 16:24, Mark 8:34, Luke 9:23; Revelation 14:4.

49 Matthew 14:28.

[50] Whitefield's decision on the timing of his ordination for professional ministry is discussed in Chapter 2.

[51] Whitefield is referring to the two churches he founded in London, the Tabernacle and Tottenham Court Road Chapel.

[52] Whitefield's earlier six visits to the American colonies were 1738, 1739–1741, 1744–1748, 1751–1752, 1754–1755, and 1763–1765.

[53] 1 Corinthians 15:58a.

[54] Whitefield's benediction is Numbers 6:24–26, a blessing given by God to the high priest Aaron and his sons to bless the people of Israel.

BIBLIOGRAPHY

Alexander, Archibald. *Biographical Sketches of the Founder and Principal Alumni of the Log College.* Princeton, NJ, 1845.

Alexander, Archibald, ed. *Sermons of the Log College: Being Sermons and Essays by the Tennents and their Contemporaries.* Ligonier, PA: Soli Deo Gloria Publications, 1993. First published as *Sermons and Essays by the Tennents and their Contemporaries* in 1855 by the Presbyterian Board of Publication.

Baker, Frank, ed. *Letters I: 1721–1739.* Vol. 25 of *The Works of John Wesley.* Oxford: Clarendon Press, 1980.

Batinski, Michael C. *Jonathan Belcher, Colonial Governor.* Lexington: University Press of Kentucky, 1996.

Bebbington, David. *Evangelicalism in Modern Britain: A History from the 1730s to the 1980s.* London: Routledge, 1993. First published 1989 by Unwin Hyman (London).

Belton, David, dir. *God in America.* Episode 1, "A New Adam." Aired October 11, 2010, on PBS. http://www.pbs.org/godinamerica/view/.

Boren, Braxton. "Whitefield's Voice." In *George Whitefield: Life, Context, and Legacy,* edited by Geordan Hammond and David Ceri Jones, 167–189. Oxford: Oxford University Press, 2016.

Brunner, Daniel L. *Halle Pietists in England: Anthony William Boehm and the Society for Promoting Christian Knowledge.* Göttingen: Vandenhoeck & Ruprecht, 1993.

Cashin, Edward J. *Beloved Bethesda: A History of George Whitefield's Home for Boys, 1740–2000.* Macon, GA: Mercer University Press, 2001.

Chamberlain, Ava. "The Grand Sower of the Seed: Jonathan Edwards' Critique of George Whitefield." *New England Quarterly* 70, no. 3 (Sept. 1997): 368–385.

Choi, Peter Y. *George Whitefield: Evangelist for God and Empire.* Grand Rapids, MI: Eerdmans, 2018.

Choinski, Michał. *The Rhetoric of the Revival: The Language of the Great Awakening Preachers.* Bristol, CT: Vandenhoeck & Ruprecht, 2016.

Claghorn, George S., ed. *Letters and Personal Writings.* Vol. 16 of *The Works of Jonathan Edwards,* edited by Harry S. Stout. New Haven: Yale University Press, 1998.

Coalter, Milton J., Jr. *Gilbert Tennent, Son of Thunder: A Case Study of Continental Pietism's Impact on the First Great Awakening in the Middle Colonies.* Contributions to the Study of Religion 18. New York: Greenwood Press, 1986.

Cummings, Archibald. *Faith Absolutely Necessary, But Not Sufficient to Salvation Without Good Works.* Philadelphia, 1740.

Dallimore, Arnold A. *George Whitefield: The Life and Times of the Great Evangelist of the Eighteenth-Century Revival.* 2 vols. London: Banner of Truth Trust, 1970.

Dwight, Sereno, ed. *The Works of President Edwards.* Vol. 1. New York, 1830.

Ecclesiastical Records, State of New York. 7 vols. Albany, NY: State of New York, 1901–1916. https://archive.org/details/ecclesiasticalre02newy/page/1334/mode/2up?q=vesey.

Edwards, Jonathan. *Copies of the Two Letters Cited by the Rev. Mr. Clap, Rector of the College at New Haven.* Boston, 1745.

Edwards, Jonathan. *A Treatise Concerning Religious Affections.* Boston, 1746.

Fiering, Norman. "The First American Enlightenment: Tillotson, Leverett, and Philosophical Anglicanism." *The New England Quarterly* 54, no. 3 (September 1981): 307–344. https://www.jstor.org/stable/365467.

Fogleman, Aaron Spencer. *Jesus is Female: Moravians and Radical Religion in Early America.* Philadelphia: University of Pennsylvania Press, 2007.

Foster, Richard J. *Meditative Prayer.* Downers Grove, IL: InterVarsity Press, 1983.

Fowler, Dorothy Ganfield, and Donna W. Hurley. *A City Church: The First Presbyterian Church in the City of New York.* 2nd ed. New York: The First Presbyterian Church in the City of New York, 2016.

Garden, Alexander. *Six Letters to the Rev. Mr. Whitefield, With Mr. Whitefield's Answer to the First Letter.* 2nd ed. Boston, 1740.

Gerbner, Katharine. *Christian Slavery: Conversion and Race in the Protestant Atlantic World.* Philadelphia: University of Pennsylvania Press, 2018.

Gibson, Edmund. *The Bishop of London's Pastoral Letter to the People of his Diocese . . . Against Lukewarmness on One Hand, and Enthusiasm on the Other.* London, 1739.

Gillies, John. *Memoirs of the Life of the Reverend George Whitefield.* London, 1772.

Gillies, John. *The Works of the Reverend George Whitefield.* 6 vols. London, 1771–1772.

Glasson, Travis. *Mastering Christianity: Missionary Anglicanism and Slavery in the Atlantic World.* Oxford: Oxford University Press, 2012.

Hammond, Geordan. "The Correspondence of George Whitefield Project: A Report and Reflection on the Early Stages." *Wesley Theological Journal* 54, no. 1 (Spring 2019): 57–70.

Henry, Stuart C. *George Whitefield: Wayfaring Witness.* New York: Abingdon Press, 1957.

Hindmarsh, D. Bruce. *The Evangelical Conversion Narrative: Spiritual Autobiography in Early Modern England.* Oxford: Oxford University Press, 2005.

Holy Bible, New International Version. Colorado Springs, CO: Biblica, 2011.

Houghton, S.M., ed. *Letters of George Whitefield for the Period 1734–1742.* Carlisle, PA: Banner of Truth Trust, 1976. Facsimile of *The Works of the Reverend George Whitefield,* ed. John Gillies, vol. 1, *A Select Collection of Letters of the Late Reverend George Whitefield.* London, 1771.

Jay, William, ed. *Memoirs of the Life and Character of the Late Reverend Cornelius Winter.* Bath, UK, 1808.

Jones, David Ceri. "'So Much Idolized by Some, and Railed at by Others': Towards Understanding George Whitefield." *Wesley and Methodist Studies* 5 (2013): 3–29.

Jordan, Albert F. "The Chronicle of Peter Böehler, Who Led John and Charles Wesley to the Full Light of the Gospel." *Transactions of the Moravian Historical Society* 22, no. 2 (1971): 100–178. https://www.jstor.org/stable/41179802.

Kenney, William Howland, III. "Alexander Garden and George Whitefield: The Significance of Revivalism in South Carolina 1738–1741." *The South Carolina Historical Magazine* 71, no. 1 (Jan. 1970): 1–16. https://www.jstor.org/stable/27566968.

Kidd, Thomas S. "Daniel Rogers' Egalitarian Great Awakening." *The Journal of The Historical Society* 7, no. 1 (March 2007): 111–135.

Kidd, Thomas S. *George Whitefield: America's Spiritual Founding Father.* New Haven, CT: Yale University Press, 2014.

Kidd, Thomas S. *The Great Awakening: The Roots of Evangelical Christianity in Colonial America.* New Haven, CT: Yale UP, 2007.

Koch, Philippa. "Slavery, Mission, and the Perils of Providence in Eighteenth-Century Christianity: The Writings of Whitefield and the Halle Pietists." *Church History* 84, no. 2 (June 2015): 369–393.

Kolchin, Peter. *American Slavery, 1619–1877.* Rev. ed. New York: Hill and Wang, 2003.

Lambert, Frank. "'I Saw the Book Talk': Slave Readings of the First Great Awakening." *The Journal of African American History* 87 (1992): 12–25.

Lambert, Frank. *"Pedlar in Divinity": George Whitefield and the Transatlantic Revivals, 1737–1770.* Princeton, NJ: Princeton University Press, 1994.

Laycock, J.W. "Great Britain's Indebtedness Under God to George Whitefield." *Proceedings of the Wesley Historical Society* 10, no. 1 (March 1915): 26–28. https://www.biblicalstudies.org.uk/pdf/whs/10-1.pdf.

"Letters of George Whitefield: From the Collection of Mr. George Stampe." *Proceedings of the Wesley Historical Society* 10, no. 1 (March 1915): 17–25. https://www.biblicalstudies.org.uk/pdf/whs/10-1.pdf.

Lyles, Albert M. *Methodism Mocked: The Satiric Reaction to Methodism in the Eighteenth Century.* London: Epworth Press, 1960.

Mahaffey, Jerome Dean. *The Accidental Revolutionary: George Whitefield and the Creation of America.* Waco, TX: Baylor University Press, 2011.

Mahaffey, Jerome Dean. *Preaching Politics: The Religious Rhetoric of George Whitefield and the Founding of a New Nation.* Waco, TX: Baylor University Press, 2007.

Marrant, John. *A Narrative of the Lord's Wonderful Dealings with John Marrant.* 2nd ed. London, 1785.

Marsden, George M. *Jonathan Edwards: A Life.* New Haven, CT: Yale University Press, 2003.

Minkema, Kenneth P. "Whitefield, Jonathan Edwards, and Revival." In *George White-field: Life, Context, and Legacy*, edited by Geordan Hammond and David Ceri Jones, 115–131. Oxford: Oxford University Press, 2016.

Parr, Jessica M. *George Whitefield: Race, Revivalism, and the Making of a Religious Icon*. Jackson, MS: University Press of Mississippi, 2015.

Pears, Thomas C. *Documentary History of William Tennent and the Log College*. Philadelphia: Department of History of the Office of the General Assembly of the Presbyterian Church in the USA, 1940.

Podmore, Colin. *The Moravian Church in England, 1728–1760*. Oxford: Clarendon Press, 1998.

Pusey, Edward B., trans. *The Confessions of Saint Augustine*. New York: Simon & Schuster, 1997.

The Querists, Or, An Extract of Sundry Passages Taken Out of Mr. Whitefield's Printed Sermons, Journals, and Letters. Philadelphia, 1740.

Roberts, Richard Owen. *Whitefield in Print: A Bibliographic Record of Works by, for, and against George Whitefield*. Wheaton, IL: R.O. Roberts, 1988.

Scougal, Henry. *The Life of God in the Soul of Man: Or, The Nature and Excellency of the Christian Religion*. London, 1677. Reprint, with an introduction by J.I. Packer. Ross-shire, Scotland: Christian Heritage, 2021.

Scribner, Vaughn. "Transatlantic Actors: The Intertwining Stages of George Whitefield and Lewis Hallam, Sr., 1739–1756." *Journal of Social History* 50, no. 1 (Fall 2016): 1–27. https://doi.org/10.1093/jsh/shw006.

Sloat, William A., II. "George Whitefield, African-Americans, and Slavery." *Methodist History* 33, no. 1 (October 1994): 3–13.

Smith, Lisa. *The First Great Awakening in Colonial American Newspapers: A Shifting Story*. Lantham, MD: Lexington Books, 2012.

Smith, Lisa. *Godly Character(s): Insights for Spiritual Passion from the Lives of 8 Women in the Bible*. Baltimore, MD: Square Halo Books, 2018.

Spurgeon, C.H. *"The Modern Whitfield": Sermons of the Rev. C.H. Spurgeon, of London; with an Introduction and Sketch of his Life by E.L. Magoon*. New York: Sheldon, Blakeman, 1856.

Stevens, Abel. *The Women of Methodism: Its Three Foundresses, Susanna Wesley, the Countess of Huntingdon, and Barbara Heck*. New York: Carlton & Porter, 1866.

Stout, Harry S. *The Divine Dramatist: George Whitefield and the Rise of Modern Evangelicalism*. Grand Rapids, MI: Eerdmans, 1991.

Three Letters to the Reverend Mr. George Whitefield. Philadelphia, 1739.

Tyerman, Luke. *The Life of the Rev. George Whitefield*. 2 vols. London: Hodder and Stoughton, 1876.

Ward, W. R. *The Protestant Evangelical Awakening*. Cambridge: Cambridge University Press, 1992.

Wesley, John. *A Sermon on the Death of the Rev. Mr. George Whitefield.* London, 1770.

Wheatley, Phillis. *Poems on Various Subjects, Religious and Moral.* London, 1773.

Whitefield, George. *A Continuation of the Reverend Mr. Whitefield's Journal, After his Arrival at Georgia, To a Few Days after his Second Return Thither from Philadelphia.* London, 1741.

Whitefield, George. *A Continuation of the Reverend Mr. Whitefield's Journal, From a few Days after his Return to Georgia to his Arrival at Falmouth, on the 11th of March 1741.* London, 1741.

Whitefield, George. *A Continuation of the Reverend Mr. Whitefield's Journal, From his Arrival at London, to his Departure from thence on his Way to Georgia.* London, 1739.

Whitefield, George. *A Continuation of the Reverend Mr. Whitefield's Journal, From his Embarking after the Embargo, To his Arrival at Savannah in Georgia.* London, 1740.

Whitefield, George. *The First Two Parts of his Life, with his Journals, Revised, Corrected, and Abridged.* London, 1756.

Whitefield, George. *A Further Account of God's Dealings with the Reverend Mr. George Whitefield.* London, 1747.

Whitefield, George. *A Journal of a Voyage from London to Savannah in Georgia.* London, 1738.

Whitefield, George. *The Last Will and Testament, of the Late Reverend and Renowned George Whitefield.* London, 1771.

Whitefield, George. *A Letter From the Rev. Mr. Whitefield, to Some Church Members of the Presbyterian Persuasion, in Answer to Certain Scruples Lately Proposed in Proper Queries Raised on Each Remark.* Philadelphia, 1740.

Whitefield, George. *The Nature and Necessity of our New Birth in Christ Jesus, in Order to Salvation.* London, 1737.

Whitefield, George. *A Sermon by the Reverend Mr. George Whitefield, Being His Last Farewell to His Friends.* London, 1769.

Whitefield, George. *A Short Account of God's Dealings with the Reverend Mr. George Whitefield.* London, 1740.

Whitefield, George. *Three Letters from the Reverend Mr. G[eorge] Whitefield.* Philadelphia, 1740.

Whitefield, George. *The Wise and Foolish Virgins: A Sermon Preached at Philadelphia, 1739.* Philadelphia, 1739.

Wigginton, Caroline, and Abram Van Engen, eds. *Feeling Godly: Religious Affections and Christian Contact in Early North America.* Amherst, MA: University of Massachusetts Press, 2021.

Wilcox, William B., ed. *The Papers of Benjamin Franklin.* Vol. 18, *January 1 through December 31, 1771.* New Haven, CT: Yale UP, 1974. https://franklinpapers.org/framed-Volumes.jsp.

"William Carey, Father of Modern Protestant Missions." Christian History. *Christianity Today*, October 22, 2022. https://www.christianitytoday.com/history/people/missionaries/william-carey.html.

Witzig, Fred E. *Sanctifying Slavery and Politics in South Carolina: The Life of the Reverend Alexander Garden, 1685–1756*. Columbia, SC: The University of South Carolina Press, 2018.

Wood, Betty. *Slavery in Colonial America, 1619–1776*. Lanham, MD: Rowman & Littlefield, 2005.

Wood, Betty. *Slavery in Colonial Georgia, 1730–1775*. Athens, GA: University of Georgia Press, 1984.

LISA SMITH earned her PhD in early American literature and teaches at Pepperdine University in Malibu, California. Her book *The First Great Awakening in Colonial American Newspapers: A Shifting Story* examines newspaper coverage of the revival. Lisa's first book with Square Halo Books, *Godly Character(s): Insights for Spiritual Passion from the Lives of 8 Women in the Bible,* explores how eight women in the Bible impacted their communities and culture.

Other Square Halo Books *featuring* Lisa Smith

GODLY CHARACTER(S): INSIGHTS FOR SPIRITUAL PASSION FROM THE LIVES OF 8 WOMEN IN THE BIBLE

Igniting spiritual passion doesn't have to be a mysterious process. Lisa Smith shows that by conforming our character to God's design, we can awaken in our hearts a sincere love for him. That rekindled affection can drive us to deeper intimacy with God and lead to greater joy in our daily lives. "As much as this book is about character and stories of particular women, it is also a look at a set of eight people who knew and loved their Lord—people who allowed themselves to be shaped by Him over and above their culture and their circumstances. It is my hope that Lisa's insights into these 'great eight' propel you towards habits of godliness—putting you in a place to receive grace and fall more deeply in love with your savior—and that in His love you might be re-shaped and re-formed."—Robert William Alexander, author of *The Gospel-Centered Life at Work*

ORDINARY SAINTS: LIVING EVERYDAY LIFE TO THE GLORY OF GOD

Lisa Smith and over forty other writers celebrate Square Halo's twenty-fifth anniversary with essays on such topics as knitting, home repair, pipes, traffic, chronic pain, mentoring, pretzels, and naps. "A delightfully organic fleshing out of the 'every moment holy' idea. Real people communing with a real God in the midst of real lives."—Douglas McKelvey, author of *Every Moment Holy*

SQUAREHALOBOOKS.COM